Discovering
In His Own Words
William Tyndale

A one-year program to
establish a 500-year perspective
on his translation of the Bible
into the English tongue.

"Grace, peace, and increase of knowledge in our Lord Jesus
Christ be with thee, dear reader, and with all that
call on the name of the Lord unfeignedly
and with a pure conscience."
(William Tyndale)

Copyright 2016 by Philip M. Hudson.
The book author retains sole copyright to his contributions to this book.

Published 2016.
Printed in the United States of America.

All rights reserved.

No portion of this book may be reproduced, stored in a retrieval system, or transmitted in any form or by any means – electronic, mechanical, photocopy, recording, scanning, or other – except for brief quotations in critical reviews or articles, without the prior written permission of the author.

ISBN 978-1-943650-13-2

Library of Congress Control Number 2016941154

Illustrations - Google Images.

This book was published by BookCrafters
Parker, Colorado.
bookcrafterscolorado@gmail.com

This book may be ordered from
www.bookcrafters.net
and other online bookstores.

BookCrafters

"Sweet religion makes a rhapsody of words."
(William Shakespeare)

Table of Contents

Preface..1
Introduction..5
Calendar...27
Appendix One: Scriptures in Chronological Order...409
Appendix Two: Equivalent Scriptures in the King James Translation................415
Appendix Three: Additional Familiar Tyndale Biblical Phrases........................461
Appendix Four: Reflections...469
About the Author..475
Also by the Author..477

"Sweet religion makes a rhapsody of words."
William Shakespeare

Table of Contents

Introduction 1
Chorden 3
Appendix One: Scriptures in Chronological Order 168
Appendix Two: Quotations, Scripture and a King James Translation 170
Appendix Three: Additional Tamil and Tyndale Bible at Lambeth 172
A Final Few Reflections 174
About the Author 176
Also by the Author 177

Preface

One day, a priest visiting Little Sodbury
openly attacked Tyndale's beliefs. He replied:
"If God spare my life, before very long I shall cause
a plough boy to know the scriptures better than you do!"

It will warm the cockles of my heart, if you enjoy reading this book half as much as I have enjoyed writing it. I appreciate that it can be a daunting task to immerse oneself in a quest to understand a man like William Tyndale, and to embrace his translations of the Old and New Testaments. So the thought crossed my mind that if I could take some of his more memorable scriptural turns of phrase and link them to related quotations from his writings, perhaps I could succeed in reducing familiarity with this icon of the Reformation to bite-sized chunks that would be more agreeable to our twenty-first century palates. It seemed important to me that I commence this undertaking well in advance of the 500th anniversary of the publication of the 1526 edition of his Bible. In fact, I have worked on this homage for the better part of a year, to give myself a ten-year window of opportunity, and to be ready for the fireworks that are sure to accompany the quincentennial celebration that will take place in 2026.

Organizing the book, I have employed two devices that have proven to be successful in the past. First, I have labored to give both literal and figurative form and symmetry to the thoughts and scriptures expressed, and second, I have utilized a simple yearly calendar format to reduce the scholarly work-load, to make daily study less intimidating, and to invite regular and consistent reflection. I believe that these strategies work well, because the layout facilitates intellectual and spiritual equilibrium by shaping and sculpting Tyndale's thoughts in order to more easily comprehend and personalize the daily struggles of a man who lived in an almost unimaginably different time and place. I hope that I have succeeded in familiarizing the reader with one whose bones have been mouldering in the dust for centuries.

In the process, the ancient scriptures acquire a relevancy that might have otherwise been elusive. In an odd way, the reflections of Tyndale, who lived half a thousand years ago, have animated holy writ that is two millennia and more old. I have been struck by the realization that we are fighting the same battles waged by Tyndale so long ago, and if there is one lesson to be learned from history, it is that we do not learn from history.

Tyndale's conflicts belong to the ages, but the issues with which we grapple are essentially the same, and are similar to those addressed by the Savior, and by His apostles and prophets in Old and New Testaments times, as well as by His disciples during the Reformation and the Dispensation of the Fulness of Times. In this sense, Tyndale was a visionary whose contributions to our understanding of the battles between good and evil have transcended time. He clothed in words the great questions of our day. John F. Kennedy once said of the wartime rhetoric of British Prime Minister Sir Winston Churchill: "He sent the English language to war." If so, Churchill owed the force of his eloquence to William Tyndale.

I think of Tyndale when I read the dialogue between Edmund Dantès and the priest Abbé Faria that occurred deep within the dungeons of the Chateau d'If, in Alexandere Dumas' novel "The Count of Monte Cristo." "What are you thinking of?" asked the Abbé smilingly, imputing the deep abstraction in which his visitor was plunged to the excess of his awe and wonder. "I was reflecting, in the first place," replied Dantès, "upon the enormous degree of intelligence and ability you must have employed to reach the high perfection to which you have attained. What would you not have accomplished if you had been free?" "Possibly nothing at all," replied the priest. "The overflow of my brain would probably, in a state of freedom, have evaporated in a thousand follies; misfortune is needed to bring to light the treasures of the human intellect. Compression is needed to explode gunpowder. Captivity has brought my mental faculties to a focus; and you are well aware that from the collision of clouds electricity is produced - from electricity, lightning, from lightning, illumination."

Finally, at the end of the tale, Dantès observes: "Only a man who has felt ultimate despair is capable of feeling ultimate bliss. It is necessary to have wished for death, in order to know how good it is to live. Live, then, and be happy, and never forget that, until the day God deigns to reveal the future to man, the sum of human wisdom will be contained in these words: wait and hope."

This approach has provided me with a working construct around which I have wrapped my mind. I have begun to appreciate William Tyndale as I never have before, and although my understanding is still incomplete, I feel that I have made progress on the road to a personal discovery of the man, his times, and his seasons. As 2026 approaches, I hope that the world will pause long enough to contemplate, and then to celebrate, the anniversary of the publication of his Bible, and will then find time during the next ten years to compose itself in respectful preparation for the commemoration in 2036 of the 500th anniversary of his martyrdom. I hope this little treatise will better prepare us to do so.

This book is more an appreciation than a history. Frankly, it adds very little to the body of work that has been previously written about William Tyndale. But I hope that it may, in a small way, contribute to his long overdue and richly deserved recognition. Just as he did, I have a confident expectation that, through study, the Holy Spirit will enlarge our grasp of the solemnities of eternity and illuminate our minds with understanding. I started this journey simply wanting to create a vehicle for the expression of my indebtedness to the man, but I ended with feelings of even greater inadequacy, and with a realization that I can scarcely articulate my thanks for his example of courage and conviction that has led, after all these years, to my own better understanding of the scriptures. This has, in turn, brought me closer to our Savior Jesus Christ. It strikes me that it is I who am the ploughboy to whom he referred. This is his real legacy, that he has touched so many people, and it is for this that I am sure he would like to be remembered.

We all owe a debt of gratitude to William Tyndale, who has influenced the lives of countless millions. He was a mentor to Hugh Latimer, who with Nicholas Ridley, was burned at the stake on October 16, 1555, in defense of his similar beliefs, at the behest of "Bloody Mary," the Catholic queen of England. Latimer is said to have urged his companion: "Play the man, Master Ridley; we shall this day light such a candle, by God's grace, in England, as I trust shall never be put out!" Because of Tyndale, that torch is still burning brightly as a beacon of hope over all of Christendom. Perhaps this book will encourage you to find your own way to enhance the brilliance of that eternal flame. A thousand points of light, when taken together, cast a very long shadow.

Introduction

"If I prove a timid friend to truth,
I am afraid that I will not survive
to be read by those to whom
these times are ancient."
(Dante)

To really appreciate this book and the New Testament, you need to know something beforehand about William Tyndale (1494 – 1536) and the times in which he lived. In his preface to "Obedience of a Christian Man," published in Antwerp, Belgium, on October 2, 1528, he wrote: "Prepare thy mind, therefore, unto this little treatise; and read it discreetly; and judge it indifferently. And when I allege any scripture, look thou on the text whether I interpret it right: which thou shalt easily perceive by the circumstance and process of them, if thou make Christ the foundation and the ground, and build all on him, and referrest all to him; and findest also that the exposition agreeth unto the common articles of the faith and open scriptures."

It behooves all of us to brush up on our religious historical scholarship as we prepare ourselves to commemorate the 500th anniversary of the publication of his Bible, the first to be translated and printed in the English language (1526), and the prototype for the King James Version, published 85 years later (in 1611). We owe it to Tyndale to know something about his life, and about his ultimate sacrifice, his martyrdom for the cause, on October 6, 1536.

Every time we open our Bibles, we should say a silent prayer in our minds, thanking God for William Tyndale, and for men and women like him, who either inspired him or dedicated themselves to follow his example. But he would have been uncomfortable with our tributes. His was a simple faith that was expressed without ambiguity. On one occasion, he wrote: "Give to every man, therefore, his duty: tribute to whom tribute belongeth; custom to whom custom is due; fear to whom fear belongeth; honour to whom honour pertaineth. Owe nothing to any man; but to love one another. For he that loveth another fulfilleth the law. For these commandments, thou shalt not commit adultery, thou shalt not kill, thou shalt not steal, thou shalt not bear false witness, thou shalt not desire, and so forth, if there be any other commandment, are all comprehended in this saying: Love thine neighbour as thyself. Love hurteth not his neighbour. Therefore, is love the fulfilling of the law."

A bumper sticker that has enjoyed popularity for years declares: "If you can read this, thank a teacher." In fact, we should display bumper stickers that proclaim: "If you can read the Bible, thank William Tyndale!" When you finish reading this book, I hope that you will have gained insight into the character of this great man, and will be better able to appreciate his incalculable contribution to our understanding of God through his interpretation of scripture as set forth in the English tongue, which was the language of the people.

He has brought a love of the scriptures within the grasp of untold millions. He urged: "Be strong in the Lord, and in the power of his might. Put on the armour of God that ye may stand steadfast against the crafty assaults of the devil. For we wrestle not against flesh and blood: but against rule, against power, and against worldly rulers of the darkness of this world, and against spiritual wickedness in heavenly things." The epic battle between light and darkness was constantly before his eyes, and he was ever mindful of the eternal consequences of the exercise of agency, in an age when simply engaging the principle of free will was dangerous, and particularly so when it related to ecclesiastical matters of faith, and when it was severely curtailed by what he perceived as the unrighteous dominion, and even the tyranny, of the state church.

If Tyndale seemed to rail against the establishment, he was on solid footing. At the very least, the careful lists of grievances that have survived in his writings provide a vivid illustration of a mind-set forged by circumstance, and put in perspective his dogged determination to set things right. "Who slew the prophets?" he asked. "Who slew Christ? Who slew his Apostles? Who the martyrs and all the righteous that ever were slain? The kings and the temporal sword at the request of the false prophets." There was no confusion in his mind regarding the individuals or institutions that squirmed uncomfortably in the cross-hairs of his criticism. He pulled no punches, even as he charted and negotiated very dangerous territory, for his was a stark and brutal world where to dare to disparage the Church was to invite institutional opposition, ecclesiastical persecution, spiritual excommunication, and even temporal death by burning at the stake, all at the hands of secular authorities who received their sanction by the very leaders of a Church whose heavenly mandate was to selflessly minister to and protect the flock.

In many ways, as we become more familiar with Tyndale, we are struck by his similarities to Joseph Smith, another martyr for the cause. Neither one was inclined to complain to God about his lot in life. On only one occasion is it recorded that Joseph ever did so. He was quickly put in his place by the Savior, Who responded to his entreaties: "My son, peace be unto thy soul; thine adversity and thine afflictions shall be but a small moment; And then, if thou endure it well, God shall exalt thee on high; thou shalt triumph over all thy foes. Thy friends do stand by thee, and they shall hail thee again with warm hearts and friendly hands. Thou art not yet as Job; thy friends do not contend against thee, neither charge thee with transgression, as they did Job." (D&C 121:7-10). It is unclear whether, at the bitter end, Tyndale was as Job, without friends upon whom he could rely, or who could provide for him even a few small comforts. We do know that after his betrayal, from his cold and dreary cell in the castle of Vilvoorde, near Brussels, where he spent the last six months of his life, he wrote: ""My overcoat and my shirts are worn out. All I ask is to be allowed to have a lamp in the evening, for it is indeed wearisome sitting alone in the dark."

Joseph Smith could have related well to one of Tyndale's observations: "Adversity also received I of the hand of God as a wholesome medicine, though it be somewhat bitter." Smith wrote from bonds in Liberty Jail: "O God, where art thou? And where is the pavilion that covereth thy hiding place? How long shall thy hand be stayed, and thine eye, yea thy pure eye, behold from the eternal heavens the wrongs of thy people and of thy servants, and thine ear be penetrated with their cries? Yea, O Lord, how long shall they suffer these wrongs and unlawful oppressions, before thine heart shall be softened toward them, and thy bowels be moved with compassion toward them?" (D&C 121:1-3).

With philosophical resignation, Tyndale confessed: "The world loveth that which is his, and hateth that which is chosen out of the world to serve God in the Spirit." Both

Tyndale and Smith were molded through adversity by the hand of God to be creative and inventive vessels. Both knew by first-hand experience the workings of the Spirit, and willingly yielded themselves to its influence. Tyndale wrote: "As our strength abateth, groweth the strength of Christ in us: when we are clean emptied of our own strength, then are we full of Christ's strength."

Joseph would have concurred. In a similar vein, he wrote: "Let thy bowels also be full of charity towards all men, and to the household of faith, and let virtue garnish thy thoughts unceasingly; then shall thy confidence wax strong in the presence of God; and the doctrine of the priesthood shall distil upon thy soul as the dews from heaven. The Holy Ghost shall be thy constant companion, and thy scepter an unchanging scepter of righteousness and truth; and thy dominion shall be an everlasting dominion, and without compulsory means it shall flow unto thee forever and ever." (D&C 121:45-46).

Both were refined in the crucible of opposition, a condition that Tyndale repeatedly and eloquently described: "Lo, persecution and adversity for the truth's sake is God's scourge, and God's rod, and pertaineth unto all his children indifferently: for when he said he scourgeth every son, he maketh none exception." On another occasion, he observed: "The weakness of the flesh is the strength of the Spirit. And by flesh understand wit, wisdom, and all that is in a man before the Spirit of God come. And of like testimonies is all the scripture full." Joseph recorded the comforting words of the Savior that must have been a spiritual impression with which Tyndale was surely intimately familiar: "Thy days are known, and thy years shall not be numbered less; therefore, fear not what man can do, for God shall be with you forever and ever." (D&C 122:9).

But what of Tyndale's legacy. As of November 2014, the full Bible, in large part based on His daring work, has blossomed into translations in no fewer than 531 languages, and 2,883 languages have at least some portion of the Bible in the vernacular. The King James Version dates from 1611, and stems directly from Tyndale's Bible. Since that time, familiar and widely used translations have included the New International Version, the New Living Translation, the New American Standard Bible, the New Revised Standard Version, and the New Jerusalem Bible.

In fact, 84% of the K.J.V. New Testament, and 76% of the K.J.V. Old Testament, is verbatim Tyndale. "In so great diversity of spirits," he asked, "how shall I know who lieth, and who sayeth truth? Whereby shall I try and judge them? Verily by God's word, which only is true. But how shall I that do, when (the Catholic Church) wilt not let me see scripture?" More than any other bold individual, he single-handedly remedied that deplorable situation. Certainly, he must have been among "the noble and great ones" that had been singled out in the pre-earth existence, to come to earth to address an entire laundry list of injustices preparatory to the Restoration of the Gospel in the Last Days. (Abraham 3:22).

Reading the Tyndale Bible can give us a new appreciation of the 7th Article of Faith of The Church of Jesus Christ of Latter-day Saints: "We believe the Bible to be the word of God as far as it is translated correctly." Tyndale would have been quite satisfied to use that declaration of belief as his springboard for action, for he scathingly wrote of the ecclesiastical misanthropes of his day: "O crafty jugglers and mockers with the word of God! Know ye not that scriptures sprang out of God?" He characterized church leaders, from the pope to the parish priest, as a generation of vipers. "How can ye say well," he asked, "when ye yourselves are evil? (Matthew 12:34).

Tyndale personified He to whom Paul referred, when he taught the Athenians: "In Him we live, and move, and have our being." (Acts 17:28). He recognized the stirrings of the spirit within his breast, and knew beyond the shadow of a doubt that we are quickened and are alive because of Jesus Christ, and Him alone.

The United States Constitution (June 21, 1788) with its Bill of Rights (December 15, 1791), was ratified roughly 250 years after Tyndale's martyrdom, but it can trace its origins right back to his dogged determination to make scripture the ultimate source of knowledge that would be available to the common man. The First Amendment includes freedom of religion and freedom of speech, and reads: "Congress shall make no law respecting an establishment of religion, or prohibiting the free exercise thereof; or abridging the freedom of speech, or of the press." Even the articulation of those eternal principles was only possible because of the groundbreaking efforts of William Tyndale. In 1528, at the dawn of the Reformation in mainland Europe, he challenged the English clergy: "But how shall I (conform my life to the teachings of Jesus Christ), when ye will not let me have his testimonies, or witnesses, in a tongue which I understand? Will ye resist God? Will ye forbid him to give his Spirit unto the lay as well as unto you? Hath he not made the English tongue? Why then forbid ye him to speak in the English tongue?"

Tyndale presaged the Declaration of Independence (1776), and Thomas Paine's "The Right of Man" (1791). The Declaration asserts: "We hold these truths to be self-evident, that all men are created equal, that they are endowed by their Creator with certain unalienable rights, that among these are life, liberty and the pursuit of happiness. That to secure these rights, governments are instituted among men, deriving their just powers from the consent of the governed… And for the support of this Declaration, with a firm reliance on the protection of divine providence, we mutually pledge to each other our lives, our fortunes and our sacred honor." The framers of the Declaration cast their lot with those who would defy authority to insist upon the exercise of "the rights of man." Surely, as men of intelligence, reason, and of faith, with a sense of history, they would not have been unaware of the precedent established by William Tyndale, or of the example he set when he lay his life on the altar of sacrifice in the defense of principles of freedom that he held sacred.

Tyndale would probably have considered himself a true Catholic, for he never wavered from his faith. It was only the bishops, monks, and friars with whom he took umbrage, evidenced by his characteristic vitriolic responses to Sir Thomas More and others of the establishment who challenged his beliefs and convictions. He influenced Hugh Latimer and Nicholas Ridley, who, at Oxford (on October 16, 1555, nearly twenty years after his martyrdom,) were burned at the stake in defense of their similar beliefs, at the behest of "Bloody Mary, the Catholic queen of England. Latimer is said to have urged his companion: "Play the man, Master Ridley; we shall this day light such a candle, by God's grace, in England, as I trust shall never be put out." Nineteen years earlier, Tyndale's last words had been: "Lord, open the king of England's eyes." That prayer was answered just two short years later, when newly Protestant King and Defender of the Faith Henry VIII (by the 1534 Act of Supremacy, two years before Tyndale's martyrdom!) ordered that the Bible of Miles Coverdale be used in every parish in the land. Largely based on Tyndale's work, the Coverdale Bible was a large volume, meant to grace a pulpit, unlike Tyndale's small pocket-sized New Testament, designed to be held in the hand as a prized personal possession, to be referred to regularly. Amazingly, in 1539, just three years after his martyrdom, Tyndale's edition of the Bible became officially approved for printing and distribution in England!

Martin Luther (1483-1546) was Tyndale's German contemporary. He and the Dutch Renaissance humanist, Catholic priest, social critic, teacher, and theologian Erasmus (1466-1536) provided fuel for the fire his faith. Perhaps they gave him the courage to ask his English religious contemporaries to act on the Savior's penetrating question: "Can ye not discern the signs of the times?" (Matthew 16:3). The times were surely changing in Europe, with the initiation of the Protestant Reformation with its 95 Theses, propositions for debate concerned with the question of indulgences, written (in Latin) and posted by Luther on the door of the Schlosskirche, Wittenberg, Germany, on Oct. 31, 1517.

Tyndale's familiarity with Luther's theses and Erasmus' philosophy helped him to see things in a new light. In his mind, the persecution and accusations of heresy that followed his challenge of dogma were not crises, but instead, were wonderful opportunities. I am sure that, if he had been given a choice, he would have lived in no other time or place. He was no "Man for All Seasons," reacting involuntarily to political and ecclesiastical pressures, following the path of least resistance, or bowing to expediency. Rather, he must have been supremely confident that he had been raised up to perform a specific work. He was as one who had been foreordained to "walk before the Lord in the land of the living." (Tyndale Bible, Psalms 116:9)

His perspective on the scriptures is, even today, refreshing and stimulating. He was a polyglot who was fluent in eight languages, and his mastery of these tongues was so powerful that it was said that when speaking any of them, one listening would be hard pressed to discern if it was his native tongue. The greater point is that he was able to see scriptural source material in German, Latin, Hebrew, and Greek with equal intimacy, and utilize that understanding as the key to knowledge. Tyndale carefully and meticulously used a number of reference works when carrying out his translations of both the New and Old Testaments. When translating the New Testament, he referred to the third edition (1522) of Erasmus' Greek New Testament. He also used Erasmus' Latin New Testament, as well as Luther's German version and the Latin Vulgate. It is believed that he refrained from using Wycliffe's manuscript Bible as a source text because he didn't want its English usage that reflected pre-Renaissance terminology and would likely be deemed to be archaic. Tyndale wanted his Bible to be easily understandable in the language of the people. (See below).

John Wycliffe had been an English philosopher, theologian, reformer, seminary professor at Oxford University, and dissident within the Roman Catholic church. He is generally recognized as being the first to translate, or more likely to oversee the translation, of the Bible into Middle English, in 1382 (?), around 60 years before the invention of the printing press. All copies were handwritten manuscripts that were verbatim translations of St. Jerome's Latin Vulgate Bible, inasmuch as in the 14th century, Greek and Hebrew texts were not generally available. Wycliffe has been called the "Morning Star of the Reformation" because he at least orchestrated, and certainly presaged, the growing opposition in Europe to ecclesiastical abuses. (Interestingly, there still exist as many as 250 manuscripts, complete or partial, containing Wycliffe's translation in its revised forms).

His unauthorized translation of the Bible into English was banned by the Church in 1408, and Wycliffe, who had died on New Year's Eve, 1384, was so vilified by the papacy that on October 8, 1427, over 41 years after his death, on the orders of the Council of Constantine (the same council that had ordered Jan Hus / John Huss burned at the stake in 1415) he was condemned on 260 counts of heresy, and his bones were exhumed, burned, and dumped in the River Swift. The council probably thought that by doing so, Wycliffe might be forgotten. A later chronicler observed: "They burned his bones to ashes and cast them into the Swift, a neighboring brook running hard by. Thus, the brook conveyed his ashes into the Avon, the Avon into the Severn, the Severn into the narrow seas, and then into the main ocean. And so, the ashes of Wycliffe are symbolic of his doctrine, which is now spread throughout the world."

Today, Wycliffe's translation is difficult to read. For example, he translated James 1:5-8 as: "And if ony of you nedith wisdom, axe he of God, which yyueth to alle men largeli, and vpbreidith not; and it schal be youun to hym. But axe he in feith, and doute no thing; for he that doutith, is lijk to a wawe of the see, which is moued and borun a boute of wynde. Therfor gesse not the ilke man, that he schal take ony thing of the Lord. A man dowble in soule is vnstable in alle hise weies."

On the other hand, reading that same scripture from Tyndale's translation, we can easily recognize and relate to its poetical flow, and we can thank him for the rendition that provided the scriptural impetus for the King James Translators, whose version drove Joseph Smith to the Sacred Grove nearly three centuries later: "If any that is among you lack wisdom, let him ask of God, which giveth to all men without doubleness, and casteth no man in the teeth: and it shall be given him: but let him ask in faith, and waver not. For he that doubteth is like the waves of the sea, tossed of the wind, and carried with violence. Neither let that man think that he shall receive any thing of God. A wavering minded man is unstable in all his ways." (Tyndale Bible, James 1:5-8).

It is interesting to see how the phraseology of the scriptures evolved, from even before Wycliffe, through Tyndale and the King James Version. Consider below the textual variants in only a few of the earliest English translations of John 3:16, that is today rendered in the familiar King James Version as: "For God so loved the world, that he gave his only begotten Son, that whosoever believeth in him should not perish, but have everlasting life."

> **1st Ed. King James Version (1611)**: "For God so loued the world, that he gaue his only begotten Sonne: that whosoeuer beleeueth in him, should not perish, but haue euerlasting life."
>
> **Rheims (1582)**: "For so God loued the vvorld, that he gaue his only-begotten sonne: that euery one that beleeueth in him, perish not, but may haue life euerlasting."
>
> **Geneva (1560)**: "For God so loueth the world, that he hath geuen his only begotten Sonne: that none that beleue in him, should peryshe, but haue euerlasting lyfe."

Great Bible (1539): "For God so loued the worlde, that he gaue his only begotten sonne, that whosoeuer beleueth in him, shulde not perisshe, but haue euerlasting lyfe."

Tyndale (1534): "For God so loveth the worlde, that he hath geven his only sonne, that none that beleve in him, shuld perisshe: but shuld have everlastinge lyfe."

Wycliff (1380): "for god loued so the world; that he gaf his oon bigetun sone, that eche man that bileueth in him perisch not: but haue euerlastynge liif,"

Anglo-Saxon Proto-English Manuscript (995 AD): "God lufode middan-eard swa, dat he seade his an-cennedan sunu, dat nan ne forweorde de on hine gely ac habbe dat ece lif."

Interestingly, even the Book of Doctrine and Covenants of The Church Of Jesus Christ of Latter-day Saints (February 4, 1831) renders the verse differently: "Who so loved the world that he gave his own life, that as many as would believe might become the sons of God." (D&C 34:3).

In the twenty-first century, it is sobering to reflect upon the sacrifices of our own forefathers, who shed their blood, that they might articulate and protect the freedoms of religious expression and free speech that were purchased so long ago, at the cost of the best blood of England; that of Wycliffe, Tyndale, Latimer, Ridley, and other martyrs. To safeguard the freedom of speech that we too frequently take for granted, today we often take our cases to impartial courts, but it was not always so. Every time we open our mouths to express our opinion, every time we read a controversial book, every time we post our thoughts of social media, every time we do a Google search on an interesting topic, we have men like Tyndale and his contemporaries to thank, who gave their lives to first establish, and then to protect, and finally to preserve our expressions and our desire for unhindered scholarship, that is all in the comfort of our native tongue. "If any man hear my voice and open the door, I will come in unto him and will sup with him, and he with me." (Tyndale Bible, Revelation 3:20). So that a divine communication might freely flow, Tyndale opened that door by squarely addressing the question: "How can we whet God's Word our children and household, when we are violently kept from it and know it not?"

It must have been so painful for Tyndale to witness the persecution of true believers that he could not stand by as a silent witness to the martyrdom of parents who only wanted their children to become familiar with the Lord's Prayer or with the Ten Commandments. Therefore, he determined to make the scriptures within reach of even the illiterate ploughboys who dotted England's rural countryside. He wrote: "Here seest thou that it is God's gift, to suffer for Christ's sake. Happy are ye if ye suffer for the name of Christ; for the glorious Spirit of God resteth in you. Is it not an happy thing, to be sure that thou art sealed with God's Spirit to everlasting life? And, verily, thou art sure thereof, if thou suffer patiently for his sake. Tribulation maketh feeling; or it maketh us feel the goodness of God, and his help, and the working of his Spirit. Lo, Christ is never strong in us till we be weak. As our strength abateth, so groweth the strength of Christ in us. Therefore, very gladly will I rejoice in my weakness, that the strength of Christ may dwell in me." Confronted with that quality of conviction, how could the authorities ever hope to successfully compete?

On another occasion, Tyndale wrote: "Behold, God setteth before us a blessing and also a curse: a blessing, if we suffer tribulation and adversity with our Lord and Savior Christ; and an everlasting curse, if, for a little pleasure's sake, we withdraw ourselves from the chastising and nurture of God, wherewith he teacheth all his sons, and fashioneth them after his godly will, and maketh them perfect, and maketh them apt and meet vessels to receive his grace and his Spirit, that they might perceive and feel the exceeding mercy which we have in Christ, and the innumerable blessings and the unspeakable inheritance, whereto we are called and chosen, and sealed in our Savior Jesus Christ, unto whom be praise for ever." There is no indication that Tyndale ever wavered in that determination or conviction during a relentless persecution that lasted for well over a decade.

When we study his translations and writings, we sense the portent of his own martyrdom, but more significantly, we are enveloped in the fire of his words that brim over with an enthusiastic expectation of unspeakable joy. He was as Jeremiah, who wrote: "But his word was in mine heart as a burning fire shut up in my bones, and I was weary with forebearing, and I could not stop." (K.J.V. Jeremiah 20:9). Or, as Tyndale wrote in his Old Testament translation: "But the word of the Lord was a very burning fire in my heart and in my bones, which when I would have stopped, I might not." (Tyndale Bible, Jeremiah 20:9).

He made little or no distinction between the anticipation of eternal happiness in the resurrection and the realization of joy, or more properly, hope, during his sojourn through this vale of tears. His faith was firmly based on that hope, which gave him the ability to see things as they really are. Consequently, he enjoyed a confidence that was not dependent upon circumstances. "Forasmuch, then, as we must needs be baptized in tribulations, and through the Red sea, and a great and a fearful wilderness, and a land of cruel giants, into our natural country; yea, and inasmuch as it is a plain earnest that there is no other way into the kingdom of life than through persecution, and suffering of pain, and of very death, after the ensample of Christ; therefore, let us arm our souls with the comfort of the scriptures: how that God is ever ready a hand, in time of need, to help us; and how that such tyrants and persecutors are but God's scourge, and His rod to chastise us." Faced with that sense of determination, his tormenters could never gain the upper hand, for in his mind they were special friends sent from God to try him and to prove him, and to make sure that he was worthy of his hire.

He may have been something of a fatalist, but it cannot be disputed that he was somehow completely at ease with the memory of his former life and the purpose of his call, and that he never wavered in his zealous determination to fulfill a mission whose purpose was clearly defined in his own mind. He persevered because he was sure of his election as a servant of the Lord Jesus Christ, and it seems that, particularly in his darkest hours, his Master had already invited him to come and "sup with Him." (Tyndale Bible, Revelation 3:20). The Savior had granted His faithful servant a peace that surpasses our understanding. "Let us receive all things of God," he encouraged, "whether it be good or bad: let us humble ourselves under his mighty hand, and submit ourselves unto his nurture and chastising, and not withdraw ourselves from his correction."

Before his martyrdom, Joseph Smith had said: "I am going like a lamb to the slaughter; but I am calm as a summer's morning; I have a conscience void of offense towards God, and towards all men. I shall die innocent, and it shall yet be said of me: he was murdered in cold blood." (D&C 135:4). The conduct of William Tyndale's life expressed a similar peace born of confident expectation. "He will not work until all be past remedy," Tyndale wrote, "and brought unto such a case, that men may see, how that his hand, his power, his mercy, his goodness and truth, hath wrought altogether. He will let no man be partaker with him of his praise and glory. His works are wonderful, and contrary unto man's works. Who ever, saving he, delivered his own Son, his only Son, his dear Son, unto the death, and that for his enemies' sake, to win his enemy, to overcome him with love, that he might see love, and love again, and of love do likewise to other men, and overcome them with well doing?" The Catholic Church in England did not stand a chance, in the face of such passionate logic, conviction, and determination.

As Will Durant wrote of early Christianity, so could it have been similarly said of William Tyndale: The evidence and memory of his ministry could have just quietly faded away, but as time passed and events unfolded, there was instead "no greater drama in human record than the sight of a few Christians, scorned and oppressed by a succession of emperors, (or popes!) bearing their trials with a fierce tenacity, multiplying quietly, building order while their enemies generated chaos, fighting the sword with the word, brutality with hope, and at last defeating the strongest state that history had known (that was, in Tyndale's mind, the Vatican state of the Holy Roman Empire). Caesar and Christ had met in the arena, and Christ had won."

Tyndale knew what he was up against, but he eagerly sought out the foe on the field of battle. For him, it was a war of words, an ideological conflict with the contestants engaged in a fight for spiritual life, and not temporal death. In a sense, he may have had a tactical advantage, because he positioned himself as the protagonist, while the ecclesiastical establishment was cast as the unpopular antagonist. Tyndale was able to choose his field of battle by defining the parameters of the debate. In the arena of public opinion, he was destined to win, although the eventual outcome would be agonizingly slow in an era when the interactive communication of ideas was in its infancy.

Although he took the fight to his adversaries, the constant sparring was on the home turf with which he was ever comfortable, where he could be nourished and refreshed, and receive validation from the spiritual compost and scriptural foundations of his rhetoric. Its vigor may have added fuel to the fire, but it surely kept things lively. "So sore have our false prophets brought the people out of their wits, and have wrapped them in darkness, and have rocked them asleep in blindness and ignorance!" he exclaimed. "Now ye preach nothing but lies, and, therefore, are of the devil, the father of all lies, and of him are ye sent." His politically incorrect protestations were the 16th century equivalents of modern day "sound-bites" that would be sure to catch the attention of those who watched the "5 o-clock news," garnering the support of a people starved for the word of God, while forcing his opponents to respond as silly-sounding robots in the early Renaissance arena of public opinion.

Because of his contributions to our understanding of the nature of God, we know today to Whom we must look if we are to obtain eternal life. The word of God has become firmly entrenched in our minds, hearts, and society, and is now readily available to billions of our brothers and sisters. As Tyndale translated the Psalms, he might have identified with David, who wrote: "Quicken me, O Lord, for thy name's sake: for thy righteousness' sake bring my soul out of trouble." (Tyndale Bible, Psalms 143:11). The same could be said of his translation of Paul's epistle to the Ephesians: "God, who is rich in mercy, for his great love wherewith he loved us, even when we were dead in sins, hath quickened us together with Christ." (Tyndale Bible, Ephesians 2:4-5).

Tyndale may have thought of his own revelatory experiences, when he discovered the following quotation from Job among his source texts: "For when God doth once command a thing, there should no man be curious, to search whether it be right. In dreams and visions of the night season, when slumbering cometh upon men, that they fall a sleep in their beds, he roundeth them in the ears, he informeth them, and sheweth them plainly." (Tyndale Old Testament Job 33:4-16). The later King James Version beautifully renders these same verses: "For God speaketh once, yea twice, yet man perceiveth it not. In a dream, in a vision of the night, when deep sleep falleth upon men, in slumberings upon the bed; then he openeth the ears of men, and sealeth their instruction."

These verses are reminiscent of Joseph Smith's experiences when, during the quiet hours of the evening, he was visited numerous times by angels. Although there is no existing record that Tyndale enjoyed similar visions, we would like to believe that this gentle spiritual giant was also attended and comforted by angels. Tyndale must have been encouraged, as was one latter-day lyricist who was also familiar with trials, tribulations, and persecution, who wrote: "Gird up your loins, fresh courage take, our God will never us forsake!" (William Clayton). As one having authority, Tyndale declared: "A true messenger must do his message truly; and say neither more nor less than he is commanded."

As we near the 500th anniversary of the publication of those 3,000 precious copies of Tyndale's Bible, published by Peter Schoeffer in the German city of Worms, in 1526, we can once again thank him for expressions such as: "gave up the ghost," "a shining light," "my brother's keeper," "they laughed him to scorn," "be of good cheer," enter ye in at the strait gate," "blessed are the meek, "fight the good fight," "riotous living," "the powers that be," "suffer fools gladly," "wandering stars," "fallen from grace," "eye hath not seen," "that old serpent," "bottomless pit," "live and let live," "cast the first stone," "stiff-necked," "Passover," "atonement," and "wept bitterly," to name just a few. (See Appendix Four). Today, only three copies survive from that initial printing, but his legacy lives on in countless translations of the Bible, and its ripple effect has worked its way into the English language as a whole. It has been said that, in the shaping of modern English, Tyndale has been even more influential as a wordsmith than Shakespeare.

In the words of Steven Lawton: "With his New Testament, William Tyndale became the father of the Modern English language. He shaped its syntax, grammar, and vocabulary more than any man who ever lived; more than the author Geoffrey Chaucer, the playwright William Shakespeare, or the poets Percy Shelley and John Keats. At the dawn of the sixteenth-century, the English language was crude and unrefined, lacking precision and standardization, a strange mixture of Anglo-Saxon and Norman features with an ancient Latin vocabulary. Tyndale proved to be its change agent. As he translated the Bible, giving careful thought to words, phrases, and clauses, he shaped the language at its transition point from Middle English to Early Modern English. The speech of a nation was constructed in his mind and flowed from his pen. In providing the English Bible, Tyndale became the father of Modern English."

Think of Winston Churchill, who delivered an address of hope to the oppressed of Europe, in January 1940: "The day will come when the joybells will ring again throughout Europe, and when victorious nations, masters not only of their foes, but of themselves, will plan and build in justice, in tradition, and in freedom, a house of many mansions where there will be room for all." Vintage Tyndale, underlining mine. (See Tyndale's Bible, John 14:2). Or, Thomas Jefferson: "I have sworn upon the altar of god eternal hostility against every form of tyranny over the mind of man." (K.J.V. Psalms 43:4, underlining mine, see Tyndale's Old Testament, Psalms 43:4). Or, John F. Kennedy: "The rights of man come not from the generosity of the state but from the hand of God." (K.J.V. Mark 16:19, underlining mine, See Tyndale's New Testament, Mark 16:19).

We can all thank Tyndale for providing the Bible that has become our platform for provident living. In the words of John Quincy Adams: "My custom is to read four or five chapters of the Bible every morning immediately after rising. It seems to me the most suitable manner of beginning the day. It is an invaluable and inexhaustible mine of knowledge and virtue." Or, Abraham Lincoln: "I am profitably engaged in reading the Bible. Take all of this Book upon reason that you can, and the balance by faith, and you will live and die a better man." Or, Grover Cleveland: "The reception of the teachings of Christ results in the purest patriotism, in the most scrupulous fidelity to public trust, and in the best type of citizenship." Or, Ronald Reagan: "Of the many influences that have shaped the United States into a distinctive nation and people, none may be said to be more fundamental and enduring than the Bible."

Would Tyndale be encouraged by the progress that has been made during the past 500 years, to put the vernacular scriptures in the hands of the people, and to facilitate the understanding of God's word so that it is now almost universal? According to the Gideon Society, there have been somewhere in the neighborhood of six billion Bibles published since the original 3,000 copies of the Tyndale Bible were smuggled by ship from the Continent into England, hidden in bales of cloth. Three of those original copies remain. They are the Stuttgart Copy, that was only recently discovered, and that is now owned by the Wurttemberg State Library in Stuttgart, Germany. It is complete with both its title page and the original binding. A second copy is owned by the British Library. Its 706 page New Testament is pocket-sized, bound in crimson leather, and is richly illuminated. It was acquired in 1994, at a cost of one million pounds sterling (U.S. $1,420,000.00 in 2015). It would be hard to put a proper price on one of Tyndale's Bibles, but a million dollars seems like a good starting point. The only other known copy of Tyndale's New Testament, safeguarded in St. Paul's Cathedral, London, has 59 leaves missing.

When considering the life of William Tyndale, one is reminded of the words of Tom Paine, who wrote: "Tyranny, like hell, is not easily conquered; yet we have this consolation with us, that the harder the conflict, the more glorious the triumph. What we obtain too cheap, we esteem too lightly. 'Tis dearness only that gives everything its value. Heaven knows how to put a proper price upon its goods; and it would be strange, indeed, if so celestial an article as freedom should not be highly rated." ("The Political Works of Thomas Paine," p. 55).

Tyndale would have been encouraged by the spread of Protestantism, as well as by the reforms of the Catholic Counter-Reformation, beginning with the Council of Trent, that were fueled by the spread of information made possible by the invention of the printing press by Johannes Gutenberg, around 1440. Tyndale would have been thrilled by the progress made at the Second Vatican Council, convened on October 11, 1962, by Pope John XXIII. One of the changes implemented by that council has been the use of vernacular languages, instead of Latin, in the Mass. This process only began 430 years after Tyndale's death, so he might have judged the reform to be too little and too late. But I think he would have, nevertheless, been overjoyed to participate in a Mass conducted in a language other than Latin, and also to see that the Church had finally severely restricted the practical application of indulgences. But he would still be fighting to put an end to confession, transubstantiation, and the dogma relating to purgatory and intercession by Saints.

While he would have been particularly pleased to know that, as the Reformation gained momentum, there was a Catholic Anti-Reformation, he would have been more encouraged by the later Ages of Reason and Enlightenment made possible by the Renaissance, (although he would have been dismayed by their rationality), and finally by the Restoration of the Gospel, that was more in line with his philosophy of direct and personal interaction with God, by the people.

He would have been bewildered by the rationality of the Last Days, and particularly by the new irreligion spawned by man's unrestrained, unfocused, and undisciplined reason. But he would not have judged his sacrifices to have been wasted, or squandered on an undeserving or uncaring people. He welcomed each opportunity that God gave to him to suffer for the Savior, thinking himself particularly blessed that Jesus Christ would think so much of him that He would give him opportunities to experience his own personal Gethsemane. He was utterly consumed in Christ. The way before him was clarified by the Spirit, and as he spent the last year of his life in the darkest of dungeons, the narrow confines of his small cell must have been illuminated with an undeniable celestial light that only he could discern. "Adversity also receive I of the hand of God," he wrote, "as a wholesome medicine, though it be somewhat bitter."

In Latter-day Saint circles, it has often been said that the Restoration could not have taken place without the groundwork that had been laid by the architects of the Reformation. But it is not often acknowledged or even recognized that the Reformation itself might have fizzled were it not for brave men like William Tyndale. "And as pertaining unto them that despise God's word, counting it as a fantasy or a dream; and to them also that for fear of a little persecution fall from it, set this before thine eyes; how God, since the beginning of the world, before a general plague, ever sent his true prophets and preachers of his word, to warn the people, and gave them time to repent. But they, for the greatest part of them, hardened their hearts, and persecuted the word that was sent to save them. And then God destroyed them utterly, and took them clean from the earth. As thou seest what followed the preaching of Noe in the old world; what followed the preaching of Lot among the Sodomites; and the preaching of Moses and Aaron among the Egyptians; and that suddenly, against all possibility of man's wit."

Tyndale may have been anti-establishment, but he was no rebel without a cause. He knew precisely what his mission was, and he was incredibly centered. In spite of a variety of temporal deprivations, his intellect and his emotional and spiritual stability remained remarkably intact. He wrestled with no inner conflict, nd suffered no crisis of confidence. "So ought every preacher to preach God's word purely, and neither to add nor minish." He made no bones about the fact that he was a sinner, and freely acknowledged his utter inability to work his way into heaven. He steadfastly believed in salvation by the grace of the Lord Jesus Christ. That commitment is evident in his translation of Ephesians: "God, who is rich in mercy, for his great love wherewith he loved us, even when we were dead in sins, hath quickened us together with Christ." (Tyndale Bible, Ephesians 2:4-5).

"Another conclusion is this," he taught, "that no person, neither any degree, may be exempt from this ordinance of God: neither can the profession of monks and friars, or any thing that the pope or bishops can lay for themselves, except them from the sword of the emperor or kings, if they break the laws. For it is written, 'Let every soul submit himself unto the authority of the higher powers.' Here is no man except; but all souls must obey. The higher powers are the temporal kings and princes; unto whom God hath given the sword, to punish whosoever sinneth. God hath not given them swords to punish one, and to let another go free, and sin unpunished."

We owe him a debt of gratitude that he picked his battles so carefully, and focused his energies on the larger issues of life. "He that avengeth himself on every trifle," he wrote, "is not meet to preach the patience of Christ, how that a man ought to forgive and to suffer all things. He that is overwhelmed with all manner riches, and doth but seek more daily, is not meet to preach poverty. He that will obey no man is not meet to preach how we ought to obey all men."

Tyndale had a grasp of the first principles and ordinances of the Gospel, which are those sacraments that are necessary for salvation. Of the Savior, he wrote: "Outwardly he disguised him not; but made him like other men, and sent him into the world to bless us, and to offer himself for us a sacrifice of a sweet savor, to kill the stench of our sins, that God henceforth should smell them no more, nor think on them any more; and to make full and sufficient satisfaction, or amends, for all them that repent, believing the truth of God, and submitting themselves unto his ordinances, both for their sins that they do, have done, and shall do."

The problem, as Tyndale saw it, was that "without a promise can there be no faith. The sacraments which Christ himself ordained, which have also promises, and would save us if we knew them and believed them, them minister they in the Latin tongue." He argued that "Peter in the second of the Acts practiced his keys; and by preaching the law brought the people into the knowledge of themselves, and bound their consciences, so that they were pricked in their hearts, and said unto Peter and to the other apostles, 'What shall we do?' Then brought they forth the key of the sweet promises, saying, 'Repent, and be baptized every one of you in the name of Jesus Christ, for the remission of sins, and ye shall receive the gift of the Holy Ghost. For the promise was made to you, and to your children, and to all that are afar, even as many as the Lord shall call. Of like ensamples is the Acts full, and Peter's epistles, and Paul's epistles, and all the scripture."

Of the first of the principles of the Gospel, he wrote: "Faith cometh by hearing, and hearing cometh by the word of God. And how shall they hear without a preacher, and how shall they preach except they be sent?" He reasoned: "Faith, that loveth God's commandments, justifieth a man. If thou believe God's promises in Christ, and love his commandments, then art thou safe. If thou love the commandment, then art thou sure that thy faith is unfeigned, and that God's Spirit is in thee. Faith justifieth before God in the heart; and love springeth of faith, and compelleth us to work; and the works justify before the world, and testify what we are, and certify us that our faith is unfeigned, and that the right Spirit of God is in us."

Of the second of the principles of the Gospel, he wrote: "Contrition and repentance are both one, and nothing else but a sorrowful and a mourning heart." And also: "If

God make him feel in his heart that lusts and appetites are damnable, and give him power to hate and resist them; then is he free, even with the freedom wherewith Christ maketh free, and hath power to do the will of God."

Of the first of the ordinances of the Gospel, he wrote: "Ask the people what they understand by their baptism or washing? And thou shalt see, that they believe how that the very plunging into the water saveth them. But of the promises they know not, nor what is signified thereby." How he wished the people could read and understand their covenants, that "Christ cleansed the congregation in the fountain of water through the word."

Of forgiveness of sin without confession, or ear-shrift, to a priest, he wrote: "Believe the promise, we are sure by God's word, that he is loosed and forgiven in Christ. When a man feeleth that his heart consenteth unto the law of God, and feeleth himself meek, patient, courteous, and merciful to his neighbor, altered and fashioned like unto Christ; why should he doubt but that God hath forgiven him, and chosen him, and put his Spirit in him, though he never crome his sin into the priest's ear?"

Of the second of the ordinances of the Gospel, he wrote that the 20th chapter of the Gospel of John clearly explains: "Receive the Holy Ghost. Whosoever's sins ye remit, they are remitted or forgiven; and whosoever's sins ye retain, they are retained or holden. With preaching the promises, loose they as many as repent and believe. And for that John saith, 'Receive the Holy Ghost.' I say that a steadfast faith, or belief in Christ and in the promises that God hath sworn to give us for his sake, bringeth the Holy Ghost, as all the scriptures make mention." He knew that the scriptures, translated into a language that the common man could understand, would be his most formidable weapons. "And in the last of Matthew, saith he: 'All power is given me in heaven and in earth; go, therefore, and teach all nations, baptizing them in the name of the Father, and of the Son, and of the Holy Ghost; teaching them to observe whatsoever I commanded you.'"

Of the sacrament of the Lord's Supper, he wrote somewhat wistfully: "No more doth it hurt to say that the body and blood are not in the sacrament." On the contrary, he felt the power of the Lord's encouragement: "This do in the remembrance of me." (Tyndale Bible, 1 Corinthians 11:24). "We have a promise," he explained, "that Christ, and his body, and his blood, and all that he did and suffered, is a sacrifice, a ransom, and a full satisfaction for our sins; that God for his sake will think no more on them, if we have power to repent and believe."

Of Christ's ability to save our souls, he wrote: "Who dried up the Red sea? Who slew Goliath? Who did all those wonderful deeds which thou readest in the Bible?

Who delivered the Israelites evermore from bondage, as soon as they repented and turned to God? Faith verily, and God's truth, and the trust in the promises which he had made."

He wrote of our responsibility to bring up our children in light and truth, and emphasized that it could only be done if they were taught the Gospel in their native tongue: "Bring them up in the nurture and information of the Lord," he urged. "Teach them to know Christ, and set God's ordinance before them, saying, 'Son, or daughter, God hath created thee and made thee, through us thy father and mother; and at his commandment have we so long thus kindly brought thee up, and kept thee from all perils.'" He would have identified with Nephi of old, who had explained that "we talk of Christ, we rejoice in Christ, we preach of Christ, we prophesy of Christ, and we write according to our prophecies, that our children may know to what source they may look for a remission of their sins." (2 Nephi 25:26).

Because he was born again in the fiery crucible of experience, he wrote in a personal way of enduring to the end. "When all is at peace, and no man troubleth us, we think that we are patient and love our neighbors as ourselves. But let our neighbor hurt us in word or deed, and then find we it otherwise. Then fume we, and rage, and set up the bristles, and bend ourselves to take vengeance. If we loved with godly love, for Christ's kindness' sake, we should desire no vengeance; but pity him, and desire God to forgive and amend him, knowing well that no flesh can do otherwise than sin, except that God preserve him."

He alluded to being Born Again: "Ye are born anew, not of mortal seed, but of immortal seed, by the word of God, which liveth and lasteth ever." Of our ultimate salvation and exaltation, he wrote: "Moreover, let us arm our souls with the promises both of help and assistance, and also of the glorious reward that followeth. The tribulations of the righteous are many, and out of them all, will the Lord deliver them. The Lord keepeth all the bones of them, so that not one of them shall be bruised. The Lord shall redeem the souls of his servants."

Because of his profound understanding of the scriptures as they must have fallen from the lips of the prophets, he was able to counsel: "But as Christ biddeth us beware of the leaven of the Pharisees, so beware of their counterfeited keys, and of their false net; which are their traditions and ceremonies, their hypocrisy and false doctrine, wherewith they catch, not souls unto Christ, but authority and riches unto themselves. Let Christian kings, therefore, keep their faith and truth, and all lawful promises and bonds, not one with another only, but even with the Turk or whatsoever infidel it be. For so it is right before God; as the scriptures and ensamples of the Bible testify." Thus, he was able to see more clearly his mission to bring the people of England to the truth.

The reward of both cultural and religious evolution is the elaboration of new and reformed behavior. Tyndale's Bible will stand forever as one of the talismans of civilization, and he joins the Sumerian mathematicians, the Greek philosophers, the architects of Angkor Wat, the mystics of the East, the engineers of the Renaissance, and the framers of the Declaration of Independence, to name only a few who have been part of a cooperative effort carried out over millennia on the grand scale of a world stage, punctuated by innumerable acts and curtain calls, and who all have personified a marvelous plasticity of mind that is at the very heart of the ascent of our species.

I think of William Tyndale when I read "Lays of Ancient Rome," by Thomas Babbington Mccaulay: "Then out spake brave Horatius, the Captain of the Gate: 'To every man upon this earth, death cometh soon or late. And how can man die better, than facing fearful odds, for the ashes of his fathers, and the temples of his gods?" (Stanza 27).

All scriptures cited are from William Tyndale's 1526 Bible, Worms, Germany edition.

These scriptures are listed in Appendix One, in the order in which they appear in the Bible.

Differences between these citations and the equivalent verses in the 1611 King James Version, are noted in Appendix Two.

Additional familiar expressions from Tyndale's translations comprise Appendix Three.

Post Tenebras Lux

"Greater love than this hath no man,
than that a man bestow his life for his friends."
(John 15:13)

January 1

"Be of good
cheer, it is I. Be not
afraid. And he went up
unto them into the ship, and the
wind ceased, and they were sore
amazed in themselves beyond
measure, and marveled."
(Mark 6:50-51)

"I beg your Lordship that if I am to remain
here through the winter, you will request the
commissary to have the kindness to send me from
the goods of mine which he has, a warmer cap, for I
suffer greatly from cold in the head, and am afflicted by a
perpetual catarrh (a cold) which is much increased in this
cell. But most of all, I beg your clemency to be urgent
with the commissary, that he will kindly permit me
to have the Hebrew Bible, Hebrew grammar, and
Hebrew dictionary, that I may pass the time in
study. I will be patient abiding the will of
God, to the glory of the grace of my
Lord Jesus Christ, whose spirit I
pray may ever direct your
heart. Amen."

January 2

"Speak thou that which becometh
wholesome learning, that the
elder men be sober, honest,
discreet, sound in the
faith, in love, and
in patience."
(Titus 2:1-2)

"Where
a congregation
is gathered together in
Christ, one alone may preach,
and else no man openly; but that
every man teach his household after
the same doctrine. But if the preacher
preach false, then whosoever's heart
God moveth, to the same it shall be
lawful to rebuke and improve the
false teacher with the clear and
manifest scripture, and that
same is no doubt a true
prophet, sent of God.
For the scripture is
God's, and theirs
that believe."

January 3

"And
Eliah came unto
all the people and said:
Why halt ye between two
opinions? If the Lord be very
God, follow him, or if Baal
be he, follow him. And the
people answered him
not one word."
(1 Kings 18:21)

"They begin
their divinity not at the
scripture, but every man taketh a
doctor, the one contrary unto the other,
as divers fashions and monstrous shapes,
none like another, among our sects of religion.
Every university, and almost every man, hath a
sundry divinity. Whatsoever opinions every man
findeth with his doctor, that is his gospel, and
that only is true to him, and that holdeth all
his life long. Every man, to maintain his
doctor, corrupteth the scripture, and
fashioneth it after his own
imagination."

January 4

"I
say unto you,
Moses gave you not
bread from heaven, but
my Father giveth you the
true bread from heaven. For
he is the bread of God, which
cometh down from heaven, and
giveth life unto the world."
(John 6:32-33)

"And, therefore,
when the pope describeth
God after his covetous complexion,
and that God forgiveth the everlasting
pain, and will yet punish me a thousand
years in the pope's purgatory, that leaven
savoureth not in my mouth. I understand
my Father's words as they sound, and
after the most merciful manner, and
not after the pope's leaven and
captivating wits, to believe
that every poet's fable
is a true story."

January 5

"Be ye followers of God
as dear children, and walk in
love even as Christ loved us, and gave
himself for us, an offering and a sacrifice of a
sweet savour to God. So that fornication and all
uncleanness, or covetousness, be not once named
among you, as it becometh saints; neither filthiness,
neither foolish talking, neither jestings, which are not
comely, but rather giving of thanks. For this ye
know, that no whoremonger, either unclean
person, or covetous person, hath any
inheritance in the kingdom of
Christ, and of God."
(Ephesians 5:1-5)

"So sore
have our false
prophets brought the
people out of their wits,
and have wrapped them
in darkness, and have
rocked them asleep
in blindness and
ignorance."

January 6

"Lord,
thou art God
which hast made
heaven and earth,
the sea, and all
that in them
is."
(Acts 4:24)

"Though
it seem unlikely,
or so impossible unto
natural reason, yet believe
steadfastly that he will do it;
and then shall he, according to
his old use, change the course of
the world, even in the twinkling
of an eye, and come suddenly
upon our giants, as a thief in
the night, and compass
them in their wiles
and worldly
wisdom."

January 7

"The wicked hath nothing to
hope for, and the candle of the ungodly
shall be put out. My son, fear thou the Lord
and the king, and keep no company with the
slanderous. For their destruction shall
come suddenly, and who knoweth
the fall of them both?"
(Proverbs 24:20-22)

"God, which
is also righteous, hath
always poured his plagues upon
them without delay; which plagues the
hypocrites ascribe unto God's word, saying:
See what mischief is come upon us since this
new learning came up, and this new sect, and this
new doctrine. But the prophet answered them that
their idolatry went unto the heart of God, so that he
could no longer suffer the maliciousness of their
own imaginations or inventions, and that the
cause of all such mischiefs was because
they would not hear the voice of
the Lord and walk in his
law, ordinances, and
testimonies."

January 8

"Behold,
I stand at the
door and knock. If
any man hear my voice
and open the door, I will
come in unto him and
will sup with him,
and he with me."
(Revelation 3:20)

"Paul
commandeth that
no man once speak in the
congregation, but in a tongue that all
men understand, except that there be an
interpreter by. He commandeth to labor for
knowledge, understanding, and feeling,
and to beware of superstition, and
persuasions of worldly wisdom,
philosophy, and of hypocrisy
and ceremonies, and of all
manner disguising, and
to walk in the plain
and open
truth."

January 9

"I heard the voice
of much people in heaven
saying: Alleluia. Health, and glory,
and honour, and power be unto our
Lord God, for true and righteous are his
judgments, for he hath judged the great
whore which did corrupt the earth with
her fornication, and hath avenged the
blood of his servants of her hand.
And again they said, Alleluia,
and smoke rose up for
ever more."
(Revelation 19:1-3)

"If men
should continue
to buy prayer four
or five hundred years
more, as they have done,
there would not be a foot of
ground in all Christendom, nor
any worldly thing, which they,
that will be called spiritual,
should not possess."

January 10

"The
first day of
unleavened bread,
the disciples came to
Jesus saying unto him:
Where wilt thou that we
prepare for thee to eat the
ester lamb? And he said: Go
into the city, unto such a man,
and say to him, the master saith
my time is almost come. I will
keep mine ester at thy house
with my disciples."
(Matthew 26:17-18)

"The
sacraments preach
God's word unto us, and
therefore justify, and minister
the Spirit to them that believe; as
Paul through preaching the Gospel
was a minister of righteousness,
and of the Spirit, unto all that
believed his preaching."

January 11

"How shall
he that occupieth
the room of the unlearned
say 'amen' at thy giving of thanks?
seeing he understandeth not what thou
sayest? Thou verily givest thanks well, but
the other is not edified. I thank my God
I speak with tongues more then ye all.
Yet had I lever in the congregation to
speak five words with my mind to
the information of other, rather
than ten thousand words
with the tongue."
(1 Corinthians 14:16-19)

"When we call men our heads,
that we do because of their names, parson,
vicar, bishop, or pope, but only because of the
word which they preach. If he will not obey the
scriptures, then have his brethren authority by
the scriptures to put him down, and send
him out of Christ's church among the
heretics, which prefer their false
doctrine above the true
word of Christ."

January 12

"Let
us leave the
doctrine pertaining
to the beginning of a
Christian man, and go unto
perfection, and now no more lay
the foundation of repentance from
dead works, and of faith toward
God, of baptism, of doctrine,
and of laying on of hands,
and of resurrection from
death, and of eternal
judgment."
(Hebrews 6:1-2)

"God hath
given one man
riches, to help another
at need. When thy neighbor
need, and thou help him not,
being able, thou withholdest
thy duty from him, and
art a thief before
God."

January 13

"Ye have
heard of the
patience of Job, and
have known what end
the Lord made. For the
Lord is very pitiful,
and merciful."
(James 5:11)

"Whenever we
submit ourselves unto
the chastising of God, and
meekly knowledge our sins for
which we are scourged, and amend
our living, then will God take the rod
away. That is, he will give the rulers
a better heart. Or, if they continue
their malice and persecute you
for well-doing, and because
ye put your trust in God,
then will God deliver
you out of their
tyranny, for
his truth's
sake."

January 14

"Beware
of false prophets,
which come to you in
sheep's clothing, but inwardly
they are ravening wolves. Ye shall
know them by their fruits."
(Matthew 7:15-16)

"Faith cometh not
of our free-will, but is
the gift of God, given us by
grace, ere there be any will in our
hearts to do the law of God. And why
God giveth it not every man, I can give no
reckoning of his judgments. But well I know,
I never deserved it, nor prepared myself unto it,
but ran another way clean contrary in my blindness,
and sought not that way. But he sought me, and found
me out, and showed it me, and therewith drew me to
him. And I bow the knees of my heart unto God
night and day, that he will show it all other
men; and I suffer all that I can, to be a
servant, to open eyes. For well I
know they cannot see
of themselves."

January 15

"They…lightly
regarded the counsel of the
most highest. Their heart was
vexed with labor. They fell down,
and there was none to help them. So
they cried unto the Lord in their trouble,
and he delivered them out of their distress."
(Psalms 107:11-13)

"He will not
work until all be past
remedy, and brought unto
such a case that men may see, how
that his hand, his power, his mercy, his
goodness and truth, hath wrought altogether.
He will let no man be partaker with him of his
praise and glory. His works are wonderful, and
contrary unto man's works. Who ever, saving he,
delivered his own Son, his only Son, his dear Son,
unto the death, and that for his enemies' sake,
to win his enemy, to overcome him with
love, that he might see love, and love
again, and of love to do likewise to
other men, and to overcome
them with well doing?"

January 16

"Let no man deceive you with
vain words. For through such things
cometh the wrath of God upon the children
of unbelief. Be not therefore companions with
them. Ye were once darkness, but are now light
in the Lord. Walk as children of light."
(Ephesians 5:6-8)

"O, how sore
differeth the doctrine
of Christ and his apostles
from the doctrine of the pope
and of his apostles! For if any man will
obey neither father nor mother, neither lord
nor master, neither king nor prince, the same
needeth but only to take the mark of the beast,
that is, to shave himself a monk, friar, or priest,
and is then immediately free and exempted from
all service and obedience due unto man. He
that will obey no man (as they will not)
is most acceptable unto them. The
more disobedient that thou art
unto God's ordinances, the
more apt and meet art
thou for theirs."

January 17

"Grace be with you
and peace, from him which is,
and which was, and which is to come,
…and from Jesus Christ which is a faithful
witness, and first begotten of the dead, and Lord
over the kings of the earth. Unto him that loved us
and washed us from our sins in his own blood, and
made us kings and priests unto God his Father, be
glory, and dominion for evermore, amen. Behold
he cometh with clouds, and all eyes shall see
him, and they also which pierced him. And
all kindreds of the earth shall wail. Even
so, amen. I am Alpha and Omega, the
beginning and the ending, saith
the Lord almighty, which
is, and which was, and
which is to come."
(Revelation 1:4-8)

"I know by my own experience,
that all flesh is in bondage, and cannot
but sin. Therefore, am I merciful, and
desire God to loose the bonds of
sin, even in mine enemy."

January 18

"How can I
see the evil that
shall happen unto my
people, and how can I look
upon the destruction
of my kindred?"
(Esther 8:6)

"Howbeit,
it is no new thing unto
the word of God to be railed
upon, neither is this the first time
that hypocrites have ascribed to God's
word the vengeance whereof they themselves
were ever cause. For the hypocrites, with their false
doctrine and idolatry, have evermore led the wrath and
vengeance of God upon the people, so sore that God could
no longer forbear nor defer his punishment. Yet God, who
is always merciful, before he would take vengeance, hath
sent his true prophets and true preachers to warn the
people, that they might repent. But the people, and
particularly the heads and rulers, through comfort
and persuading of the hypocrites, have ever
waxed more hard-hearted than before,
and have persecuted the word of
God and his prophets."

January 19

"For ye suffer fools
gladly, because that ye
yourselves are wise."
(2 Corinthians 11:19)

"Seeing that it has
pleased God to send to
our English people (as many
as sincerely desire it) the scriptures in
their mother tongue, but also that there are
false teachers and blind leaders in every place,
and in order that you not be deceived by any man,
I believed it very necessary to prepare this pathway
into the scripture for you. I do it so that you might walk
surely, and always know the true from the false. I write to
put you in remembrance of certain points, namely to well
understand what these words mean: The Old Testament,
the New Testament, the law, the Gospel, Moses, Christ,
nature, grace, working, believing, deeds and faith,
lest we ascribe to the one that which belongs to
the other, and make Christ to be Moses, or the
Gospel to be the law, or despise grace and
rob from faith, or fall from meek learning
into idle disputes, brawling, and
scolding about words."

January 20

"Where
wast thou, when
I laid the foundations
of the earth? Tell plainly, if
thou hast understanding. Who
hath measured it, knowest thou? Or,
who hath spread the line upon it? Where
upon stand the pillars of it? Or, who laid the
corner stone? Where wast thou, when the
morning stars praised me together,
and all the children of
God rejoiced?"
(Job 38:4-7)

"We see also by stories, how your
confession, penance, and pardons, are come
up, and whence your purgatory is sprung. And
your falsehood in the sacraments we see by open
scripture. And all your works we rebuke with
the scripture, and therewith prove that
the false belief that ye couple to
them may not stand with the
true faith that is in our
Saviour Jesus."

January 21

"The word also that cometh
out of my mouth shall …accomplish
my will. …And so shall ye go forth with
joy, and be led with peace. The mountains
and hills shall sing with you for joy, and all the
trees of the field shall clap their hands. For thorns,
there shall grow fir trees, and the myrtle tree
in the stead of briers. And this shall be
done to the praise of the Lord, and
for an everlasting token that
shall not be taken away."
(Isaiah 55:11-13)

"We
need not to
use filthy lucre in the
Gospel, to chop and change,
and to play the taverners, altering
the word of God, as they do their wines
to their most advantage, and to fashion God's
word after every man's mouth, or to abuse
the name of Christ, to obtain thereby
authority and power to feed
their slow bellies."

January 22

"He is
despised and rejected of
men; a man of sorrows, and
acquainted with grief; and we
hid as it were our faces from
him. He was despised, and
we esteemed him not."
(Isaiah 53:3)

"Last of all, he
sent his own Son to
them, and they waxed more
hardhearted than ever before.
And see what a fearful example of his
wrath and cruel vengeance he hath made
of them to all the world, now almost fifteen
hundred years. Unto the old Britons also, which
dwelled where our nation doth now, preached Gildas,
and rebuked them of their wickedness, and prophesied
what vengeance would follow, except they repented.
But they waxed hardhearted, and God sent his
plagues and pestilences among them, and
sent their enemies upon them on
every side, and destroyed
them."

January 23

"I am
that bread of life.
He that cometh to me,
shall not hunger. And he
that believeth on me,
shall never thirst."
(John 6:35)

"As Christ compareth the
understanding of scripture to a
key, so compareth he it to a net, and
unto leaven, and unto many other things
for certain properties. I marvel, therefore,
that they boast not themselves of their net and
leaven, as well as of their keys, for they are all
one thing. But as Christ biddeth us beware
of the leaven of the Pharisees, so beware
of their counterfeited keys, and of their
false net, which are their traditions
and ceremonies, their hypocrisy
and false doctrine, wherewith
they catch, not souls unto
Christ, but authority
and riches unto
themselves."

January 24

"I will patiently abide God my
Savior. My God shall hear me. O,
thou enemy of mine, rejoice not at
my fall, for I shall get up again,
and though I sit in darkness,
yet the Lord is my light."
(Micah 7:7-8)

"And as the
father hath always, in
time of correction, the rod
fast in his hand, so that the rod
doth nothing but as the father moveth
it, even so, hath God all tyrants in his hand,
and letteth them not do whatsoever they would,
but as much only as he appointeth them to do, and
as far forth as it is necessary for us. And as, when the
child submitteth himself unto his father's correction
and nurture, and humbleth himself altogether unto
the will of his father, then the rod is taken away.
When we are come unto the knowledge of
the right way, and have forsaken our
own will, and offer ourselves unto
the will of God, then turneth
he away the tyrants."

January 25

"The Lord himself shall descend from
heaven with a shout, and the voice of the
archangel, and trump of God. And the dead
in Christ shall arise first. Then shall we which
live and remain be caught up with them also
in the clouds, to meet the Lord in the air.
And so shall we ever be with the Lord.
Wherefore, comfort yourselves one
another with these words."
(1 Thessalonians 4:16-18)

"As pertaining to good
deeds therefore, do the best thou canst,
and desire God to give thee strength to do
better daily. But in Christ put thy trust, and in the
pardon and promises that God hath made thee for
his sake, and on that rock build thine house, and
there dwell. For there only shalt thou be sure
from all storms and tempests, and from
all wily assaults of our wicked spirits,
which study with all falsehood to
undermine us. And the God of
all mercy give thee grace so
to do, unto whom be
glory for ever!"

January 26

"When we have food and raiment, let us be content. They that will be rich, fall into temptation, snares, and many foolish and noisome lusts, which drown men in perdition, and destruction. For covetousness is the roote of all evil, which while some lusted after, they erred from the faith, and tangled themselves with many sorrow… Follow righteousness, godliness, love, patience, and meekness. Fight the good fight of faith. Lay hand on eternal life, whereunto thou art called, and hast professed a good profession before many witnesses."
(1 Timothy 6:8-12)

"My overcoat
is worn out, and my
shirts also are worn out.
And I ask to be allowed
to have a lamp in the
evening. It is indeed
wearisome sitting
alone in the
dark."

January 27

"Rejoice in hope. Be
patient in tribulation. Continue in
prayer. Distribute unto the necessity
of the saints. Bless them which persecute
you. Bless, but curse not. Be merry with them
that are merry. Weep with them that weep. Be of
like affection, one towards another. Be not high
minded, but make yourselves equal to them
of the lower sort. Be not wise in your own
opinions. Recompense to no man evil
for evil. Provide aforehand things
honest in the sight of all men. If
it be possible, yet on your part
have peace with all men."
(Romans 12:12-18)

"He now that
is renewed in Christ,
keepeth the law without
compulsion of any ruler
or officer, save by
the leading of
the Spirit
only."

January 28

"Take my yoke on you,
and learn of me, for I am
meek and lowly in heart,
and ye shall find ease
unto your souls."
(Matthew 11:29)

"Our
deeds serve
in three ways. First
they assure us that we are
heirs of everlasting life and that
the Spirit of God, which is the deposit
thereof, is in us, in that our hearts consent to
the law of God and we have power in our members
to do it, though imperfectly. Secondarily, we tame the
flesh therewith and kill the sin that still remains in us, and
thereby we grow daily more and more perfect in the Spirit,
ensuring lusts do not choke the word of God sown in us,
nor quench the gifts and working of the Spirit, and
that we do not lose the Spirit again. And thirdly,
we do our duty to our neighbors therewith,
and help them in their need, to our own
comfort also, and draw all men
to honor and praise God."

January 29

"Whatsoever things
are true, whatsoever
things are honest, whatsoever
things are just, whatsoever things
are pure, whatsoever things pertain to
love, whatsoever things are of honest report,
if there be any virtuous thing, if there be any
laudable thing, those same have ye in your
mind, which ye have both learned and
received, heard and also seen in me.
Those things do, and the God of
peace shall be with you."
(Philippians 4:8-9)

"If
we keep the
commandments
of love, then are we
sure that we fulfill the
the law in the sight of
God, and that our
blessing shall be
everlasting
life."

January 30

"And they all
died in faith, and received
not the promises, but saw them afar
off, and believed them, and saluted them, and
confessed that they were strangers and pilgrims on
the earth. They that say such things, declare that they
seek a country. Also, if they had been mindful of that
country, from whence they came, they had leisure
to have returned again. But now they desire a
better, that is to say a celestial. Wherefore,
God is not ashamed of them, even to
be called their God, for he hath
prepared for them a city."
(Hebrews 11:13-16)

"If thou repent and
believe the promises,
then God's truth justifieth
thee, that is, forgiveth thee thy
sins, and sealeth thee with his
Holy Spirit, and maketh thee
heir of everlasting life,
through Christ's
descryings."

January 31

"An
abundant
spirit, knowledge
and wisdom to expound
dreams, open secrets, and to
declare hard doubts, was
found in him: Yea,
even in Daniel."
(Daniel 5:12)

"That
forbidding
the lay people to
read the scripture is not
for the love of your souls is
evident, inasmuch as they permit
you to read Robin Hood, Hercules,
Bevis of Hampton and Troilus, with a
thousand histories and fables of love
and wantonness, and of ribaldry,
as filthy as heart can think, to
corrupt the minds of youth
withal, clean contrary
to the doctrine
of Christ."

"Tender mercies"
(Psalms 51:1)

February 1

"Let us
run with patience,
unto the battle that is set
before us, looking unto Jesus, the
author and finisher of our faith, which
for the joy that was set before him, abode
the cross, and despised the shame, and is set
down on the right hand of the throne of God.
Consider, therefore, how that he endured
such speaking against him of sinners,
lest ye should be wearied and
faint in your minds."
(Hebrews 12:1-3)

"Therefore, is a
Christian called to suffer
even the bitter death for his
hope's sake, and because he
does no evil. Kings and rulers,
be they ever so evil, are yet a
great gift of the goodness of
God, and defend us from
a thousand things that
we see not."

February 2

"Thenceforth shall no man teach
his neighbour or his brother, and
say: Know the Lord. But they shall
all know me, from the lowest unto
the highest, sayeth the Lord. For
I will forgive their misdeeds,
and will never remember
their sins any more."
(Jeremiah 31:34)

"A word
is there in Greek,
called presbyter, in Latin
senior, in English an elder, and
is nothing but an officer to teach.
This needeth no anointing of man. They
of the Old Testament were anointed with
oil, to signify the anointing of Christ, and
of us through Christ, with the Holy Ghost.
Thiswise is no man priest, but he that is
chosen, save as in time of necessity
every person christeneth, so may
every man teach his wife and
household, and the wife
her children."

February 3

"Woe be to you
scribes and Pharisees,
dissemblers, for ye tithe
mint, anise, and cumin, and
leave the weightier matters of
the law undone: Judgment,
mercy, and faith. These
ought ye to have done,
and not to have left
the other undone."
(Matthew 23:23)

"A
Christian man
receiveth all things
of the hand of God, both
good and bad, both sweet and
sour, both wealth and woe. If
any person do me good, to
God give thanks. He gave
wherewith, and gave a
commandment, and
moved his heart
so to do."

February 4

"If any that is among you lack wisdom, let him ask of God, which giveth to all men without doubleness, and casteth no man in the teeth, and it shall be given him. But let him ask in faith, and waver not. For he that doubteth is like the waves of the sea, tossed of the wind, and carried with violence. Neither let that man think that he shall receive any thing of God. A wavering minded man is unstable in all his ways."
(James 1:5-8)

"Because we be blind, God hath appointed in the scriptures how we should serve him and please him. As pertaining unto his own person, he is pleased when we believe his promises and holy testament, which he hath made unto us in Christ, and, for the mercy which he there showed us, love his commandments."

February 5

"Despise not the chastening of the Lord, neither faint
when thou are rebuked of him. For whom the Lord
loveth, him he chasteneth, and yet delighteth
in him even as a father in his own son."
(Proverbs 3:11-12)

"Whom
God chooseth to
reign with Christ, him
sealeth he with his mighty
Spirit, and poureth strength into
his heart, to suffer afflictions also with
Christ for bearing witness unto the truth. And
this is the difference between the children of God
and of salvation, and between the children of the devil
and of damnation: That the children of God have power in
their hearts to suffer for God's word, which is their life and
salvation, their hope and trust, and whereby they live in
the soul and spirit before God. And the children of the
devil in time of adversity fly from Christ, whom they
followed feignedly, their hearts not sealed with
his holy and mighty Spirit, and get them to
the standard of their right father the
devil, and take his wages, the
pleasures of this world."

February 6

"Let the word
of God dwell in you
plenteously in all wisdom.
Teach and exhort your own
selves, in psalms, and hymns,
and spiritual songs which
have favour with them,
singing in your hearts
to the Lord."
(Colossians 3:16)

"Another comfort hast thou, that,
as the weak powers of the world defend
the doctrine of the world, so the mighty power
of God defendeth the doctrine of God, which thing
thou shalt evidently perceive, if thou call to mind the
wonderful deeds which God hath ever wrought for
his word in extreme necessity, since the world
began, beyond all man's reason, which are
written for our learning, and not for our
deceiving, that we through patience
and comfort of the scripture might
have hope. The nature of God's
word is to fight against
hypocrites."

February 7

"Ye say,
today shall
be foul weather,
and that because the
sky is tremulous and red.
O, ye hypocrites, ye can
discern the fashion of
the sky, and can ye
not discern the
signs of the
times?"
(Matthew 16:3)

"Are not the shepherd's hook
and the bishop's crose false signs? Is not
that white rochet, that the bishops and canons
wear, so like a nun, and so effeminate, a false sign?
What other things are their sandals, gloves, and mitres,
than false signs, as Christ warned us to beware of wolves
in lamb's skins, and bade us look rather unto their fruits
and deeds, than to wonder at their disguisings. So, too,
these things run throughout our holy religions,
and thou shalt find them likewise
clothed in falsehood."

February 8

"If ye
fulfil the royal law
according to the scripture
which saith: 'Thou shalt love
thine neighbour as thyself,' ye
do well. But if ye regard one person
more than another, ye commit sin,
and are rebuked of the law as
transgressors. Whosoever
shall keep the whole
law, and yet fail in
one point, he is
guilty in all."
(James 2:8-10)

"No
man
can amend
himself, except
God pour his Spirit
unto him. Have we not a
commandment to love
our neighbors as
ourselves?"

February 9

"I testify
unto every man that
heareth the words of prophecy of
this book: If any man shall add unto
these things, God shall add unto him the
plagues that are written in this book. And
if any man shall minish of the words of
the book of this prophecy, God shall
take away his part out of the book
of life, and out of the holy city,
and from those things which
are written in this book."
(Revelation 22:18-19)

"Paul, in every
epistle, warneth us that
we put no trust in works, and to
beware of persuasions or arguments
of man's wisdom, of superstitiousness,
of ceremonies of pope holiness, and
of all manner disguising. And he
exhorteth us to cleave fast
to the naked and pure
word of God."

February 10

"And thou shalt
make a mercy seat of
pure gold two cubits and
an half long, and a cubit
and an half broad."
(Exodus 25:17)

"The law of God, which is the
key wherewith men bind, and the
promises, which are the keys wherewith
men loose, have our hypocrites also taken
away. They will suffer no man to know God's
word, but burn it, and make heresy of it. Yea,
and because the people begin to smell their
falsehood, they make it treason to the king,
and breaking of the king's peace, to have
so much as their pater noster in English.
And instead of God's law, they bind
with their own law, and instead
of God's promises, they loose
and justify with pardons
and ceremonies, which
they themselves have
imagined for their
own profit."

February 11

"I have fought a good
fight, and have fulfilled my
course, and have kept the faith. From
henceforth is laid up for me a crown of
righteousness, which the Lord that is
a righteous judge shall give me
at that day. Not to me only,
but unto all them that
love his coming."
(2 Timothy 4:7-8)

"A Christian man is not saved by works,
but by his faith in the promises before all good
works; though that the works (when we work God's
commandment with a good will, and not works of our
own imagination) declare that we are safe, and that
the Spirit of him that hath made us safe is in us.
Yea, and as God, through preaching of faith,
doth purge and justify the heart, even so
through working of deeds doth he
purge and justify the members,
making us perfect both in
body and soul, after
the likeness of
Christ."

February 12

"It is a fearful
thing to fall into the
hands of the living God."
(Hebrews 10:31)

"The only power of
excommunication is this: If any
man sin openly, and amendeth not
when he is warned, then ought he to be
rebuked openly before all the parish. And the
priest ought to prove by the scripture, that all such
have no part with Christ. For Christ serveth not, but
for them that love the law of God, and consent that it is
good, holy, and righteous, and repent, sorrowing and
mourning for power and strength to fulfill it. And
we ought to pity him, and to have compassion
on him, and with all diligence to pray unto
God for him, to give him grace to repent
and to come to the right way again,
and not to use such tyranny over
God and man, commanding
God to curse. And if he
repent, we ought with
all mercy to receive
him again."

February 13

"When they had dined, Jesus
said to Simon Peter…lovest thou me more
than these? He said unto him: Yea Lord, thou
knowest that I love thee. He said unto him: Feed
my lambs. He said to him again the second time…
lovest thou me? He said unto him: Yea Lord thou
knowest that I love thee. He said unto him: Feed
my sheep. He said unto him the third time…
lovest thou me? Peter sorrowed because
he said to him the third time, lovest
thou me, and said unto him: Lord,
thou knowest all things, thou
knowest that I love thee.
Jesus said unto him:
Feed my sheep."
(John 21:15-17)

"Christ
said to Peter,
the last chapter
of John: Feed my
sheep, and not:
Shear thy
flock."

February 14

"The prophets teach falsely, and priests
follow them, and my people hath
pleasure therein. What will
come thereof at the last?"
(Jeremiah 5:31)

"They say
the scriptures
cannot be translated
into our rude tongue. It is
not so rude, as they are false liars.
For the Greek tongue agreeth more
with the English than with the Latin. And
the properties of the Hebrew tongue agreeth
a thousand times more with English than with the
Latin. The manner of speaking is both one, so that in a
thousand places thou needest not but to translate it into the
English, word for word, when thou must seek a compass in
the Latin, and yet shall have much work to translate it
well-favoredly, so that it have the same grace and
sweetness, sense and pure understanding with
it in the Latin, as it hath in the Hebrew.
A thousand parts better may it be
translated into the English,
than into the Latin."

February 15

"Then opened he their wits, that
they might understand the scriptures."
(Luke 24:45)

"Scripture ought to be
in the mother tongue, and
the reasons that our spirits make
for the contrary are but sophistry to fear
thee from the light, that thou mightiest follow
them blindfold, and be their captive to honor their
ceremonies, and to offer to their belly. First, God gave
the children of Israel a law by the hand of Moses in their
mother tongue, and all the prophets wrote in their mother
tongue, and all the psalms were in the mother tongue.
And there was Christ but figured, and described in
ceremonies, in riddles and parables, and in dark
prophecies. What is the cause that we may not
have the Old Testament, with the New also,
which is the light of the old, and wherein
is openly declared that which there was
darkly prophesied? I can imagine no
cause verily, except it be that we
should not see the work of
antichrist, and juggling
of hypocrites."

February 16

"Though I spake with the
tongues of men and angels, and yet had
no love, I were even as sounding brass, and as a
tinkling cymbal. And though I could prophesy, and
understood all secrets, and all knowledge, yea, if
I had all faith so that I could move mountains
out of their places, and yet had no love, I
were nothing. And though I bestowed
all my goods to feed the poor, and
though I gave my body even that
I burned, and yet had no love,
it profiteth me nothing."
(1 Corinthians 13:1-3)

"And as
for that other
solemn doubt, as they
call it, whether Judas was a
priest or no? I care not what
he then was, but of this, I
am sure, that he is now
not only a priest, but
also a cardinal and
and pope."

February 17

"All that will live godly in Christ Jesus must suffer persecutions. But the evil men and deceivers shall wax worse and worse, while they deceive, and are deceived themselves. But continue thou in the things which thou hast learned."
(2 Timothy 3:12-14)

"Tribulation is a blessing that cometh from God, as witnesseth Christ: 'Blessed are they that suffer persecution for righteousness' sake, for theirs is the kingdom of heaven.' Is not this a comfortable word? Who ought not rather to choose, and desire to be blessed with Christ, in a little tribulation, than to be cursed perpetually with the world for a little pleasure?"

February 18

"What availeth it, my brethren,
though a man say he hath faith, when
he hath no deeds? Can faith save him? If a
brother or a sister be naked or destitute of daily
food, and one of you say unto them: Depart in
peace, God send you warmness and food,
notwithstanding ye give them not those
things which are needful to the body,
what helpeth it them? Even so
faith, if it have no deeds,
is dead in itself."
(James 2:14-17)

"Whosoever doth knowledge
his sins, receiveth forgiveness. This
confession is necessary all our lives long, as is
repentance. As thou understandest repentance,
so understand this confession, for it is likewise
included in the sacrament of baptism. For we
always repent, and always knowledge or
confess our sins unto God, and yet
despair not, but remember
that we are washed in
Christ's blood."

February 19

"Forasmuch as Christ
hath once suffered for sins,
the just for the unjust, for to bring
us to God, and was killed, as pertaining
to the flesh, but was quickened in the spirit. In
which spirit, he also went and preached unto the
spirits that were in prison, which were in time
past disobedient, when the long suffering
of God abode exceeding patiently in the
days of Noah, while the ark was a
preparing, wherein few, that
is to say 8 souls, were
saved by water."
(1 Peter 3:18-20)

"Dumb
ceremonies
are no sacraments,
but are superstitiousness.
Christ's sacraments preach the
faith of Christ, as his apostles did, and
thereby justify. Antichrist's dumb ceremonies
preach not the faith that is in Christ; as his
apostles, bishops and cardinals, do not."

February 20

"In the last
days shall come
perilous times. For the
men shall be lovers of their
own selves, covetous, boasters,
proud, cursed speakers, disobedient
to father and mother, unthankful, unholy,
churlish, stubborn, false accusers, rioters, fierce,
despisers of them which are good, traitors, heady,
high minded, greedy upon voluptuousness
more than the lovers of God, having a
similitude of godly living, but have
denied the power there of."
(2 Timothy 3:1-5)

"God chose us, and elected us
before the beginning of the world, created
us anew, and put his Spirit in us. If we have
no lust to do good works, how is God's Spirit
in us? If the Spirit of God be not in us, how
are we his sons? How are we his heirs,
and heirs annexed with Christ of the
eternal life, which is promised to
all them that believe in him?"

February 21

"If a man covet the office of
a bishop, he desireth a good work. Yea,
and a bishop must be faultless, the husband
of one wife, sober, of honest behavior, honestly
appareled, harbourous, apt to teach, not drunken,
no fighter, not given to filthy lucre, but gentle,
abhorring fighting, abhorring covetousness;
one that ruleth his own house honestly,
having children under obedience, with
all honesty. For if a man cannot rule
his own house, how shall he care
for the congregation of God."
(1 Timothy 3:1-5)

"What
protestations
should I make unto
our prelates, those stubborn
Nimrods who so mightily fight
against God and resist his Holy Spirit,
enforcing with all craft and subtlety to
quench the light of the New Testament;
those promises and appointments
made between God and us?"

February 22

"Behold
how great a thing
a little fire kindleth, and
the tongue is fire, and a world
of wickedness. So is the tongue
set among our members, that it
defileth the whole body, and
setteth a fire all that we
have of nature, and
is itself set afire,
even of hell."
(James 3:5-6)

"If to seek
glory and honor
be a sure token that a
man speaketh of his own self,
and doth his own message, and
not his master's, then is the doctrine
of our prelates of themselves, and not
of God. Be ye learned, therefore, ye
that judge the earth, lest God be
angry with you, and ye perish
from the right way."

February 23

"We have also
a more sure word
of prophecy, whereunto
if ye take heed, as unto a light
that shineth in a dark place, ye do
well, until the day dawn and the day
star arise in your hearts. So that ye
first know this, that no prophecy
in the scripture hath any private
interpretation. For the scripture
came never by the will of man,
but holy men of God spake
as they were moved by
the Holy Ghost."
(2 Peter 1:19-21)

"Our hypocrites boast
themselves of the authority of
Peter, and of Paul, and the other
Apostles, clean contrary unto
the deeds and doctrine
of Peter, Paul, and
of all the other
Apostles."

February 24

"When we
were in the flesh,
the lusts of sin which
were stirred up by the law,
reigned in our members, to bring
forth fruit unto death. But now are we
delivered from the law, and dead from it,
whereunto we were in bondage, that we
should serve in a new conversation
of the spirit, and not in the old
conversation of the letter."
(Romans 7:5-6)

"Take heed, wicked
prelates, blind leaders of
the blind, indurate and obstinate
hypocrites. For no man by sprinkling
himself with holy water, and with eating
holy bread, is more merciful than before,
or forgiveth wrong, or becometh at one
with his enemy, or is more patient,
and less covetous, and so forth,
which are the sure tokens
of the soul-health."

February 25

"I am the light of the world. He that
followeth me shall not walk in
darkness, but shall have
the light of life."
(John 8:12)

"He that
bideth in the
world, as monks call
it, hath more faith than
the cloisterer, for he hangeth
on God in all things. He must trust
God to send him good speed, good luck,
favor, help, a good master, a good neighbor,
a good servant, a good wife, a good chapman
merchant, to send his merchandise safe to
land, and a thousand like. He loveth also
more, which appeareth in that he doeth
service always unto his neighbor. To
pray one for another are we equally
bound, and to pray is a thing that
we may always do, whatsoever
we have in hand and that to
do may no man hire
another."

February 26

"Ye are a chosen generation, a royal priesthood,
an holy nation, and a peculiar people, that
ye should show the virtues of him that
called you out of darkness into
his marvelous light."
(1 Peter 2:9)

"As for our pain
taking, God rejoiceth not
therein as a tyrant, but pitieth us,
and as it were mourneth with us, and is
alway ready and at hand to help us, if we
call, as a merciful father and a kind mother.
Neverthelater he suffereth us to fall into many
temptations and much adversity. Yea, himself
layeth the cross of tribulation on our backs, not
that he rejoiceth in our sorrow, but to drive sin
out of the flesh, which can none otherwise be
cured, as the physicians do many things
which are painful to the sick, not that
they rejoice in the pains of the poor
wretches, but to persecute and to
drive out the diseases which
can no otherwise be
healed."

February 27

"Jesus went about all
Galilee, teaching in their
synagogues, and preaching
the Gospel of the kingdom, and
healing all manner of sickness, and all
manner diseases among the people. And his
fame spread abroad throughout all Syria. And
they brought unto him all sick people, that were
taken with divers diseases and gripings, and
that were possessed with devils, and them
which were lunatic, and those that had
the palsy. And he healed them."
(Matthew 4:23-24)

"We do
not wish to
abolish teaching
and to make every
man his own master, but
if the curates will not teach
the Gospel, the layman must
have the scripture, and read
it for himself, taking God
for his teacher."

February 28

"Whereof, we have many
things to say which are hard
to be uttered, because ye are dull
of hearing. For when as concerning
the time, ye ought to be teachers, yet
have ye need again that we teach you
the first principles of the word of
God, and are become such as
have need of milk, and
not of strong meat."
(Hebrews 5:11-12)

"It is not enough to talk of the scripture
only, but we must also desire God, day and
night, instantly to open our eyes, and to understand
and feel wherefore the scripture was given, that we may
apply the medicine of the scripture, every man to his own
sores; unless then we intend to be idle disputers, and
brawlers about vain words, ever gnawing upon the
bitter bark without, and never attaining unto
the sweet pith within; and persecuting
one another in defending of lewd
imaginations, and phantasies
of our own invention."

February 29

"Beware,
lest any man
come and spoil you
through philosophy and
deceitful vanity, through
the traditions of men, and
ordinances after the world,
and not after Christ, in that
ye are buried with him
through baptism."
(Colossians 2:8 &12)

"The
plunging
into the water
signifieth that we die,
and are buried with Christ,
as concerning the old life of sin.
And the pulling out again signifieth
that we rise again with Christ in a
new life, full of the Holy Ghost,
which shall teach us and guide
us, and work the will
of God in us."

"O ye of little faith."
(Matthew 16:8)

March 1

"Another said: I will follow thee Lord. But let
me first go bid them farewell, which are at home
at my house. Jesus said unto him: No man that
putteth his hand to the plough, and looketh
back, is apt to the kingdom of God."
(Luke 9:61-62).

"If any man have
resisted ignorantly, let him look on
the truth after he come to knowledge.
Also, if any man clean against his heart, but
overcome with the weakness of the flesh, for fear
of persecution, have denied, let him, if he repent, come
again, and take better hold, and not despair, or take it for a
sign that God hath forsaken him. For God oft-times taketh his
strength even from his very elect, when they either trust in
their own strength, or are negligent to call to him for his
strength. And that doth he to teach them, and to make
them feel that in that fire of tribulation, for his
word's sake, nothing can endure and abide
save his work and that strength only
which he hath promised. For the
which strength he will have
us to pray unto him
night and day."

March 2

"Jethro said: Blessed be
the Lord which hath delivered
you out of the hand of the Egyptians
and out of the hand of Pharaoh, which
hath delivered his people from under the
power of the Egyptians. Now I know that
the Lord is greater than all gods."
(Exodus 18:10-11)

"The promise
of God is the anchor that
stayeth us in all temptations. If all
the world be against us, God's word is
stronger than the world. If the world kill
us, that shall make us alive again. If it be
possible for the world to cast us into hell,
from thence yet shall God's word bring
us again. Hereby seest thou that it is
not the work, but the promise, that
justifieth us through faith. Now
where no promise is, there can
no faith be, and therefore no
justifying, though there
be never so glorious
works."

March 3

"Think not,
that I am come
to send peace into
the earth. I came not to
send peace, but a sword.
For I am come to set a man
at variance against his father,
and the daughter against her
mother, and the daughter in
law against her mother in
law. And a man's foes
shall be they of his
own household."
(Matthew 10:34-36)

"Let the temporal
powers, to whom God
hath given the sword to take
vengeance, look before they leap,
that they may see what they do. Let
the causes first be disputed before
them, that he that is accused
may have room to answer
for himself."

March 4

"That comforter
which is the Holy Ghost
(whom my Father will send in
my name) shall teach you all
things, and bring all things
to your remembrance,
whatsoever I have
told you."
(John 14:26)

"Though the
scripture be an outward
instrument, and the preacher
also, to move men to believe, yet
the chief and principal cause why a
man believeth, or he believeth not, is
within. For the Spirit of God teacheth
his children to believe, and the devil
blindeth his children, and keepeth
them in unbelief, and maketh
them to consent unto lies,
and think good evil,
and evil good."

March 5

"They shall fall before thee with their
faces flat upon the earth, and lick
up the dust of thy feet, that
thou mayest know how
that I am the Lord."
(Isaiah 49:23)

"If God
promise riches, the way
thereto is poverty. Whom he
loveth, him he chasteneth; whom
he exalteth, he casteth down; whom
he saveth, he damneth first. He bringeth
no man to heaven, except he send him to hell
first. If he promise life, he slayeth first; when he
buildeth, he casteth all down first. He is no patcher
and cannot build on another man's foundations. He
will not work until all be past remedy, and brought
unto such a case, that men may see how that his
hand, his power, his mercy, his goodness and
truth, hath wrought altogether. He will let
no man be partaker with him of his
praise and glory. His works are
wonderful, and contrary
unto man's works."

March 6

"Whoso
listeth to love life,
and to see good days,
let him refrain his tongue
from evil, and his lips, that
they speak not guile. Let him
eschew evil and do good. Let
him seek peace, and ensue it.
For the eyes of the Lord are
over the righteous, and
his ears are open unto
their prayers."
(1 Peter 3:10-12)

"Let a man's
wife make herself a
sister of the chatter house,
and answer her husband, when he
bids her hold her peace. My brethren
keep silence for me, and see whether she
shall so escape. And be thou sure that God
is more jealous over His commandments
than man is over his, or than any
man is over his wife."

March 7

"All things
are given unto me
of my Father. And no
man knoweth the Son, but
thy Father, neither knoweth any
man the Father, save the Son, and
he to whom the Son will open
him. Come unto me, all ye
that labor, and are laden,
and I will ease you."
(Matthew 11:27-28)

"When I translated the New
Testament, unto the latter end I added
an epistle, in the which I desired them that
were learned to amend if ought were found
amiss. But our malicious and wily hypocrites,
which are so stubborn and hard hearted in their
wicked abominations that it is not possible for
them to amend anything at all, say that it is
impossible to translate the scripture into
English; some, that it is not lawful
for the lay people to have it
in their mother tongue."

March 8

"Who
told thee that thou
wast naked? Hast thou
eaten of the tree of which
I bade thee that thou
shouldest not eat?"
(Genesis 3:11)

"What prayers pray our
clergy for us, which stop us
and exclude us from Christ, and
seek all the means possible to keep us
from knowledge of Christ? They compel
us to hire friars, monks, nuns, canons, and
priests, and to buy their abominable merits,
and to hire the saints that are dead to pray for
us. For the very saints have they made hirelings
also, because that their offerings come to their
profit. What pray all those? That we might
come to the knowledge of Christ, as the
apostles did? Nay, For it is plain case,
that all they which enforce to keep
us from Christ, pray not that
we might come to the
knowledge of him."

March 9

"And the kings
of the earth, and the
great men, and the rich men
and the chief captains, and the
mighty men, and every bondman, and
every free man, hid themselves in dens,
and in rocks of the hills, and said to the
hills, and rocks: Fall on us, and hide
us from the presence of him that
sitteth on the seat, and from
the wrath of the lamb."
(Revelation 6:15-16)

"Whosoever
ascribeth eternal life unto the
deserving and merit of works, must
fall in one of two inconveniences: either
must he be a blind Pharisee, not seeing
that the law is spiritual and he carnal,
and look and rejoice in the outward
shining of his deeds, despising
the weak, and, in respect
of them, justify himself;
or else he must needs
despair."

March 10

"Make
thy tent
wider, and
spread out the
hangings of thine
habitation. Spare not,
lay forth thy cords, and
make fast thy stakes."
(Isaiah 54:2)

"If we resist evil rulers, we shall,
no doubt, bring ourselves into more evil
bondage, and wrap ourselves in much more
misery and wretchedness. Understand also, that
whatsoever thou doest unto them, be it good or bad,
thou doest unto God. When thou pleasest them, thou
pleasest God. When thou displeasest them, thou
displeasest God. When they are angry with
thee, God is angry with thee. Neither is it
possible for thee to come to the favor
of God again. No, though all the
angels of heaven pray for thee,
until thou have submitted
thyself unto thy father
and mother again."

March 11

"The
spirit of the Lord
spake in me, and his
words were on my tongue.
The God of Israel spake unto
me, and the strength of Israel said:
He that beareth rule over men, he that
ruleth justly in the fear of God. And he
shall be as the morning light, when the
sun shineth in a morning in which are
no clouds to let the brightness, and
as the grass of the earth is by
the virtue of the rain."
(2 Samuel 23:-2-4)

"Evangelion,
which we call the
Gospel, is a Greek word that
signifies good, merry, glad
and joyful tidings - tidings
that make a man's heart
glad and make him
sing, dance, and
leap for joy."

March 12

"And the
very same made some
apostles, some prophets, some
evangelists, some shepherds, some
teachers; that the saints might have
all things necessary to work and minister
withal, to the edifying of the body of Christ,
till we every each one grow up unto a perfect
man, after the measure of age which is in the
fullness of Christ. That we henceforth be no
more children wavering and carried with
every wind of doctrine, by the wiliness
of men and craftiness, whereby they
lay a wait for us to deceive us."
(Ephesians 4:11-14)

"Deacon, priest, bishop,
cardinal, and pope be names of
offices and service, or should be, and
not sacraments. There is no promise
coupled therewith. If they minister
their offices truly, it is a sign that
Christ's Spirit is in them. If not,
that the devil is in them."

March 13

"Ye shall
hear of wars,
and of the noise of
wars, but see that ye be
not troubled, for all these
things must come to pass, but
the end is not yet. For nation shall
rise against nation, and realm against
realm, and there shall be pestilence,
and hunger, and earthquakes in
all quarters. All these are the
beginning of sorrows."
(Matthew 24:6-8)

"Thy deeds testify
what thou art, and certify thy
conscience that thou art received to
mercy, and sanctified in Christ's
passions and sufferings, and
shalt hereafter, with all
them that follow God,
receive the reward
of eternal
life."

March 14

"Then
answered
Jesus and said unto
them: Verily, verily, I say
unto you, the son can do
no thing of himself, but
that he seeth the father
do. For whatsoever he
doeth, that doeth
the son also."
(John 5:19)

"The
morality of
clean blood ought to
be one of the first lessons
taught us by our pastors and
teachers. The physical is the
substratum of the spiritual,
and this fact ought to give
to the food we eat, and
the air we breathe,
a transcendent
significance."

March 15

"See
that ye love
not the world,
neither the things
that are in the world.
If any man love the world,
the love of the Father is not in
him. For all that is in the world
(as the lust of the flesh, the lust of
the eyes, and the pride of goods) is
not of the Father, but of the world.
And the world vanisheth away,
and the lust thereof; but he
that fulfilleth the will of
God, abideth ever."
(1 John 2:15-17)

"Moreover the rich,
and they that have wisdom
with them, must see the poor set
a-work, that as many as are able may
feed themselves with the labor of their
own hands, according to the scripture
and commandment of God."

March 16

"Then shall they also answer him saying: Master, when saw we thee an hungered, or a thirst, or harborless, or naked, or sick, or in prison, and have not ministered unto thee? Then shall he answer them and say: Verily I say unto you, in as much as ye did it not to one of the least of these, ye did it not to me."
(Matthew 25:44-45)

"Christ threateneth them that forsake him, for whatsoever cause it be, whether for fear, either for shame, either for loss of honor, friends, life, or goods. In Mark 8, he saith: Whosoever is ashamed of me, or of my words, among this adulterous and sinful generation, of him shall the Son of Man be ashamed when he cometh in the glory of his Father with his holy angels."

March 17

"Watch and pray,
that ye fall not into
temptation. The spirit
is willing, but the
flesh is weak."
(Matthew 26:41)

"We take heart from
Tyndale's success against the
odds, and we recognize that there
is victory even in losing battles. The
courage I speak of is to have a new hope
and a renewed desire to continue the work
and push through to the very end, and trust, as
he trusted, that God will provide, even if it is left
to others to continue the task. Let not your hearts be
troubled. Work as you have never worked before, aspire
as you have never aspired before, and risk as you have
never risked before, as long as you have days left you.
And if you dare to trust God as Tyndale did, then
He will see you through the work, and the trial,
and if it becomes necessary, the burning. Or,
as vernacular English would put it, to the
bitter end." (Gordon Jackson).

March 18

"There are
many disobedient,
and talkers of vanity, and
deceivers of minds, namely
they of the circumcision, whose
mouths must be stopped, which
pervert whole houses, teaching
things which they ought not,
because of filthy lucre."
(Titus 1:10-11)

"They preach
also that the wagging of the
bishop's hand over us blesseth us, and
putteth away our sins. If the wagging of the
bishop's hand over me be so precious a thing
in the sight of God that I am thereby blessed,
how then am I full blessed with all spiritual
blessing in Christ? Or if my sins be full
done away in Christ, how remaineth
there any to be done away by such
fantasies? The apostles knew
no ways to put away sin,
or to bless us, but by
preaching Christ."

March 19

"When they heard
this, they were pricked
in their hearts, and said unto
Peter, and unto the other apostles:
Ye men and brethren, what shall we
do? Peter said unto them: Repent and
be baptized every one of you in the
name of Jesus Christ, for the
remission of sins, and ye
shall receive the gift of
the Holy Ghost."
(Acts 2:37-38)

"So
was it
the manner
to call Peter chief
of the Apostles for
his singular activity
and boldness, and not
that he should be lord
over his brethren,
contrary to his
doctrine."

March 20

"I am the vine, and
ye are the branches. He
that abideth in me, and I
in him, the same bringeth
forth much fruit. For
without me can ye
do nothing."
(John 15:5)

"Every soul that beareth
fruit in Christ shall be purged of
the Father to bear more fruit day by
day, not in the pope's purgatory, where no
man feeleth it, but here in this life such fruit as is
unto his neighbour's profit; so that he which hath
his hope in Christ purgeth himself here, as Christ
is pure, and ever yet the blood of Jesus only doth
purge us of all our sins, for the imperfectness of
our works. The forgiveness of sins is to remit
mercifully the pain that I have deserved. I
do believe that the pain that I suffer here
in my flesh is to subdue my body,
that I might serve my neighbour,
and not to make satisfaction
unto God for my sins."

March 21

"My soul
abideth only
upon God, for he is
my God. He only is my
strength, my salvation, my
defense, so that I shall not fall.
In God is my health, my glory, my
might, and in God is my trust. O put
your trust in him always, pour out
your hearts before him, for God is
our hope. As for men, they are
but vain; men are deceitful.
Upon the weights, they
are altogether lighter
than vanity itself."
(Psalms 62:5-9)

"By grace, I understand
the favor of God, and the gifts
and working of his Spirit, as love,
kindness, patience, obedience,
mercifulness, despising of
worldly things, peace,
concord, and such."

March 22

"Put on tender mercy, kindness, humbleness of mind, meekness, long suffering, forbearing one another, and forgiving one another, if any man have a quarrel to another. Even as Christ forgave you, even so do ye. Above all these things, put on love, which is the bond of perfectness, and the peace of God rule in your hearts, to the which peace ye are called in one body. And see that ye be thankful."
(Colossians 3:12-15)

"Bodily service must be done to man in God's stead. We must give obedience, honor, toll, tribute, custom, and rent unto whom they belong. Then, if thou have ought more to bestow, give unto the poor, which are left here in Christ's stead, that we show mercy on them."

March 23

"Therefore, brethren,
stand fast and keep the
ordinations which ye have
learned, whether it were by our
preaching, or by our pistel. Our Lord
Jesus Christ himself, and God our Father,
which hath loved us, and hath given us
everlasting consolation, and good
hope through grace, comfort your
hearts, and establish you in all
saying, and good doing."
(2 Thessalonians 2:15-17)

"I am fellow with Paul, and joint
heir with him, of all the promises of God, and
God's truth heareth my prayer as well as Paul's. I
also now could not but love Paul, and wish him good,
and pray for him, that God would strengthen him in
his temptations and give him victory, as he would
do for me. Nevertheless, in the congregation
there are many with weak and young
consciences which they who have
the office to preach, ought to
teach, and not deceive."

March 24

"In your
faith, minister virtue,
and in virtue knowledge,
and in knowledge temperancy,
and in temperancy patience, in patience
godliness, in godliness brotherly kindness,
in brotherly kindness love. For if these things
be among you, and are plenteous, they will
make you that ye neither shall be idle
nor unfruitful unto the knowledge
of our Lord Jesus Christ."
(2 Peter 1:5-8)

"When we come
first to faith, then Christ
forgiveth us and blesseth us. If a
man repent truly, and come to faith,
and put his trust in Christ, then as oft as he
sinneth of frailty, at the sigh of the heart is his
sin put away in Christ's blood. For Christ's blood
purgeth ever and blesseth ever. For yet have we
an Advocate with the Father, Jesus Christ
which is righteous, and he is it that
obtaineth grace for our sins."

March 25

"It goeth
with the righteous
as with the ungodly;
with the good and clean as
with the unclean; with him that
offereth as with him that offereth
not; like as it goeth with the
virtuous, so goeth it also
with the sinner."
(Ecclesiastes 9:2)

"Persecution and
tyranny maketh the righteous
feel the working of God's Spirit in
them, that their faith is unfeigned. I
say that no man is so great a sinner, if he
repent and believe, but that he is righteous in
Christ and in the promises. Yet if thou look on
the flesh and unto the law, there is no man
so perfect that is not found a sinner, nor
any man so pure that he hath not
somewhat yet to be purged.
This shall suffice at this
time, as concerning
obedience."

March 26

"God, it is thou that
hast made heaven and earth
with thy great power and high arm,
and there is nothing too hard for thee.
Thou shewest mercy upon thousands, thou
recompensest the wickedness of the fathers,
into the bosom of the children that come
after them. Thou art the great and
mighty God, whose name is
the Lord of Hosts."
(Jeremiah 32:17-18)

"How shall they believe
that hear not? And how shall
they hear without a preacher? For look
on the promises of God, and so are all our
preachers dumb, or if they preach them, they
so sauce them and leaven them, that no stomach
can brook them, nor find any savor in them.
For they paint us such an ear-confession
as is impossible to be kept, and more
impossible that it should stand
with the promises and
testament of God."

March 27

"See thou have the
example of the wholesome words
which thou heardest of me, in faith and
love which is in Jesus Christ. That good
thing which was committed to thy
keeping, keep in the Holy Ghost
which dwelleth in us."
(2 Timothy 1:13-14)

"What
shall make us
love? Verily, that shall
faith do. If thou behold how
much God loveth thee in Christ, and
from what vengeance he hath delivered
thee for his sake, and of what kingdom he
hath made thee heir, then shalt thou see cause
enough to love thy very enemy without respect
of reward, either in this life or in the life to
come, but because that God will so have
it, and Christ hath deserved it. Yet
thou shouldest feel in thine heart
that all thy deeds to come are
abundantly recompensed
already in Christ."

March 28

"And
Israel stretched
out his right hand
and laid it upon Ephraim's
head which was the younger,
and his left hand upon Manasse's
head, crossing his hands, for
Manasse was the elder."
(Genesis 48:14)

"It was the
Holy Ghost who
commanded the Apostles to
separate Paul and Barnabas to
go and preach. Then they fasted
and prayed, and put their hands
on their heads, and prayed for
them, that God would go with
them, and strength them, and
courage them also, bidding
them to be strong in God,
and to warn them to be
faithful and diligent
in the work of
God."

March 29

"I thank him that hath made me
strong in Christ Jesus our Lord, for he
counted me true, and put me in office, when
before I was a blasphemer, and a persecuter,
and a tyrant. Nevertheless, I obtained mercy
because I did it ignorantly, in unbelief.
But the grace of our Lord was more
abundant, with faith and love,
which is in Christ Jesus."
(1 Timothy 1:12-14)

"The
judgment
of him that hath
no lust to hear the
truth, is to hear lies,
and to be established and
grounded therein through
false miracles. And he that
will not see, is worthy to
be blind; and he that
biddeth the Spirit of
God go from him,
is worthy to be
without it."

March 30

"From that time,
many of his disciples
went away from him, and
companied no more with him. Then
said Jesus to the twelve: Will ye also
go away? Simon Peter answered him:
Master to whom shall we go? Thou
hast words of eternal life, and we
have believed and known that
thou art Christ, the Son of
the Living God."
(John 6:66-69)

"Man's wisdom is plain
idolatry. Neither is there any other
idolatry than to imagine of God after man's
wisdom. God is not man's imagination, but that
only which he saith of himself. God is nothing
but his law and his promises; that is to say,
that which he biddeth thee to do, and
that which he biddeth thee believe
and hope. God is but his word,
as Christ saith, my words
are spirit and life."

March 31

"And I, John,
saw that holy city new
Jerusalem come down from
God out of heaven prepared as a bride
garnished for her husband. And I heard a
great voice from the throne, saying: Behold, the
tabernacle of God is with men, and he will dwell
with them. And they shall be his people, and God
himself shall be with them and be their God. And
God shall wipe away all tears from their eyes.
And there shall be no more death, neither
sorrow, neither crying, neither shall
there be any more pain, for the
old things are gone."
(Revelation 21:2-4)

"If God's
word bear record
that I say truth, why
should any man doubt
but that the Father of
truth and of light,
hath sent
me."

"The lost sheep
of the house of Israel"
(Matthew 10:6)

April 1

"Ye shall not think,
that I am come to disannul
the law, other the prophets. No,
I am not come to disannul them,
but to fulfil them. For truly I say
unto you, till heaven and earth
perish, one jot or one tittle of
the law shall not scape,
till all be fulfilled."
(Matthew 5:17-18)

"Tyndale would have
had difficulty saying when
the holy muse was speaking and when
his own DNA was at work. The word of God
and the word of man seem to have coincided in a
perfect partnership so that the word of the divine and
of the poet were simultaneous, when righteousness
and truth kissed each other. I would still imagine,
however, that had Tyndale lived, he would have
continued to revise his New Testament; but
there are some passages, some phrases,
some words, that he would never
have dared to tamper with."
(Gordon Jackson)

April 2

"We have
heard say no doubt
that there are some which walk
among you inordinately, and work
not at all, but are busybodies. Them
that are such, we command and exhort
in the name of our Lord Jesus Christ,
that they work with quietness, and
eat their bread. Brethren, be not
weary in well doing."
(2 Thessalonians 3:11-13)

"As faith
entereth, the power
of God looseth the heart
from the captivity and bondage
under sin, and knitteth him to God,
and coupleth him to his will. It altereth
him, changeth him clean, fashioneth, and
forgeth him anew; giveth him power to
love, and to do that which before was
impossible for him either to love
or do; and turneth him unto
a new nature."

April 3

"Come to the waters, all ye
that be thirsty, and ye that have no
money. Come, buy, that ye may have to
eat. Come, buy wine and milk, without any
money, or money worth. Wherefore do ye lay
out your money for the thing that feedeth not,
and spend your labour about the thing that
satisfieth you not? Hearken rather unto
me, and ye shall eat of the best, and
your soul shall have her pleasure
in plenteousness."
(Isaiah 55:1-2)

"May an increase of
knowledge be with thee and
with all that call on the name of
the Lord with a pure conscience.
Let it not make thee despair, neither
yet discourage thee, O reader, that it
is forbidden thee in pain of life and
goods, or that it is made breaking
of the king's peace, or treason
unto his highness, to read the
word of thy soul's health."

April 4

"All
scripture given
by inspiration of God
is profitable to teach, to
improve, to inform, and
instruct in righteousness,
that the man of God may
be perfect, and prepared
unto all good works."
(2 Timothy 3:16-17)

"God's
word through
faith bringeth the Spirit
into our hearts and also life.
The word also purgeth us and
cleanseth us. Christ is our peace, our
redemption or ransom for our sins, our
righteousness and satisfaction. And
we, for the great and infinite love
which God hath to us in Christ,
love him again, love also
his laws, and love
one another."

April 5

"They shall see his face,
and his name shall be in their
foreheads. And there shall be no
more night there, and they need
no candle, neither light of the
sun, for the Lord God giveth
them light, and they shall
reign for evermore."
(Revelation 22:4-5)

"Washing
alone helpeth not, but
through the word it purifieth and
cleanseth us, as thou readest how Christ
cleanseth the congregation in the fountain of
water through the word. The word is the promise
that God hath made. Now, as a preacher, in preaching
the word of God, sayeth that the hearers believe, so doth
the washing, in that it preacheth and representeth unto
us the promise that God hath made unto us in Christ.
Washing comfirmeth that we are cleansed. Christ's
blood-shedding was a satisfaction for the sin
of all that repent and believe, who
submit themselves unto the
will of God."

April 6

"The people which sat in
darkness saw great light."
(Matthew 4:16)

"A
translator
hath great need
to study well the
sense both before and
after, and then also he hath
need to live a clean life and be
full devout in prayers, and have
not his wit occupied about worldly
things, that the Holy Spirit, author of all
wisdom and knowledge and truth, dress him
for his work and suffer him not to err. By this
manner, with good living and great travail,
men can come to true and clear translating,
and true understanding of holy writ, seem
it ever so hard at the beginning. God grant
to us all grace to know well, and to keep
well holy writ, and to suffer joyfully
some pain for it at the last." (John
Purvey, a contemporary of
William Tyndale).

April 7

"I pray
that the God of
our Lord Jesus Christ
and the Father of glory
might give unto you the spirit
of wisdom, and open to you the
knowledge of himself, and lighten the
eyes of your minds, that ye might know
what thing that hope is, whereunto he hath
called you, and how glorious the riches of his
inheritance is upon the saints, and what is the
exceeding greatness of his power to usward,
which believe according to the working
of that his mighty power, which he
wrought in Christ when he raised
him from death and set him on
his right hand in heavenly
things, above all rule,
power, and might."
(Ephesians 1:17-20)

"Let every man, of whatsoever craft or
occupation he be of, serve his brethren."

April 8

"Preach the Gospel to all
creatures. Whosoever believeth, and is
baptized, shall be safe, and whosoever that
believeth not, shall be damned. And these signs
shall follow them that believe: In my name they shall
cast out devils, and shall speak with new tongues,
and shall kill serpents. And if they drink any
deadly thing, it shall not hurt them. They
shall lay their hands on the sick,
and they shall recover."
(Mark 16:15-18)

"The
priest, before
he baptizeth, asketh,
saying: 'Believest thou in
God, the Father Almighty, and
in his Son Jesus Christ, and in the
Holy Ghost, and that the congregation
of Christ is holy?' They say: 'Yea.' Then
the priest upon this faith, baptizeth the
child in the name of the Father, and
of the Son, and of the Holy Ghost,
for the forgiveness of sins."

April 9

"And his heart did melt upon them, and he healed of them those that were sick."
(Matthew 14:14)

"A Christian man
is but a passive thing,
a thing that suffereth only,
and doth nought, as the sick, in
respect of the surgeon or physician,
doth but suffer only. The surgeon lanceth
and cutteth out the dead flesh, searcheth the
wounds, seareth, burneth, seweth or stitcheth,
and layeth to caustics, to draw out the corruption,
and, last of all, layeth to healing plaisters, and maketh
it whole. The physician likewise giveth purgations and
drinks to drive out the disease, and then with restoratives
bringeth health. If the sick resist the razor, the searching
iron, and so forth, doth he not resist his own health and
is cause of his own death? So likewise is it if we resist
evil rulers, which are the rod and scourge wherewith
God castiseth us; the instruments wherewith God
searcheth our wounds; and bitter drinks to drive
out the sin and to make it appear, and caustics
to draw out by the roots the core of the pocks
of the soul that fretteth inward."

April 10

"I saw the Lord sitting upon
an high and glorious seat, and
his train filled the palace. From above
flakerd the Seraphims, where of every one
had six wings. With twain each covered his
face, with twain his feet, and with twain
did he fly. They cried also each one to
other on this manner: Holy, holy,
holy, is the Lord of Hosts."
(Isaiah 6:1-3)

"To see inwardly
that the law of God is
spiritual and to hunger and thirst
after strength to do the will of God
from the ground of the heart, and to
cleave yet to the promises of God, and to
believe that for Christ's blood sake thou art
received to the inheritance of eternal life, is a
wonderful thing the world knoweth not of.
But whosoever feeleth that, though he
fall a thousand times in a day, doth
yet rise again a thousand times,
and is sure that the mercy
of God is upon him."

April 11

"We
labor and suffer
rebuke, because we
believe in the living God,
which is the Saviour of all
men, but specially of those
that believe. Such things
command and teach."
(1 Timothy 4:10-11)

"Therefore,
have I delectation
in infirmities, in rebukes,
in need, in persecutions, and
in anguish for Christ's sake, for
when I am weak, then am I strong.
The weakness of the flesh is the strength
of the Spirit. And by flesh, understand wit,
wisdom, and all that is in a man before the
Spirit of God come, and whatsoever
springeth not of the Spirit of God,
or of God's word. And of
like testimonies is all
the scripture
full."

April 12

"Whosoever
shall say, Thou
fool, shall be in
danger of hell fire."
(Matthew 5:22)

"If the
sacraments
justify as they
say, I understand by
justifying, forgiveness
of sins. Then do they wrong
unto the sacraments, inasmuch as
they rob the most part of them, through
confession, of their effect, and of the cause
wherefore they were ordained. For no man
may receive the body of Christ, no man may
marry, no man may be oiled or anoiled as
they call it, no man may receive orders,
except he be first shriven. Now if
the sins be forgiven by shrift
aforehand, there would be
nought left for the
sacraments
to do."

April 13

"A new
commandment
I write unto you: He that
saith how that he is in the light,
and yet hateth his brother, is in
darkness even until this time.
He that loveth his brother,
abideth in the light, and
there is none occasion
of evil in him."
(1 John 2:8-10)

"I am
bound to love the
Turk with all my might and
power; yea, and above my power,
even from the ground of my heart, after
the ensample that Christ loved me, neither
to spare goods, body, or life, to win him to
Christ. And what can I do more for thee,
if thou gavest me all the world? If
I see need, there can I not but
pray, if God's Spirit
be in me."

April 14

"And seeing also
that we have an high priest
which is ruler over the house of God, let
us draw nye with a true heart in a full faith
sprinkled in our hearts, from an evil conscience,
and washed in our bodies with pure water, and let
us keep the profession of our hope, without wavering,
for he is faithful that promised. And let us consider
one another to provoke unto love, and to good
works. And let us not forsake the fellowship
that we have among ourselves, as the
manner of some is, but let us exhort
one another, and that so much
the more, because ye see that
the day draweth nye."
(Hebrews 10:21-25)

"A forgiveness of
sins comes not by any
deservings of our deeds, but
by faith, or by believing the
promises of God, and
by the merits of
Christ only."

April 15

"And he took
bread, gave thanks,
and brake it, and gave
it unto them, saying: This is
my body which is given for you.
This do in the remembrance of me.
Likewise also, when they had supped,
He took the cup saying: This is the
cup, the New Testament, in my
blood, which shall for
you be shed."
(Luke 22:19-20)

"Christ
ordained the
sacrament to be
a perpetual memory
that his body was broken
for our sins upon the cross,
that all that repent should
receive, as often as they
eat of it, forgiveness
of sin through
faith."

April 16

"Blessed are they which suffer persecution for righteousness sake, for theirs is the kingdom of heaven. Blessed are ye when men revile you, and persecute you, and shall falsely say all manner of evil sayings against you for my sake. Rejoice, and be glad, for great is your reward in heaven. For so persecuted they the prophets which were before your days."
(Matthew 5:10-12)

"Knowledge maketh thee safe, that is, it declareth that thou art safe already, certifieth thine heart, and maketh thee feel that thy faith is right, and that God's Spirit is in thee, as all other good works do. For if, when it cometh unto the point, thou hadst no lust to work, nor power to confess, how couldest thou presume to think that God's Spirit were in thee?"

April 17

"When ye be come over
Jordan unto the land which the
Lord thy God giveth thee, set up
great stones…and write upon them
all the words of this law, when thou art
come over, that thou mayst come into
the land which the Lord thy God
giveth thee, a land that floweth
with milk and honey, as the
Lord God of thy fathers
hath promised thee."
(Deuteronomy 27:2-3)

"If thou hast done thy duty to thine
household and hast an abundance of the
blessings of God, that owest to the poor
that cannot labor, or would labor and can
get no work, and are destitute of friends.
If thy neighbors which thou knowest be
served, and thou yet have superfluity,
and hearest necessity to be among
the brethren a thousand miles
off, to them art thou
a debtor."

April 18

"Where two or three are gathered
together in my name, there am
I in the middes of them."
(Matthew 18:20)

"Christ was
poor, to make
other men rich, and
bound, to make others free.
He left also with His disciples
the law of love. Now love seeketh
not her own profit, but her neighbor's.
The spirituality (the clergy), therefore, are
condemned by all the laws of God, who through
falsehood and disguised hypocrisy have sought
so great profit, so great riches, so great authority
and so great liberties, and have so beggared the
laymen, and so brought them into subjection
and bondage, and so despised them, that
they have set up franchises in all towns
and villages, for whosoever robs,
murders, or slays them, and
even for traitors unto the
king's person
also."

April 19

"First cast
out the beam out
of thine own eye, and
then shalt thou see clearly
to pluck out the mote out
of thy brother's eye."
(Matthew 7:5)

"It began at Abel, hath
ever since continued, and shall, I
doubt not, until the last day. And the
hypocrites have always the world on their
side. They had the rulers of the Jews on their
side; they had Pilate and the emperor's power on
their side; they had Herod also on their side. Moreover
they brought all their worldly wisdom to pass, and all
that they could think, or imagine, to serve for their
purpose. They excommunicated all that believed
in him, and put them out of the temple. They
found the means to have him condemned
by the emperor's power, and made it
treason to Caesar to believe in him.
They obtained to have him
hanged as a thief or
a murderer."

April 20

"If the gentiles,
which have no law, do of
nature the things contained in the
law, then they having no law, are a law
unto themselves, which shew the deed of
the law written in their hearts. While their
conscience beareth witness unto them,
and also their thoughts, accusing
one another, or excusing at the
day when God shall judge
the secrets of men."
(Romans 2:14-16)

"Christ's
kingdom is
altogether spiritual,
and the bear of rule in it is
clean contrary unto the bear
of rule temporally. Wherefore,
none may have any temporal
jurisdiction, or minister a
temporal office that
requires violence
to compel
withal."

April 21

"Preach the word,
be fervent, be it in season, or out of
season. Improve, rebuke, exhort with all long
suffering. For the time will come, when they will
not suffer wholesome doctrine, but after their own
lusts shall they whose ears itch get them an heap
of teachers, and shall turn their ears from the
truth, and shall be given unto fables. But
watch thou in all things, and suffer
adversity, and do the work of an
evangelist. Fulfil thine office
unto the utmost."
(2 Timothy 4:2-5)

"If
I see my
brother sin, I
may between him
and me rebuke him, and
damn his deed by the law of
God. I may also comfort him
with the promises of God,
and save him if he
believes."

April 22

"Ye serpents
and generation of vipers,
how shall ye scape the damnation
of hell? Wherefore, behold, I send unto
you, prophets, wise men, and scribes, and
of them some shall ye kill and crucify,
and some shall ye scourge in your
synagogues, and persecute
from city to city."
(Matthew 23:33-34)

"Repentance and faith begin at our
baptism, and when we first profess the
laws of God. They continue unto our life's
end, and grow as we grow in the Spirit, for the
more perfect we are, the greater is our repentance
and the stronger our faith. And thus, as the Spirit and
doctrine on God's part, and repentance and faith on our
part, beget us anew in Christ, they also make us grow
ever more perfect and save us unto the end, and
never leave us until all sin be put off and we
are clean purified and full formed and
fashioned after the similitude and
likeness of the perfection of
our Savior Jesus."

April 23

"Let us keep our profession.
For we have not an high priest
which cannot have compassion on
our infirmities, but was in all points
tempted in like manner, but yet without
sin. Let us, therefore, go boldly unto the seat
of grace, that we may receive mercy, and
find grace to help in time of need."
(Hebrews 4:14-16)

"The gifts
of grace are given to
him as much to do his brother
service as for himself, and as much
for the love God has for the weak as for
him to whom God has given such gifts. And
whosoever withdraws anything he has from his
neighbor's need, robs his neighbor and is a thief.
And he that is proud of the gifts of God and by
reason of them thinks himself better than his
feeble neighbor, and does not rather (as the
truth is) acknowledge himself to be, by
reason of them, a servant to his poor
neighbor, has Lucifer's spirit in
him, and not Christ's."

April 24

"Hear Israel,
the Lord thy God
is Lord only, and thou
shalt love the Lord thy God
with all thine heart, with all thy
soul and with all thy might. And
these words which I command
thee this day shall be in thine
heart and thou shalt whet
them on thy children."
(Deuteronomy 6:4-7)

"What should
be the cause that we,
which walk in the broad
day, should not see as well
as they that walked in the night,
or that we should not see as well at
noon, as they did in the twilight?
Came Christ to make the world
more blind? By this means,
Christ is the darkness
of the world, and
not the light."

April 25

"Nevertheless,
the people that have
dwelt in darkness, shall see
a great light. As for them that
dwell in the land of the shadow
of death, upon them shall
the light shine."
(Isaiah 9:2)

"I would have
thought no one so blind as
to have to ask why light should be
shown to them who walk in darkness. Nor
would I have thought any man would be so
malicious that he would begrudge another
so necessary a thing, or so mad as to assert
that good is the natural cause of evil, and
that darkness proceeds out of light, and
that lying is grounded in truth and
verity. I would think he would
assert the very contrary, that
light destroys darkness
and truth reproves
all manner of
lying."

April 26

"Let no filthy
communication proceed out of
your mouths, but that which is good to
edify withal, when need is, that it may have
favor with the hearers. And grieve not the Holy
Spirit of God, by whom ye are sealed unto the day
of redemption. Let all bitterness, fierceness and
wrath, roaring and cursed speaking, be put
away from you, with all maliciousness.
Be ye courteous one to another, be
merciful, forgiving one another,
even as God for Christ's
sake forgave you."
(Ephesians 4:29-32)

"The prayer of
faith, and the deeds
thereof that spring of love,
are accepted before God. The
prayer is good, according to
the proportion of faith, and
the deed, according to
the measure of
love."

April 27

"God
himself our
Father, and our Lord
Jesus Christ, guide our
journey unto you, and the
Lord increase you, and make
you flow over in love one
toward another, and
toward all men."
(1 Thessalonians 3:11-12)

"When we have the
assurance that we are beloved sons
and heirs with Christ, and have God's
Spirit in us, the consent of our hearts is unto
the law of God. Which law is all perfection, and
the mark whereat we ought to shoot. And he that
hitteth that mark, so that he fulfilleth the law with all
his heart, soul, and might, and with full love and
lust, without all let or resistance, is pure gold,
and needeth not to be put any more in the
fire. He is straight and right; he is full
fashioned like Christ, and can have
no more added unto him."

April 28

"And
they brought that
which Moses commanded
before the tabernacle of
the congregation."
(Leviticus 9:5)

"Let us
see the pith of
a ceremony or two, to
judge thereby. In conjuring
of holy water, they believe that
whosoever be sprinkled therewith may
receive health as well of body as of soul.
And likewise in making holy bread, and so
forth in the conjurations of other ceremonies.
Now we see by daily experience, that half
their prayer is unheard. For no man
receiveth health of body thereby.
No more do they of soul. Yea,
we see also by experience,
that no man receiveth
health of soul
thereby."

April 29

"And
there was great
battle in heaven. Michael
and his angels fought with the
dragon and the dragon fought and his
angels, and prevailed not, neither was
their place found any more in heaven.
And the great dragon, that old serpent
called the devil and Sathanas, was
cast out, which deceiveth all the
world. And he was cast into
the earth, and his angels
were cast out also."
(Revelation 12:7-9)

"Antichrist bindeth
the angels, for we read of
popes that have commanded
the angels to fetch diverse
souls out of purgatory.
Howbeit, I am not yet
certified whether
they obeyed
or no."

April 30

"Unto you, it
is given to know the
mystery of the kingdom of
God. But unto them that
are without, shall all
things be done in
similitudes."
(Mark 4:11)

"Confession is
necessary unto all men
that will be saved. For Christ
saith: 'He that denieth me before
men, him will I deny before my Father
that is in heaven.' And of this confession,
saith the holy apostle Paul: 'The belief of the
heart justifieth, and to knowledge with the mouth
maketh a man safe.' This is a wonderful text for our
philosophers, or rather sophisters, our worldly-wise
enemies to the wisdom of God, our deep and
profound wells without water, our clouds
without moisture of rain; that is to say,
natural souls without the Spirit
of God and feeling of
godly things."

He is not here; he is risen.
Matthew (xxvi)

"He is not here: he is risen."
(Matthew 28:6)

May 1

"And I
saw an angel
fly in the middes
of heaven having an
everlasting Gospel to preach
unto them that sit and dwell on
the earth, and to all nations, kindreds,
and tongues, and people, saying with a
loud voice: Fear God and give honour to
him, for the hour of his judgment is
come. And worship him that made
heaven and earth and the sea,
and fountains of water."
(Revelation 14:6-7)

"Paul forbiddeth to speak in
the church or congregation, save in
the tongue that all understand. For the
layman thereby is not edified or taught.
How shall the layman say 'Amen' to thy
blessing or thanksgiving, when he
wotteth not what thou sayest?
He wotteth not whether
thou bless or curse."

May 2

"Woe be to you
scribes, and Pharisees,
hypocrites, for ye are like unto
painted tombs which appear
beautiful outwards, but
are within full of dead
men's bones and of
all filthiness."
(Matthew 23:27)

"The promises justify,
for they bring the Spirit, which
looseth the heart, giveth lust to the
law, and certifieth us of the good-will
of God. If we submit ourselves unto God,
and desire him to heal us, he will do it, and
will no more hate us, but pity us, cherish
us, be tender-hearted to us, and love
us as he doth Christ himself. Christ
is our Redeemer, Savior, peace,
atonement, and satisfaction,
and hath made amends for
all the sin which they that
repent do, have done,
or shall do."

May 3

"Above
all things, have
fervent love among you. For
love covereth the multitude of
sins. Be ye harbourous, and that
without grudging. As every man
hath received the gift, minister
the same one to another as
good ministers of the
manyfold grace
of God."
(1 Peter 4:7-10)

"A righteous
example I have set out for them in
various places, but their blind eyes have
no power to see it, for covetousness has so
blinded them. Faith alone justifies us, that is to
say, faith alone receives the mercy by which
God justifies us and forgives us. I do not
mean faith without repentance, and
faith without love for the laws of
God, and unto good works,
as wicked hypocrites
falsely accuse us."

May 4

"The day of the Lord shall
come even as a thief in the night. When
they shall say peace and no danger, then
cometh on them sudden destruction, as
the travailing of a woman with child,
and they shall not escape."
(1 Thessalonians 5:2-3)

"As for the saints, whose
prayer was, when they were
alive, that we might be grounded,
established, and strengthened in Christ
only, if it were of God that we should this wise
worship them, contrary unto their own doctrine,
I dare be bold to affirm, that by the means of their
prayers we should have been brought long ago unto
the knowledge of God and Christ again, though
that these beasts had done their worst to let
it. Let us therefore set our hearts at rest
in Christ and in God's promises, for
so I think it best, and let us take
the saints for an ensample
only, and let us do as
they both taught
and did."

May 5

"See that
ye be doers of the
word and not hearers only,
deceiving your own selves. For
if any hear the word, and do it not,
he is like unto a man that beholdeth his
bodily face in a glass. For as soon as he hath
looked on himself, he goeth his way, and hath
immediately forgotten what his fashion was.
But whosoever looketh in the perfect law
of liberty, and continueth therein (if
he be not a forgetful hearer, but a
doer of the work) he shall be
happy in his deed."
(James 1:22-25)

"The life of a Christian man is the consent of
the Spirit to the will and honor of God. His
honor is the final end of all good works.
Good works are all things that are
done within the laws of God, in
which he is honored, and
for which thanks are
given to him."

May 6

"Wherefore,
then, is thy clothing
red, and thy raiment like his
that treadeth in the winepress? I have
trodden the press myself alone, and of all
people, there was not one with me. Thus, have I
trodden down mine enemies in my wrath, and set
my feet upon them in my indignation. And their
blood sprang upon my clothes, and so have I
stained all my raiment. For that day of
vengeance that I have taken in
hand, and the year of my
deliverance is come."
(Isaiah 63:2-4)

"Whosoever avengeth himself
is damned in the deed-doing, and
falleth into the hands of the temporal
sword, because he taketh the office of God
upon him, and robbeth God of his most high
honor, in that he will not patiently abide
his judgment. When thou avengest
thyself, thou makest not peace,
but stirrest up more debate."

May 7

"But Ruth
said: Entreat me
not to leave thee, and to
return from after thee, for whither
thou goest, I will go, and where thou
dwellest, there I will dwell. Thy people
are my people, and thy God is my God.
Where thou diest, I will die, and there
will be buried. The Lord do so and
so to me, except that death
only depart thee and
me asunder."
(Ruth 1:16-17)

"The nearer unto Christ a man
cometh, the lower he must descend, and the
poorer he must wax. But the nearer unto the
pope ye come, the higher ye must climb, and
the more riches ye must gather however ye
can get them, to pay for your bulls, and
to purchase a glorious name and
license, to wear a mitre, and a
cross, a pall, and goodly
ornaments."

May 8

"He took on him
the shape of a servant, and
became like unto men, and was
found in his apparel as a man. He
humbled himself and became obedient
unto the death, even the death of the cross.
Wherefore, God hath exalted him, and given
him a name above all names, that in the
name of Jesus should every knee bow,
both of things in heaven, and things
in earth, and things under earth,
and that all tongues should
confess that Jesus Christ is
the Lord, unto the praise
of God the Father."
{Philippians 2:7-11}

"If I patiently suffer adversity for
conscience of God only, because I know
God and testify the truth, then am I sure that
God hath chosen me in Christ, and hath
put in me his Spirit as an earnest of
his promises, whose workings
I feel in my heart."

May 9

"These
things have
I spoken unto
you in proverbs. The
time will come when I
shall no more speak to you
in proverbs, but I shall show
you plainly from my Father.
At that day, shall ye ask
in mine name."
(John 16:25-26)

"The promises of God
have they either wiped clean
out, or thus leavened them with
open lies, to establish their confession
withal. And, to keep us from knowledge
of the truth, they do all thing in Latin. They
pray in Latin, they christen in Latin, they
bless in Latin, they give absolution in
Latin. Only curse they in the English
tongue, wherein they take upon
them greater authority than
ever God gave them."

May 10

"For many walk,
that they are the enemies of the
cross of Christ, whose end is damnation,
whose God is their belly and glory to their shame,
which are worldly minded. But our conversation is
in heaven, from whence we look for the Saviour
Jesus Christ, which shall change into another
fashion our vile bodies, that they may be
fashioned like unto his glorious body,
according to the working whereby
he is able to subdue all things
unto himself."
(Philippians 3:18-21)

"Princes are in God's
stead, and may not be resisted. Do they
ever so evil, they must be reserved unto the
wrath of God. Neverthelater, if they command to do
evil, we must then disobey, and say: 'We are otherwise
commanded of God.' But we are not to rise against them.
'They will kill us, then,' sayest thou. Therefore, I say,
is a Christian called to suffer even the bitter
death for his hope's sake, and because
he will do no evil."

May 11

"Walk worthy
of the Lord in all things
that please, being fruitful in
all good works and increasing in the
knowledge of God strengthened with all
might, through his glorious power, unto all
patience and long suffering, with joyfulness,
giving thanks unto the Father which hath
made us meet to be partakers of the
inheritance of saints in light."
(Colossians 1:10-12)

"Now, when we
obey patiently, and without
grudging, evil princes that oppress
us and persecute us, and are kind and
merciful to them that are merciless to us
and do the worst they can to us, and so
take all fortune patiently, and kiss
whatsoever cross God layeth
on our backs, then are we
sure that we keep the
commandments
of love."

May 12

"Understand
therefore in thine heart,
that as a man nurtureth his
son, even so the Lord thy
God nurtureth thee."
(Deuteronomy 8:5)

"He
promised
David a kingdom,
and immediately stirred
up king Saul against him to
persecute him, to tame him, to
meek him, to kill his lusts, to make
him merciful, to make him understand
that he was made king to minister and to
score his brethren, and that he should not
think that his subjects were made to
minister unto his lusts, and that it
were lawful for him to take
away from them life and
goods at his pleasure.
Oh, that our kings
were so nurtured
now-a-days!"

May 13

"Though
I be offered up
on your sacrifice and
of your serving of God in
the faith, I rejoice and rejoice
with you all. For the same
cause also, rejoice ye, and
rejoice ye with me."
(Philippians 2:17-18)

"Thou
must love Christ
above all things. But that
doest thou not, if thou be not
ready to forsake all for his sake.
If thou have forsaken all for his sake,
then art thou sure that thou lovest him.
Tribulation for righteousness is not
a blessing only, but also a gift that
God giveth unto none save his
special friends. The apostles
rejoiced that they were
counted worthy to
suffer rebuke for
Christ's sake."

May 14

"If thou be
oversene and
negligent in time
of need, then is thy
strength but small."
(Proverbs 24:10)

"He
promised the
children of Israel a
land with rivers of milk
and honey, but brought them
for the space of forty years into a
land where not only rivers of milk
and honey were not, but where so
much as a drop of water was not;
to nurture them, and to teach
them, as a father doth his son,
and to do them good at the
latter end, and that they
might be strong in their
spirit and souls, to use
his gifts and benefits
godly and after
his will."

May 15

"Likewise
must the deacons be
honest, not double tongued,
not given unto much drinking, neither
unto filthy lucre, but having the mystery of
the faith, in pure conscience. And let them first be
proved, and then let them minister, if they be found
faultless. Even so, must their wives be honest, not
evil speakers, but sober, and faithful in all things.
Let the deacons be the husbands of one wife and
such as rule their children well, and their own
households. For they that minister well, get
themselves good degree, and great liberty
in the faith, which is in Christ Jesus."
(1 Timothy 3:8-13)

"A deacon was
a servant or a minister
whose office was to help and
assist the priest, and to gather
up his duty, and to gather for
the poor of the parish, which
were destitute of friends,
and could not work."

May 16

"The
day of the Lord
will come as a thief
in the night, in the which
day the heavens shall perish
with terrible noise, and the
elements shall melt with
heat, and the earth with
the works that are
therein shall
burn."
(2 Peter 3:10)

"We speak
of the signs which
God hath ordained, that is
to say, of the sacraments
which Christ left among
us for our comfort, that
we may walk in light
and in truth, and in
feeling of the
power of
God."

May 17

"Submit yourselves to God, and
resist the devil, and he will fly from
you. Draw nye to God, and he will draw
nye to you. Cleanse your hands, ye sinners,
and purge your hearts, ye wavering minded.
Suffer afflictions. Sorrow ye and weep. Let your
laughter be turned to mourning, and your joy
to heaviness. Cast down yourselves before
the Lord, and he shall lift you up."
(James 4:7-10)

"St. Augustine made works
in defense of the word of God
against blasphemy, that thou mayest
see how that it is an old and accustomed thing
with the hypocrites, to wit God's word and the true
preachers of all the mischief which their lying doctrine
is the very cause of. After the preaching of God's word,
because it is not truly received, God sendeth great trouble
into the world, partly to avenge himself of the tyrants
and persecutors of his word, and partly to destroy
those worldly people which make of God's
word nothing but a cloak of their fleshly
liberty. They are not all good
that follow the Gospel."

May 18

"I am Alpha and
Omega, the beginning,
and the end. I will give to
him that is athirst of the well
of the water of life, free. He that
overcometh shall inherit all things,
and I will be his God, and
he shall be my son."
(Revelation 21:6-7)

"We are now ready to
suffer with Christ, and to lose
life and all for our very enemies,
to bring them unto Christ. Christ is the
cause why I love thee, why I am ready to do
the uttermost of my power for thee, and why I
pray for thee. Do, therefore, the worst thou canst
unto me; take away my goods, take away my good
name; yet as long as Christ remaineth in my heart, so
long I love thee not a whit the less, and so long art
thou as dear unto me as mine own soul, and so
long am I ready to do thee good for thine evil,
and so long I pray for thee with all my
heart. For Christ desireth it of me,
and hath deserved it of me."

May 19

"For
they shall bring
you up to the councils
and into the synagogues,
and ye shall be beaten, and
ye shall be brought before
rulers and kings, for my
sake, for a testimonial
unto them."
(Mark 13:9)

"Christ is our head, and God's word is
that wherein our life resteth. Therefore, to cleave
fast unto Christ, and unto those promises which God
hath made us for his sake, is our wisdom. 'Beware of
me,' saith he, 'for they shall deliver you up unto
their councils, and shall scourge you, and ye
shall be brought before rulers and kings
for my sake.' The brother shall betray,
or deliver, the brother to death,
and the father the son, and the
children shall rise against
father and mother,
and put them
to death."

May 20

"Husbands, love
your wives, even as Christ
loved the congregation…to make it
unto himself a glorious congregation
without spot, or wrinkle, or any such
thing; but that it should be holy
and without blame. So ought
men to love their wives
as their own bodies."
(Ephesians 5:25, 27-28)

"They call matrimony a
sacrament, because the scriptures
useth the similitude of matrimony to
express the marriage, or wedlock, that
is between us and Christ. For as a woman,
though she be never so poor, yet when she
is married, is as rich as her husband; even
so we, when we repent and believe the
promises of God in Christ, though
we be never so poor sinners,
yet are as rich as Christ;
all his merits are ours,
with all that he
hath."

May 21

"Unto me the
least of all saints
is this grace given, that
I should preach among the
gentiles the unsearchable riches
of Christ, and to give light to all men,
that they might know what is the fellowship
of the mystery, which from the beginning of the
world hath been hid in God which made all things
through Jesus Christ, to the intent that now unto the
rulers and powers in heaven might be known by
the congregation the manyfold wisdom of God,
according to that eternal purpose which he
purposed in Christ Jesus our Lord, by
whom we are bold to draw nye
in that trust, which we have
by faith on him."
(Ephesians 3:8-12)

"Tribulation is our
right baptism; and is signified
by plunging into the water. 'We that
are baptized in the name of Christ,' saith
Paul, 'are baptized to die with him.'"

May 22

"Him
being a ruler
and a Saviour hath
exalted with his right
hand, for to give repentance
to Israel and forgiveness
of sins. And we are his
records as concerning
these things."
(Acts 5:31-32)

"It is impossible to truly
believe, except a man repent, and
it is impossible to trust in the mercy that
is in Christ, or to feel it, but that a man must
immediately love God and his commandments,
and therefore disagree and disconsent unto the
flesh, and be at bate therewith, and fight against
it. And I feel that every soul that loveth the law,
and hateth his flesh, and believeth in Christ's
blood, hath his sins which he committed,
and pain which he deserved, in hating
the law and consenting unto his
flesh, forgiven him by
that faith."

May 23

"A bishop
must be…harbourous,
one that loveth goodness, of
honest behavior, righteous, holy,
temperate, and such as cleaveth
unto the true word of doctrine,
that he may be able to exhort
with wholesome learning,
and to improve them
that say against it."
(Titus 1:7)

"The office of a
bishop was a room, at the
beginning, that no man coveted,
and that no man durst take upon him,
save he only which loved Christ better
than his own life. For, as Christ saith, that
no man might be his disciple, except that
he were ready to forsake life and all,
even so might that officer be sure
that it would cost him his life
at one time or another, for
bearing record unto
the truth."

May 24

"Our
ableness
cometh of God,
which hath made us
able to minister the New
Testament, not of the letter,
but of the spirit. For the
letter killeth, but the
spirit giveth life."
(2 Corinthians 3:5-6)

"By
a priest,
then, in the
New Testament,
understand nothing
but an elder to teach the
younger, and to bring them
unto the full knowledge and
understanding of Christ, and to
minister the sacraments which
Christ ordained, which is
also nothing but to
preach Christ's
promises."

May 25

"Esdras opened the
book before all the people…
And when he opened it, all the
people stood up. And Esdras praised
the Lord, the great God. And all the people
answered, Amen, Amen, with their hands up,
and bowed themselves, and worshipped the
Lord with their faces to the ground."
(Nehemiah 8:5-6)

"Christ
saith that there shall
come false prophets in his
name, and say that they themselves
are Christ. That is, they shall so preach
Christ that men must believe in them, in their
holiness, and things of their imagination, without
God's word. Yea, and that Against-Christ, or Antichrist,
that shall come, is nothing but such false prophets, that shall
juggle with the scriptures and beguile the people with false
interpretations, as all the false prophets, scribes, and
Pharisees did in the Old Testament. How shall I
know whether ye are that Against Christ,
seeing ye will not let me know how
ye allege the scriptures?"

May 26

"Give the more
diligence for to make your
calling and election sure. For if ye
do such things, ye shall never err. Yea,
and by this means an entering in shall
be ministered unto you abundantly
into the everlasting kingdom
of our Lord and Saviour
Jesus Christ."
(2 Peter 1:10-11)

"Neither
needeth a Christian
man to run hither or thither, to
Rome, to Jerusalem, or St. James, or
any other pilgrimage near or far, to be
saved thereby, or to purchase forgiveness
of his sins. For a Christian man's health and
salvation is within him, even in his mouth.
If we believe the promises with our
hearts, and confess them with
our mouths, we are safe.
This is our health
within us."

May 27

"And
there was a
great earthquake,
such as was not since men
were upon the earth, so mighty
an earthquake and so great. And the
great city was divided into the three parts,
And the cities of nations fell. And great Babylon
came in remembrance before God, to give unto her
the cup of wine of the fierceness of wrath. Every isle
fled away, and the mountains were not found. And
there fell a great hail, as it had been talents, out of
heaven upon the men, and the men blasphemed
God, because of the plague of the hail, for it
was great and the plague of it sore."
(Revelation 16:18-21)

"O dreamers
and natural beasts,
without the seal of the
Spirit of God, but sealed
with the mark of the beast
and with cankered
consciences!"

May 28

"Brethren, count it exceeding joy when ye fall into diverse temptations, remembering how that the trying of your faith bringeth patience, and let patience have her perfect work, that ye may be perfect and sound, that nothing be lacking unto you."
(James 1:2-4)

"A Christian must suffer all things, be it never so great unright, as long as it is not against God's commandment. Neither is it lawful for him to cast any burden off his back by his own authority, till God pull it off, which laid it on for his deservings. Yet ought the kings everywhere to defend their realms from such oppression, if they were Christians, which is seldom seen, and is a hard thing verily, though not impossible."

May 29

"These
were the
noblest among
them of Thessalonia,
which received the word
with all diligence of mind,
and searched the scriptures
daily whether those things
were even so."
(Acts 17:11)

"Though that miracles bare
record unto his doctrine, yet desired he
no faith to be given either to his doctrine, or to
his miracles, without record of the scripture. When Paul
preached, the other searched the scriptures daily, whether
they were as he alleged them. Why shall not I likewise see
whether it be the scripture that thou allegest? Why shall
I not see the scripture and the circumstances, and what
goeth before and after, that I may know whether thine
interpretation be the right sense, or whether thou
jugglest, and drawest the scripture violently
unto thy carnal and fleshly purpose, or
whether thou be about to teach
me, or to deceive me?"

May 30

"He that hath ears
to hear, let him hear."
(Luke 8:8)

"We are come into
this damnable ignorance through
our own deserving, because, when the
truth was told us, we had no love thereto.
And to declare the full and set wrath of God
upon us, our prelates whom we have exalted over
us, to whom we have given almost all we had, have
persuaded the worldly princes to devour up body and
soul, and to keep us down in darkness, with violence of
sword, and with all falsehood and guile; insomuch that, if
any do but lift up his nose to smell after the truth, they
swap him in the face with a fire-brand, to singe his
smelling; or if he open one of his eyes once to
look toward the light of God's word, they
blear and daze his sight with their false
juggling, so that if it were possible,
though he were God's elect,
he could not but be kept
down, and perish for
lack of knowledge
of the truth."

May 31

"Keep therefore mine ordinances, and my
judgments, which if a man do, he shall
live thereby, for I am the Lord."
(Leviticus 18:5)

"I believe that every soul
that repenteth and loveth the law
is, through faith, a member of Christ's
church, and without spot or wrinkle. It is an
article of my belief that Christ's elect church is holy
and pure without sin, and every member of the same,
through faith in Christ, is in the full favour of God. And I
feel that the uncleanness of the soul is but the consent unto
sin and unto the flesh. And therefore I feel that every soul
that believeth and consenteth unto the law, and here in
this life hateth his flesh and the lusts thereof, and
doth his best to drive sin out of his flesh, and for
hate of the sin gladly departeth from his flesh,
when he is dead, and the lusts of the flesh
slain with death, needeth not as it were
bodily tormenting, to be purged of
that whereof he is quit already.
And if aught remain, it is
but to be taught, and
not to be beaten."

"The voice of one
that crieth in the wilderness"
(Mark 1:3)

June 1

"Now therefore ye are
no more strangers and foreigners, but
citizens with the saints, and of the household
of God, and are built upon the foundation of the
apostles and prophets, Jesus Christ being the head
cornerstone, in whom every building coupled
together groweth unto an holy temple
in the Lord, in whom ye also
are built together."
(Ephesians 2:19-22)

"Verily, he
is a true God, and
is our God as well as
theirs, and his promises
are with us, as well as with
them, and he is present with
us as well as he was with
them. If we ask, we shall
obtain. If we knock, he
will open. If we seek,
we shall find. If we
thirst, his truth
shall fulfill
our lust."

June 2

*"For the Son of Man is Lord
even of the Sabbath day."*
(Matthew 12:8)

"Inasmuch
as he is our Lord
and God, and we are his
double possession by creation
and redemption, and therefore we
ought not move heart or hand without his
commandment, it is right to have holy days
to come together. These times are to learn his will,
both the law which he will have us ruled by, and also
the promises of mercy upon which he will have us place
our trust, and to give thanks together to God for his mercy,
and to commit our infirmities to him, and to reconcile ourselves to him and to each other, if anything has come
between brother and brother that requires it. And
only for such purposes, and such as visiting the
sick and needy and redressing peace and
unity, were the holy days ordained, and
to this extent they are to be kept holy
from all manner of work that
may be conveniently let
go for the time."

June 3

"Ye have heard that it
hath been said: Thou shalt
love thy neighbour, and hate
thine enemy. But I say unto you,
love your enemies, bless them
that curse you, do good to
them that hate you."
(Matthew 5:43-44)

"He who trusts anything
except God and his Son Jesus
Christ keeps no commandment at all in
the sight of God. For he that has trust in any
creature except God and his Son Jesus, can see no
reason to love God with all his heart, nor to abstain
from dishonoring his name, nor to keep the holy day
for love of his doctrine, nor to obey lovingly the rulers
of the world, nor to love his neighbor as himself, nor to
abstain from hurting him if and when he may get some
profit by him while keeping himself safe. I may obey no
worldly power against the law to love my neighbor as
myself, if to do anything at any man's commandment
would be to the hurt of my neighbor who has not
deserved it, even if he be a Turk of a Muslim
tribe, generally fierce and marauding."

June 4

"This
is a true
saying, and by
all means worthy
to be received, that
Christ Jesus came into
the world to save sinners,
of whom I am chief."
(1 Timothy 1:15)

"Every
member of
Christ's congregation
sinneth daily, some more,
and some less. Yet the Spirit
leaveth us not, but rebuketh us,
and bringeth us home again unto
our profession, so that we never
cast off the yoke of God from
our necks, neither yield
up ourselves unto sin
for to serve it, but
fight afresh, and
begin a new
battle."

June 5

"Now
hath he
obtained a
more excellent
office, inasmuch
as he is the mediator
of a better testament,
which was made for
better promises."
(Hebrews 8:6)

"We
are all equally
beloved in Christ,
and God hath sworn to
all indifferently. According,
therefore, as every man believeth
God's promises, longeth for them, and is
diligent to pray unto God to fulfill them, so
is his prayer heard, and as good is the prayer
of a cobbler as of a cardinal, and of a butcher
as of a bishop. And the blessing of a baker
that knoweth the truth is as good as
the blessing of the pope."

June 6

"Jesus answered them and
said: My doctrine is not mine,
but his that sent me. If any man
will do his will, he shall know
of the doctrine, whether it
be of God, or whether
I spake of myself."
(John 7:16-17)

"So would it come to pass, that as
we know by natural wit what followeth of
a true principle of natural reason, even so, by the
principles of faith, and by the plain scriptures, and
by the circumstances of the text, should we judge all
men's exposition and doctrine, and should receive the
best, and refuse the worst. I would have you to teach
them also the properties and manner of speaking of
the scripture, and how to expound proverbs and
similitudes. Then, if they go abroad and walk
by the fields and meadows of all manner
doctors and philosophers, they could
catch no harm. They should discern
the poison from the honey, and
bring home nothing but that
which is wholesome."

June 7

"The Lord is my
shepherd, I can want
nothing. He feedeth me in a
green pasture, and leadeth me
to a fresh water. He quickeneth
my soul, and bringeth me forth in
the way of righteousness for his name's
sake. Though I should walk now in the
valley of the shadow of death, yet I fear
no evil, for thou art with me. Thy staff
and thy sheephook comfort me. Thou
preparest a table before me against
mine enemies. Thou anointest my
head with oil, and fillest my cup
full. Oh, let thy loving-kindness
and mercy follow me all the
days of my life, that I may
dwell in the house of
the Lord for ever."
(Psalms 23:1-6)

"And of such like consolation are all the psalms full. Would to God when ye read them, ye understood them."

June 8

"For this thing shall a
man leave father and
mother, and cleave
unto his wife."
(Matthew 19:5)

"It is a
great wrath
and vengeance, that
the father and mother
should hate their children,
even their flesh and their blood,
or that an husband should be unkind
unto his wife, or a master unto the servant
that waiteth on his profit, or that lords and
kings should be tyrants unto their subjects
and tenants, which pay them tribute, toll,
custom, and rent, laboring and toiling to
find them in honor, and to maintain
them in their estate. Is this not a
fearful judgment of God, and
a cruel wrath, that the very
prelates and shepherds of
our souls will slay us
and burn us with
fire?"

June 9

"Continue in one spirit,
and in one soul laboring as we do
to maintain the faith of the Gospel, and
in nothing fearing your adversaries, which
is to them a token of perdition, and to you
a sign of health, and that of God. For unto
you it is given that not only ye should
believe on Christ, but also suffer for
his sake, and have even the same
fight which ye saw me have,
and now hear of me."
(Philippians 1:27-30)

"King, subject,
master, servant, are
names in the world, but
not in Christ. In Christ, we
are all one, and even brethren.
No man is his own, but we are
all Christ's servants, bought
with His blood. Therefore,
ought no man to seek
himself, or his own
profit."

June 10

"Hereof are they fat and wealthy,
and are run away from me with shameful
blasphemies. They minister not the law, they
make no end of the fatherless cause, they judge
not the poor according to equity. Should I not
punish these things? sayeth the Lord. Should
I not be avenged of all such people, as
these be? Horrible and grievous
things are done in the land."
(Jeremiah 5:28-30)

"When we look on
your deeds, we see that ye
are all sworn together, and have
separated yourselves from the lay-people,
and have a several kingdom among yourselves,
and several laws of your own making, wherewith ye
violently bind the lay-people that never consented
unto the making of them. A thousand things
forbid ye, which Christ made free, and
dispense them again for money. Nor
is there any exception at all, but
for lack of money. Ye have
a secret council by
yourselves."

June 11

"Teach all nations,
baptizing them in the name
of the Father, and the Son, and
the Holy Ghost, teaching them to
observe all things whatsoever I have
commanded you. And, lo, I am
with you always, even until
the end of the world."
(Matthew 28:19-20)

"The outward plunging
of the body under water signifies
that we repent inwardly, and that we
profess to fight against sin and lusts and to kill
them every day more and more with the help of God
and with our diligence in following the doctrine of Christ
and the leading of his Spirit. It also signifies that we believe
ourselves to be washed from the infirmities and weaknesses
that yet remain in us after we have consented to the law and
yielded ourselves to be students thereof. And we believe
ourselves to be washed from all the imperfectness of
all our deeds done with cold love, and from all
actual sins which chance upon us while we
try to do differently and fight against
them, hoping to sin no more."

June 12

"For this cause,
I bow my knees unto the
Father of our Lord Jesus Christ,
that he would grant you according
to the riches of his glory, that ye may be
strengthened with might by his Spirit, that
Christ may dwell in your hearts by faith,
that ye being rooted and grounded in
love, might be able to comprehend
what is that breadth and length,
depth and height, and to know
what is the love of Christ."
(Ephesians 3:14-19)

"O
dreamers!
Yea, O devils, and
O venomous scorpions,
what poison have ye in your
tails! O pestilent leaven, that so
turneth the sweet bread of
Christ's doctrine into
the bitterness
of gall!"

June 13

"I,
therefore,
which am in bonds
for the Lord's sake, exhort
you, that ye walk worthy of the
vocation wherewith ye are called, in
all humbleness of mind, and meekness,
and long suffering, forbearing one another
through love, and that ye be diligent to keep
the unity of the spirit in the bond of peace,
being one body, and one spirit even as ye
are called in one hope of your calling.
Let there be but one Lord, one faith,
one baptism, one God and Father
of all, which is above all,
through all, and
in us all."
(Ephesians 4:1-6)

"No man
ought to preach,
but he that is
called."

June 14

"Walk as children of light.
Accept that which is pleasing to
the Lord, and have no fellowship with
the unfruitful works of darkness. For
whatsoever is manifest, that same is
light. Wherefore he saith: Awake,
thou that sleepest, and stand
up from death, and Christ
shall give thee light."
(Ephesians 5:8-14)

"They
preach that the
wagging of the bishop's
hand over us blesseth us,
and putteth away our sins. The
bishops therefore ought to bless
us in preaching Christ, and not
to deceive us and to bring the
curse of God upon us with
wagging their hands over
us. To preach is their
duty only, and not
to offer their feet
to be kissed."

June 15

"Help us, Lord our God, for we trust to thee,
and in thine name we come against this
multitude. Thou art the Lord our God,
Let not man prevail against thee."
(2 Chronicles 14:11)

"The
children of Israel
were in tribulation.
The promised land was far
off, with high walls up to the sky,
and inhabited with great giants. Yet
God's truth brought them out of Egypt
and planted them in the land of the giants.
There is no power against God, neither any
wisdom against his wisdom. He is stronger
and wiser than all his enemies. What help
Pharaoh to drown the men children? So
little, I fear, shall it at the last, help the
pope and his bishops to burn our men
children, which manfully confess
that Jesus Christ is the Lord,
and that there is no other
name given unto men
to be saved by."

June 16

> "I
> suffer
> all things
> for the elects'
> sakes, that they
> might also obtain that
> health which is in Christ
> Jesus, with eternal glory."
> (2 Timothy 2:10)

"In Christ, God loved us, his elect
and chosen, before the world began. And he
reserved us for the knowledge of his Son and of his
holy Gospel. And when the Gospel is preached to us he
opens our hearts, and gives us grace to believe, and puts
the Spirit of Christ in us. And we then know him as our
Father most merciful, and consent to the law and love
it inwardly in our heart and desire to fulfill it, and
sorrow because we cannot—which desire (sin we
of frailty ever so much) is sufficient, until more
strength be given us. The blood of Christ has
made satisfaction for the rest. The blood of
Christ has obtained for us all things that
are of God. Christ is our Satisfaction,
Redeemer, Deliverer and Savior."

June 17

"Give me also
this power, that
...he may receive the
Holy Ghost. Then said Peter
unto him: Perish thou and thy
money together. For thou wenest
that the gift of God may be obtained
with money? Thou hast neither part nor
fellowship in this business. For thy heart
is not right in the sight of God. Repent
therefore of this thy wickedness, and
pray God that the thought of thine
heart may be forgiven thee."
(Acts 8:18-22)

"Faith is the rock
whereon Christ buildeth
his congregation, against
which hellgates shall not
prevail. As soon as thou
believest in Christ, the
Holy Ghost cometh,
our sins fall away,
and devils fly."

June 18

"And the scribes
and Pharisees murmured
against his disciples, saying: Why
eat ye and drink ye with publicans
and sinners? Jesus answered and said
unto them: They that are whole, need
not of the physician, but they that
are sick. I came not to call the
righteous to repentance,
but the sinners."
(Luke 5:30-32)

"Them that are good, I love,
because they are in Christ, and the
evil also, to bring them to Christ. When
any man doeth well, I rejoice that God is
honored; and when any man doeth evil, I
sorrow because that God is dishonored.
Finally, inasmuch as God hath created
all, and Christ bought all with his
blood, therefore ought we all
to seek God and Christ,
and nothing
else."

June 19

"Thy priests break my law,
and defile my sanctuary. They put
no difference between the holy and unholy,
neither discern between the clean and unclean.
They turn their eyes from my sabbaths, and I
am unhallowed among them. Thy rulers
in thee are like ravishing wolves, to
shed blood, and to destroy souls,
for their own covetous lucre."
(Ezekiel 22:26-27)

"They say thy salvation is
in our faithful ear. This is their
hold; thereby know they all secrets.
The bishops, with the pope, have a certain
conspiration and secret treason against the world,
and by confession know they what kings and emperors
think. If aught be against them, do they never so evil, then
move they their captives to war and to fight, and give them
pardons to slay whom they will have taken out of the way.
They have, with falsehoods, taken from all kings and
emperors their rights and duties, which now they
call their freedoms, liberties, and privileges,
and have perverted the ordinances
that God left in the world."

June 20

"For by
grace are ye made safe
through faith, and that not
of your selves. For it is the gift of
God, and cometh not of works, lest any
man should boast himself. For we are his
workmanship, created in Christ Jesus
unto good works, unto the which
God ordained us before, that
we should walk in them."
(Ephesians 2:8-10)

"The clergy
have corrupted the pure
word of God. They rend and tear
the scriptures with their distinctions,
and expound them violently, contrary to the
meaning of the text. Wherefore, I have taken in
hand to expound the New Testament, to bring the
scripture unto the right sense, and to dig again
the wells of Abraham, and to purge and
cleanse them of worldly wisdom,
wherewith these Philistines
have distorted them."

June 21

"In that thou lovest the Lord thy God,
hearkenest unto his voice and cleavest unto
him. For he is thy life and the length of thy
days, that thou mayest dwell upon the
earth which the Lord sware unto
thy fathers Abraham, Isaac,
and Jacob, to give them."
(Deuteronomy 30:20)

"A greater perfection
than to love God and his will,
with all thine heart, with all thy soul,
with all thy strength, with all thy mind, is
there none, and to love a man's neighbor as
himself, is like the same. As glad as I would be
to receive pardon of mine own life, so glad ought
I to be to defend my neighbor's life, without respect
of my life or my good. A man ought to spare neither
his goods nor yet himself, for his brother's sake, after
the ensample of Christ. God chooseth us first, and
loveth us first, and openeth our eyes to see his
exceeding abundant love to us in Christ, and
then love we again, and accept his will,
and serve him in that office where
unto he hath chosen us."

June 22

"The Lord said unto
me: The prophets preach
lies unto them in my name. I
have not spoken with them, neither
gave I them any charge, neither did
I send them. Yet they preach unto
you false visions, charming
vanity, and deceitfulness
of their own heart."
(Jeremiah 14:14)

"All this
cometh to pass
in order to fulfill the
prophecy which Christ
prophesied, that there should
come in his name those who shall
say that they themselves are Christ.
That do verily the pope and our holy
orders of religion. For they, under the
name of Christ, preach themselves,
their own word, and their own
traditions, and teach the
people to believe
in them."

June 23

"And the son said
unto him: Father, I have
sinned against heaven, and
in thy sight, neither am I worthy
henceforth to be called thy son. Then
said the father to his servants: Bring
forth that best garment, and put
it on him, and put a ring on
his hand, and shoes
on his feet."
(Luke 15:21-24)

"When
the law
is preached,
all men are found
sinners, and therefore
damned, and when the
Gospel and glad tidings
are preached, then are
all that repent and
believe found
righteous in
Christ."

June 24

"Jesus called them unto
him, and said: Ye know that the
lords of the gentiles have domination
over them. And they that are great, exercise
power over them. It shall not be so among you.
But whosoever will be great among you, let him
be your minister, and whosoever will be chief,
let him be your servant. Even as the Son of
Man came, not to be ministered unto, but
to minister and to give his life for
the redemption of many."
(Matthew 20:25-28)

"Our promise
is that Christ, and his
body, and his blood, and
all that he did and suffered,
is a sacrifice, a ransom, and a
full satisfaction for our sins;
that God for his sake will
think no more on them,
if we have power
to repent and
believe."

June 25

"Ye are gone quite
from Christ as many as
are justified by the law, and
are fallen from grace. We look
for and hope to be justified by the
spirit, which cometh of faith."
(Galatians 5:4-5)

"Christ
forbade his
disciples not only
to climb above lords,
kings and emperors in
worldly rule, but also to
exalt themselves one above
another in the kingdom of God.
God's word should rule only, and
not pope's pleasure. That ought they
to preach purely and spiritually and to
fashion their lives thereafter and with all
example of godly living and long suffering,
to draw all to Christ, and not to expound
the scriptures carnally and worldly.
There is no brotherhood where
such philosophy is taught."

June 26

"Thou seest how
that faith wrought with
in his deeds, and through
the deeds was the faith made
perfect. ...Ye see then how that
of deeds a man is justified,
and not of faith only."
(James 2:22 & 24)

"Though
faith is never
without love and good
works, yet our salvation is
not imputed to love or good
works, but to faith only. For love
and works are under the law, and
the law requires perfection and
the ground and fountain of the
heart, and condemns any and
all imperfection. But faith is
under the promises, which
give pardon, grace, mercy,
favor, and whatsoever
is contained in the
promises."

June 27

"He that
endureth in the
doctrine of Christ,
hath both the Father,
and the Son."
(2 John 1:9)

'When the
children of Israel
were ready to despair for
the greatness and the multitude
of the giants, Moses comforted them
ever, saying, Remember what your Lord
God hath done for you in Egypt, his wonderful
plagues, his miracles, his wonders, his mighty hand,
his stretched out arm, and what he hath done for you
hitherto. He shall destroy them; he shall take their
hearts from them, and make them fear and flee
before you. He shall storm them, and stir up
a tempest among them, and scatter them,
and bring them to nought. He hath
sworn; he is true; he will fulfill
the promises that he hath
made unto Abraham,
Isaac, and Jacob."

June 28

"The powers that be
are ordained of God. It is
time that we should now awake
out of sleep. For now is our salvation
nearer than when we believed. The night is
passed and the day is come nye. Let us therefore
cast away the deeds of darkness, and let us put on
the armour of light. Let us walk honestly, as it were
in the daylight; not in eating and drinking, neither
in chambering and wantonness, neither in strife
and envying, but put ye on the Lord Jesus
Christ. And make not provision for the
flesh, to fulfill the lusts of it."
(Romans 13:1 & 11-14)

"A Christian perceiveth righteousness if he
loveth his enemy, even when he suffereth
persecution and torment of him, and the
pains of death. He mourneth more for
his adversary's blindness than for
his own pain, and prayeth God
to open his eyes, and to
forgive him his
sins."

June 29

"Warn
them that they submit
themselves to rule and power,
to obey the officers, that they be
prompt unto all good works, that
they speak evil of no man, that
they be no fighters, but soft,
shewing all meekness
unto all men."
(Titus 3:1-2)

"How hath the pope
authority above God's laws and to
command the angels, the saints, and even
God himself? Who gave him the authority to
command God to damn people? Paul also in
many things which God had made free, gave
pure and faithful counsel without tangling
of any man's conscience and without all
manner commanding under pain of
cursing, pain of excommunication,
pain of heresy, pain of burning,
pain of deadly sin, pain of
damnation and hell."

June 30

"Zacharias was filled with the
Holy Ghost, and prophesied saying:
Blessed be the Lord God of Israel, for
he hath visited and redeemed his people.
And hath raised up an horn of salvation unto
us, in the house of his servant David, even as he
promised by the mouth of his holy prophets
which were since the world began, that we
should be saved from our enemies, and
from the hands of all that hate us,
to show mercy towards our
fathers, and to remember
his holy promise."
(Luke 1:67-72)

"Christ's
authority, which he
gave to his disciples, was
to preach the law, and to bring
sinners to repentance, and then to
preach unto them the promises,
which the Father had made
unto all men for
his sake."

"Is the candle lighted,
to be put under a bushel?"
(Mark 4:21)

July 1

"Be not
suddenly moved
from your mind, and be
not troubled, neither by spirit,
neither by words, nor yet by letter,
which should seem to come from us,
as though the day of Christ were at hand.
Let no man deceive you by any means, for
the Lord cometh not, except there come a
departing first, and that that sinful man
be opened, the son of perdition
which is an adversary."
(2 Thessalonians 2:2-3)

"Let us set God's
promises before our
eyes, and desire him for his
mercy and for Christ's sake, to
fulfill them. And he is as true as
ever he was, and will do it as
well as ever he did, for to
us are the promises
made, as well as
to them."

July 2

"I gave you milk to drink, and not
meat. For ye then were not strong; no,
neither yet are strong. For ye are yet carnal.
As long verily as there is among you envying,
strife, and dissension, are ye not carnal,
and walk after the manner of men?"
(1 Corinthians 3:2-3)

"When the
lay and unlearned
people are taught the first
principles of our profession,
they read the scripture and they
understand and delight in it. Thereby,
the great pillars of the holy church, who
have nailed a veil of false gloss on Moses' face
to corrupt the true understanding of his law, cannot
come in, but only bark that the scriptures make heretics;
that it is not possible to understand the scripture in English
because they do not understand it in Latin. Because they
cannot have their way, with pure malice they slay their
brethren for their faith in our Savior, and thereby
show forth their bloody, wolfish tyranny,
what they are within, and whose
disciples they are."

July 3

"But God, which is rich in
mercy through his great love
wherewith he loved us, even
when we were dead by sin,
hath quickened us with
Christ. For by grace
are ye saved."
(Ephesians 2:4-5)

"We know that
whatsoever good thing is in
us, it is the gift of grace and therefore
not the result of our deserving the same,
although many things are given by God which
otherwise would not be, through our diligence in
working his laws and chastising our bodies, praying
for others and believing his promises. Still, our working
does not mean we deserve these gifts any more than the
diligence of a merchant in seeking a good ship brings the
goods safely to land, although such diligence does now
and again assist. But when we believe in God and
then do all we can in our strength, and do not
test him, then he is true to his promise to
help us. And he will perform alone
when our strength is past."

July 4

"I will be glad and
rejoice in thy mercy, for thou
hast considered my trouble; thou
hast known my soul in adversity. Thou
hast not delivered me over in to the hands of
the enemy, but hast set my feet in a large room.
Have mercy upon me, O Lord, for I am in trouble.
Mine eye is consumed for very heaviness; yea, my
soul and my body. My life is waxen old with
heaviness, and my years with mourning.
My strength faileth me, because
of mine adversity."
(Psalms 31:7-10)

"When we are reconciled to
God as his friends and heirs of eternal
life, the Spirit that he hath poured into us
testifieth that we may not live after our old deeds of
ignorance. For how is it possible that we should repent
and abhor them, and yet have lust to live in them?
We are sure, therefore, that God hath created and
made us new in Christ, and put his Spirit in
us, that we should live a new life, which
is the life of good works."

July 5

"Many
false prophets shall
arise, and shall deceive
many, and because iniquity
shall have the upper hand, the
love of many shall abate. But
he that endureth to the
end shall be safe."
(Matthew 24:11-13)

"After
thou hast
heard so many
masses, and after thou
hast received holy bread, holy
water, and a bishop's blessing, be
more kind to thy neighbor, and love
him better than before. Be more
obedient unto thy superiors;
more merciful, more ready
to forgive wrong, more
despisest the world,
and more athirst
after spiritual
things."

July 6

"I call to record this day unto you, heaven and earth, that I have set before you life and death, blessing and cursing. But choose life, that thou and thy seed may live."
(Deuteronomy 30:19)

"Worldly powers
or rulers are to be obeyed
only so far as their commandments
do not contend against the commandment
of God, and no further. Therefore, we must have
God's commandments always in our hearts. And by the
higher law we must interpret the inferior, so that we obey
nothing against the belief of one God, or against the faith,
hope, and trust that is in him only, or against the love
of God whereby we do or leave undone all things
for his sake; and further so we do nothing under
any man's commandment that is against the
reverence of the name of God, to make it
despised or less feared and followed;
and that we obey nothing to the
hindrance of the knowledge
of the blessed doctrine of
God, whose servant
the holy day is."

July 7

"Lo, I send you forth, as sheep among wolves. Be ye therefore wise as serpents, and innocent as doves. Beware of men, for they shall deliver you up to the councils, and shall scourge you... And ye shall be brought to the head rulers and kings for my sake, in witness to them and to the gentiles. But when they put you up, take no thought how, or what, ye shall speak, for it shall be given you even in that same hour, what ye shall say. For it is not ye that speak, but the spirit of your Father which speaketh in you."
(Matthew 10:16-20)

"He that is born of God cannot sin, for his seed dwelleth in him, which seed is the Holy Ghost, that keepeth a man's heart from consenting unto sin. It is a false conclusion how that a man may have a right faith joined with all kinds of abomination and sin."

July 8

"Avenge
not yourselves,
but give room unto
the wrath of God. For it
is written: Vengeance is mine,
and I will reward, saith the Lord.
Therefore, if thine enemy hunger, feed
him. If he thirst, give him drink. For
in so doing, thou shalt heap coals
of fire on his head. Be not overcome of evil, but overcome
evil with goodness."
(Romans 12:19-21)

"Have peace
with men. Kindle
love in others. Let not
another man's wickedness
make thee wicked also. Rather
overcome evil with good. That is,
with softness, kindness, and all
patience win him, even as
God. with kindness,
won thee."

July 9

"Therefore, I
say unto you, be not
careful for your life, what
ye shall eat, or what
ye shall drink."
(Matthew 6:31)

"When God's
law has brought the sinner
into knowledge of himself, and has
confounded his conscience and opened
the wrath and vengeance of God, only then
come good tidings. The Gospel reveals to him
the promises of God in Christ, and how Christ has
purchased pardon for him, has satisfied the law for him,
and has appeased the wrath of God. Thus, the poor sinner
believes, lauds, and thanks God through Christ, and breaks
out into exceeding inward joy and gladness in that he has
escaped so great a wrath, so heavy a vengeance, and so
fearful and so everlasting a death. And from then on,
he is hungry and thirsty for more righteousness,
so he might fulfill the law. And he mourns
continually, commending his weakness
unto God in the blood of our
Savior, Christ Jesus."

July 10

"And this I pray, that
your love may increase more
and more in knowledge, and in
all feeling, that ye might accept things
most excellent, that ye might be pure, and
such as should hurt no man's conscience,
until the day of Christ, filled with the
fruits of righteousness, which fruits
come by Jesus Christ unto the
glory and laud of God."
(Philippians 1:9-11)

"I uttered unto you
partly the malicious blindness of
the bishop of Rochester, his juggling, his
conveying, his foxy wiliness, his bopeep, his
wresting, ranting, and shameful abusing of the
scriptures, his oratory and alleging of heretics,
and how he would make the apostles the
authors of blind ceremonies without
signification, contrary to their
own doctrine, and has set
himself before all for
an ensample."

July 11

"Then
reproved I the
rulers and said:
Why forsake we
the house of God?
But I gathered them
together, and set them
in their place."
(Nehemiah 13:11)

"Except my
memory fail me, that
I have forgotten what I read
as a child, thou shalt find in the
English chronicle, how King Adelstone
caused the scriptures to be translated into the
tongue that was then in England, and how the prelates
exhorted him thereto. Today, when one of you preacheth
contrary to another, the one disputeth and brawleth with
the other. And one holdeth this doctor, and another
that, so that if thou hadst but of every author one
book, thou couldst not pile them up in any
warehouse in London, for every
author is one contrary
unto another."

July 12

"It is
written:
Man shall
not live by bread
only, but by every
word of God."
(Luke 4:4)

"The law is a
fretting corrosive and
sharp salve that kills our
dead flesh. It looses and draws
out our sores by the roots with all
corruption. It withdraws from a man the
trust and confidence that he has in himself
and in his own works, merits, deservings, and
ceremonies, and robs him of all his righteousness,
and makes him poor. It kills him, sends him down to
hell, and brings him to utter desperation. It prepares
the way of the Lord, as is written of John the Baptist.
For it is impossible that Christ should come to a
man who trusts in himself or in any worldly
thing, or has any righteousness of
his own, or riches of holy
works."

July 13

"He that
loveth his father
or mother more than me,
is not worthy of me. And he
that loveth his son or daughter
more than me is not meet for me.
And he that taketh not his cross and
followeth me is not meet for me. He
that findeth his life shall lose it,
and he that loseth his life for
my own sake shall find it."
(Matthew 10:37-39)

"If thou
wilt be at peace with
God, and love him, thou
must turn to his promises, and
to the Gospel, the ministration of
righteousness, For faith bringeth
pardon and forgiveness freely
purchased by Christ's blood,
and bringeth the Spirit.
The Spirit setteth us
at liberty."

July 14

"There shall
be false teachers among
you which privily shall bring
in damnable sects, even denying
the Lord that hath bought them, and
bring on their own heads swift damnation.
And many shall follow their damnable ways,
by which the way of truth shall be evil spoken
of, and through covetousness shall they with
feigned words make merchandise of you,
whose judgment is not far off, and
their damnation sleepeth not."
(2 Peter 2:1-3)

"And, thus,
are we never taught,
and are yet nevertheless
compelled, yea, compelled to
hire many costly schoolmasters.
These deeds are verily against Christ.
Shall we, therefore, judge you by your
deeds, as Christ commandeth? So
are ye false prophets, and the
disciples of antichrist."

July 15

"I am a good shepherd. A good shepherd giveth his life for his sheep."
(John 10:11)

"There
is no father
here that punisheth
his son to purge him,
when he is purged already
and hath utterly forsaken sin and
evil, and hath submitted himself unto
his father's doctrine. For to punish a man
that has forsaken sin of his own accord is not
to purge him, but to satisfy the lust of a tyrant.
Neither ought it to be called purgatory, but a
jail of tormenting, and a satisfactory. And
when the pope saith it is done to satisfy
the righteousness, as a judge, I say
we that believe have no judge of
him, but a Father. Neither shall
we come into judgment, for
Christ hath promised us
we are received under
grace, mercy, and
forgiveness."

July 16

"There
is a time
to plant, and a
time to pluck up the
thing that is planted. A
time to slay, and a time to
make whole. A time to break
down, and a time to build up. A
time to weep, and a time to laugh.
A time to mourn, and a time to dance.
A time to cast away stones, and a time to
gather stones together. A time to embrace,
and a time to refrain from embracing. A time
to win, and a time to lose. A time to spare, and
a time to spend. A time to cut in pieces, and a
time to sew together. A time to keep silence,
and a time to speak. A time to love, and a
time to hate. A time of war, and a time
of peace." (Ecclesiastes 3:2-8)

"We, for the most part, proceed
from that which is last unto that which is first,
disputing and making our arguments backward. We
begin at the effect and proceed unto the natural cause."

July 17

"And he
said unto them: But
whom say ye that I am?
Peter answered and said
unto him: Thou art
the very Christ."
(Mark 8:29)

"He is
our Redeemer,
Deliverer, Reconciler,
Mediator, Intercessor and
Advocate; our Attorney, Solicitor,
our Hope, Comfort, Shield, Protection,
Defender, Strength, Health, Satisfaction
and Salvation. His blood, his death, and
all that he ever did, is ours. And Christ
himself, with all that he is or can do, is
ours. His blood shedding, and all that
he did, does me as good service as if I
myself had done it. And God, with all
that he has, is mine through Christ
and his redeeming work, in the
same way that a husband
belongs to his wife."

July 18

"Behold, the time cometh,
sayeth the Lord God, that I shall
send an hunger into the earth; not the
hunger of bread, nor the thirst of water,
but an hunger to hear the word of the Lord,
so that they shall go from the one sea to the
other, yea from the north unto the east,
running about to seek the word of
the Lord, and shall not find it."
(Amos 8:11-12)

"They have
robbed all realms, not
of God's word only, but also
of all wealth and prosperity, and
have driven peace out of all lands, and
withdrawn themselves from all obedience to
princes, and have separated themselves from the
laymen, counting them viler than dogs, and have set
up that great idol, the whore of Babylon, the antichrist
of Rome, whom they call pope, and have conspired
against all commonwealths, and have made
them a several kingdom, wherein it
is lawful, unpunished, to work
all abomination."

July 19

"As
many as I love, I
rebuke and chasten.
Be fervent, therefore,
and repent. Behold, I stand
at the door and knock. If any
man hear my voice and open the
door, I will come in unto him, and
will sup with him, and he with me."
(Revelation 3:19-20)

"So
long as
thou findest any
consent in thine heart
unto the law of God, that
it is righteous and good, and
also displeasure that thou canst
not fulfill it, despair not, neither
doubt but that God's Spirit is
in thee, and that thou art
chosen for Christ's sake
to the inheritance
of eternal life."

July 20

"Let us behave ourselves
as the ministers of God. In much
patience, in afflictions, in necessity, in
anguish, in stripes, in prisonment, in strife,
in labour, in watch, in fasting, in pureness, in
knowledge, in longsuffering, in kindness, in
the Holy Ghost, in love unfeigned, in the
words of truth, in the power of God, by
the armour of righteousness."
(2 Corinthians 6:4-7)

"Forasmuch, then,
as we must needs be baptized
in tribulations, and through a great
and a fearful wilderness, into our natural
country; yea, and inasmuch as it is a plain earnest
that there is no other way into the kingdom of life than
through persecution and suffering of pain, and of very
death, after the ensample of Christ, therefore let us
arm our souls with the comfort of the scriptures,
how that God is ever ready at hand, in time
of need, to help us, and how that such
tyrants and persecutors are but
God's scourge, and his
rod to chastise us."

July 21

"Jesus, as soon as he was baptized, came straight out of the water. And lo, heaven was open unto him, and he saw the Spirit of God descend like a dove, and light upon him. And lo, there came a voice from heaven saying: This is my dear Son, in whom is my delight."
(Matthew 3:16-17)

"Repentance is no sacrament, as faith, hope, love, and knowledge of a man's sins, are not to be called sacraments. For they are spiritual and invisible. Now must a sacrament be an outward sign that may be seen, to signify, to represent, and to put a man in remembrance of some spiritual promise, which cannot be seen, but by faith only."

July 22

"God,
which is thy
God, anointed
thee with the oil of
gladness, above
thy fellows."
(Hebrews 1:9)

"We be
called unto a
kingdom that must be
won with suffering only,
as a sick man winneth health.
God is he that doeth all things for
us, and fighteth for us, and we do but
suffer only. Christ saith: I send you
forth as sheep among wolves. The
sheep fight not, but the shepherd
fighteth for them, and careth for
them. Be harmless as doves,
saith Christ, and wise as
serpents. These doves
imagine no defense,
nor seek to avenge
themselves."

July 23

"Take heed,
therefore, that ye
walk circumspectly, for
the days are evil. Wherefore,
understand what the will of the
Lord is, and be not drunk with wine,
wherein is excess, but be fulfilled with the
Spirit, speaking unto yourselves in psalms,
and hymns, and spiritual songs, singing
and playing to the Lord in your hearts,
giving thanks always for all things
in the name of our Lord Jesus
Christ to God the Father."
(Ephesians 5:15-20)

"Remember that his Son's blood is
stronger than all the sins and wickedness of
the world. Therewith, quiet thyself, and thereunto
commit thyself. Or else, perishest thou, though thou
hast a thousand holy candles about thee, a hundred
tons of holy water, a ship full of pardons, all the
ceremonies in the world, and all the good
works, deservings, and merits of men.
God's word only lasteth forever,
when all other things
perish."

July 24

"For whom the Lord
loveth, him he chasteneth.
Yea, and he scourgeth every
son that he receiveth."
(Hebrews 12:6)

"I feel that souls be purged
only by the word of God and doctrine of
Christ, and that he which is clean through the
doctrine needeth not but to wash his feet only, for
his head and hands are clean already. He must tame
his flesh, and keep it under, for his soul is clean already
through the doctrine. I feel also that bodily pain doth but
purge the body only, insomuch that the pain not only
purgeth not the soul, but maketh it more foul, except
that there be kind learning by, to purge the soul. So
that the more a man beateth his son, the worse he
is, except he teach him lovingly, and shew him
kindness besides; partly to keep him from
desperation, and partly that he fall not
into hate of his father and of his
commandment thereto, and
think that his father is a
tyrant, and his law
but tyranny."

July 25

"Thou mayest yet have
knowledge how thou oughtest
to behave thyself in the house of God,
which is the congregation of the living God, the
pillar and ground of truth. And without nay great
is that mystery of godliness. God was shewed
in the flesh, was justified in the spirit, was
seen of angels, was preached unto the
gentiles, was believed on in earth,
and received up in glory."
(1 Timothy 3:15-16)

"I
call God
to record against
the day we shall appear
before our Lord Jesus, that
I never altered one syllable
of God's Word against my
conscience, nor would do
this day, if all that is in
earth, whether it be
honor, pleasure, or
riches, might be
given me."

July 26

"He went forth
a little and fell down on the
ground and prayed that if it were
possible, the hour might pass from him.
And he said: Abba Father, all things
are possible unto thee. Take away
this cup from me. Nevertheless,
not that I will, but that
thou wilt be done."
(Mark 14:35-36)

"The
children
of the devil,
in time of adversity
fly from Christ, whom
they followed feignedly,
their hearts not sealed with
his holy and mighty Spirit, and
get them to the standard of their
right father the devil, and take
his wages, the pleasures of
this world, which are the
earnest of everlasting
damnation."

July 27

"The law was our schoolmaster unto the
time of Christ, that we might be made righteous
by faith. But after that faith is come, now are we no
longer under a schoolmaster. For ye are all the sons
of God, by the faith which is in Christ Jesus. For all
ye that are baptized, have put Christ on you. Now
is there no Jew, neither Greek; there is neither
bond, neither free, there is neither man,
neither woman, for all are one thing
in Christ Jesus. If ye be Christ's,
then are ye Abraham's seed,
and heirs by promise."
(Galatians 3:24-29)

"How know we that God
loveth us? Verily, by faith. Faith,
that loveth God's commandments,
justifieth a man. If thou believe God's
promises in Christ, then art thou safe.
If thou love the commandment,
then art thou sure that thy
faith is unfeigned, and
that God's Spirit
is in thee."

July 28

"The Lord God shall wipe away
the tears from all faces, and take away
the confusion of his people through
the whole world. For the Lord
himself hath said it."
(Isaiah 25:8)

"This was
commanded unto
all men. How cometh it
that God's word pertaineth
less unto us, than unto them?
Yea, how cometh it that our Moseses
forbid us and command us the contrary,
and threaten us if we do, and will not that
we once speak of God's word? How can
we whet God's word, that is, put it in
to practice, use and exercise it upon
our children and household, when
we are violently kept from it and
know it not? How can we give
a reason of our hope, when
we wot not what it is that
God hath promised, or
what to hope?"

July 29

"In so much as ye
have cast off your beauty, and
comforted yourselves with power and
nimbleness, and put your confidence therein,
therefore shall ye have this mischief again
for your destruction and fall, like as an
high wall that falleth because of some
rift, or blast, whose breaking
cometh suddenly."
(Isaiah 30:12-13)

"And as pertaining unto them
that despise God's word, counting it as
a fantasy or a dream, and to them also that for
fear of a little persecution fall from it, set this before
thine eyes, how God, since the beginning of the world,
before a general plague, ever sent his true prophets
and preachers of his word to warn the people,
and gave them time to repent. But they, for
the greatest part of them, hardened their
hearts, and persecuted the word that
was sent to save them. And then,
God destroyed them utterly,
and took them clean
from the earth."

July 30

"For our
knowledge and our
prophesying is imperfect,
but when that which is perfect is
come, then that which is imperfect shall
be done away. When I was a child, I spake
as a child, I understood as a child, I imagined
as a child, but as soon as I was a man I put away
childishness. Now we see in a glass even in a dark
speaking, but then shall we see face to face. Now
I know imperfectly, but then shall I know even
as I am known. Now abideth faith, hope,
and love, even these three, but
the chief of these is love."
(1 Corinthians 13:9-13)

"Do
you know who
taught the eagles to find
their prey? Well, that same
God teaches His hungry
children how to find
their Father in
his word."

July 31

"The
disciple is not
above his master,
nor yet the servant
above his Lord."
(Matthew 10:24)

"A Christian man
freely does all that he does,
considering only the will of God and
his neighbor's well being. If I live chaste,
it is not to obtain heaven thereby, for then I
would do wrong to the blood of Christ. Christ's
blood has already obtained that for me. Christ's
merits have made me heir of heaven. He is both
the door and the way to it. I do so freely to wait
on the Evangelion, and to avoid the trouble of
the world and occasions that might pluck me
from the Gospel, and to serve my brother
with it as well, even as one hand helps
another, or one member another,
because one feels another's
grief, and the pain of
the one is the pain
of the other."

"A well of water springing up
into everlasting life"
(John 4:14)

August 1

"Wherefore,
if the light that is in
thee be darkness, how
great is that darkness?"
(Matthew 6:23)

"Take
heed, therefore,
wicked prelates, blind
leaders of the blind, indurate
and obstinate hypocrites, take heed.
Ye will be the chiefest in Christ's flock,
and yet will not keep one jot of the right way
of his doctrine. …Ye keep thereof almost naught at
all, but whatsoever soundeth to make of your bellies,
to maintain your honour, whether in the scriptures, or in
your own traditions, or in the pope's law that ye compel the
lay-people to observe, violently threatening them with your
excommunications and curses, that they shall be damned
body and soul if they keep them not. And if that help
you not, then ye murder them mercilessly with the
sword of the temporal powers, whom ye have
made so blind that they be ready to slay
whom ye command, and will not
hear his cause examined."

August 2

"Do
all things
without murmuring
and disputing, that ye may be
faultless, and pure, and the sons of
God, without rebuke, in the midst of a
crooked and a perverse nation, among
which see that ye shine as lights in the
world, holding fast the word of life,
unto my rejoicing in the day of
Christ, that I have not run
in vain, neither have
laboured in vain."
(Philippians 2:14-16)

"Lo,
persecution and
adversity for the truth's
sake is God's scourge and
his rod, and pertaineth unto
all his children indifferently. For
when he said he scourgeth
every son, he maketh
none exception."

August 3

"And
he said unto
them: When I sent
you without wallet,
and scrip, and shoes,
lacked ye anything?
And they said:
Nothing."
(Luke 22:35)

"When a
parish of us hire
a schoolmaster to teach
our children, what reason is it
that we should pay him his wages,
and he should have license to go where
he will, and to dwell in another country,
and to leave our children untaught? Doth
not the pope so? Have we not given our
tithes of courtesy unto one, for to teach
us God's word, and cometh not the
pope, and compelleth us to pay
it violently to them that
never teach?"

August 4

"For ye
must walk after
the Lord your God,
and fear him, and keep his
commandments, and hearken
unto his voice, and serve him,
and cleave unto him."
(Deuteronomy 13:4)

"As
we are
blind, God
has appointed
in scripture how
we should serve and
please Him. Pertaining
to His own person, He is
abundantly pleased when
we believe His promises and
the holy testament which He
has made unto us in Christ,
as well as when we thank
him for his mercy when
we love and obey His
commandments."

August 5

"Bear ye one another's
burden and so fulfil
the law of Christ."
(Galatians 6:2)

"Recompense to
no man evil. For if thou
were not brought sometime
into cumbrance, whence God only
could deliver thee, thou shouldest never see
thy faith. Yea, except thou foughtest sometime
against desperation, hell, death, sin, and powers of
this world for thy faith's sake, thou shouldest never
know true devotion to Christ. Except thy brother now
and then offended thee, thou couldest not know whether
thy love were godly. For a Turk is not angry, till he be hurt
and offended. But if thou love him that doth thee evil, then is
thy love of God. Likewise if thy rulers were always kind, thou
shouldest not know whether thine obedience were pure or
no. But and if thou canst patiently obey evil rulers in all
things that are not to the dishonor of God, and when
thou hurtest not thy neighbors, then art thou sure
that God's Spirit worketh in thee, and that
thy faith is no dream, nor any
false imagination."

August 6

"Submit your
selves, every man one
to another. Knit yourselves
together in lowliness of mind.
For God resisteth the proud and
giveth grace to the humble. Submit
yourselves, therefore, under the
mighty hand of God, that
he may exalt you when
the time is come."
(1 Peter 5:5-6)

"Christ's
vicars minister
his kingdom in his
bodily absence, and have
the oversight of his flock. No
emperor, king, duke, lord, knight,
temporal judge, or any temporal
officer under false name may
have any such dominion,
or minister any such
office as requireth
violence."

August 7

"Who
shall separate us
from God's love? Shall
tribulation, or anguish, or
persecution, other hunger,
other nakedness, other
peril, other sword?"
(Romans 8:35)

"I had
perceived by
experience, how that it
was impossible to establish the
lay people in any truth, except the
scripture were plainly laid before their
eyes in their mother tongue, that they might
see the process, order, and meaning of the text."
Tyndale's mission, from which he never deviated,
was "to scatter Roman darkness, by this light." Of
the price he would pay to do so, he wrote: "The
loss of land and life, I'll reckon slight." As he
stood at the stake, he cried out: "Lord, open
the King of England's eyes!" We are told
that the strangling was bungled, and
that he suffered terribly.

August 8

"Blessed is
the man that goeth
not in the counsel of the
ungodly, that abideth not in the
way of sinners, and sitteth not in the
seat of the scornful, but delighteth in the
law of the Lord, and exerciseth himself in
his law both day and night. Such a man is like
a tree planted by the water side, that bringeth
forth his fruit in due season. His leaves shall
not fall off, and look whatsoever he doth,
it shall prosper. As for the ungodly, it is
not so with them. But they are like the
dust, which the wind scattereth
a way from the ground."
(Psalms 1:1-4)

"The Law
and the Gospel are
two keys. The Law is the
key that shutteth up all men
under condemnation, and the
Gospel is the key which opens
the door and lets them out."

August 9

"Ye
are the
salt of the
earth, but and
if the salt be once
unsavory, what can
be salted there with?
It is thence forth good
for nothing, but to be
cast out at the doors,
and that men tread
it under feet."
(Matthew 5:13)

"Nevertheless,
repent we never so
much, be we never so
well willing unto the law
of God, yet are we so weak,
and the snares and occasions
so innumerable, that we fall
daily and hourly, so that we
could not but despair, if
the reward hanged
on the work."

August 10

"They
chose Stephen,
a man full of faith
and of the Holy Ghost,
and Philip...which they
set before the apostles;
and they prayed, and
laid their hands
on them."
(Acts 6:5-6)

"The putting on of hands was
but that they spake unto them, and
told them their duty, and gave them a
charge, and warned them to be faithful in
the Lord's business, as we choose temporal
officers, and read their duty to them, and they
promise to be faithful ministers, and then are
admitted. Neither is there any other manner
or ceremony at all required in making of
our spiritual officers, than to choose an
able person, and then to rehearse him
his duty, and give him his charge,
and put him in his room."

August 11

"Choose you this
day whom you will
serve, whether the gods
which your fathers served
that were on the other side
of the flood, or the gods of
the Amorites in whose land
ye dwelt. And I, as for me
and my house, will
serve the Lord."
(Joshua 24:15)

"I consent
to the will of God
in my heart, though
through weakness I cannot
do the will of God at all times.
Yet, if I see my fault and meekly
knowledge my sin, weeping in
mine heart, and thirst after
strength, I am sure that
the Spirit of God is in
me, and his favor
upon me."

August 12

"And
I saw an
angel come
down from heaven,
having the key of the
bottomless pit, and a great
chain in his hand. And he took
the dragon, that old serpent, which
is the devil and satanas, and he bound
him a thousand years, and cast him into
the bottomless pit, and he bound him, and
set a seal on him, that he should deceive
the people no more, till the millennial
years were fulfilled. And after
that, he must be lowsed
for a little season."
(Revelation 20:1-3)

"Christ
is with us
until the world's
end. Let his little
flock be bold,
therefore."

August 13

"The publican stood afar off,
and would not lift up his eyes to
heaven, but smote his breast, saying:
God, be merciful to me, a sinner. I tell
you, this man departed home to his house
justified.... For every man that exalteth
himself, shall be brought low, and
he that humbleth himself,
shall be exalted."
(Luke 18:13-14)

"Whatever is
done to the least
of us is done to Christ,
and whatever is done to my
brother is done to me. Nor does
my brother's pain grieve me less
than my own, nor do I rejoice
less at his well-being than at
my own, if I love him as
well and as much as
myself, as the law
commands
me."

August 14

*"Let
brotherly
love continue.
Be not forgetful to
be kind to strangers.
For thereby have divers
received angels into their
houses unawares."*
(Hebrews 13:1-2)

*"If thou look on the
profession of our hearts, and on
the Spirit and forgiveness which we have
received through Christ's merits, we are full
dead. But if thou look on the rebellion of the flesh,
we do but begin to die, and to be baptized, that is, to
drown and quench the lusts, and are full baptized at
the last minute of death. And as concerning the
working of the Spirit, we begin to live, and
grow every day more and more, both in
knowledge and also in godly living,
as a child receiveth the full soul at
the first day, yet growth daily
in the operations and
works thereof."*

August 15

"When
they persecute you in
one city, fly into another. I
tell you for a truth, ye shall not
finish all the cities of Israel, till the
Son of Man be come. The disciple
is not above his master, nor yet
the servant above his lord…
And fear ye not them which
kill the body, and be not
able to kill the soul."
(Matthew 10:23-24 & 28)

"What signifieth
that the prelates are
so bloody, and clothed in
red? That we be ready every
hour to suffer martyrdom for the
testimony of God's word. Is that also
not a false sign, when no man dare,
for them, once open his mouth to
ask a question of God's word,
because they are ready
to burn him?"

August 16

"No
man
can serve
two masters.
For either he shall
hate the one, and love
the other, or else he shall
lean to the one, and
despise that other."
(Matthew 6:24)

"Christ is
our righteousness, and
in him ought we to teach all
men to trust, and not make a prey of
them to lead them captive, to sit in their
consciences, and to teach them to trust in our
holiness, good deeds and prayers, to the intent
that we should feed our idle and slow bellies
of their great labor and sweat. If I take on
me to save others by my merits, make I
not myself a Christ and a Savior?
I am indeed a false prophet,
and a true antichrist."

August 17

"O generation of vipers, who hath taught you to flee from the vengeance to come? Bring forth therefore the fruits belonging to repentance."
(Matthew 3:7-8)

"Without the promise of God, there can be no faith, nor justifying, nor forgiveness of sins, for it is more than madness to look for anything of God, save that he hath promised. How far he hath promised, so far is he bound to them that believe, and further not. To have faith, therefore, or a trust in anything, where God hath not promised, is plain idolatry, and a worshipping of thine own imagination, instead of God. To confess with the mouth is a good work, and the fruit of a true faith, as all other works are. Another confession is there, which goeth before faith, and accompanieth repentance. For whosoever repenteth, doth knowledge his sins in his heart."

August 18

"They may
know that thou
art alone, that thy
name is the Lord, and
that thou only art the
most highest over
all the earth."
(Psalms 83:18)

Tyndale's
inspired creation of the
English word 'Jehovah' has
left an inestimable literary mark
on the Christian world, past, present,
and future. In a note to the edition of the
New Testament that was first published in
Antwerp, in 1534, Tyndale wrote: "Iehovah is
God's name. Moreover, as oft as thou seeist LORD
in great letters (except there be any error in the
printing) is in Hebrew Iehovah." Note that
there was no 'J' in English at this time;
the 'J' is the product of a stylized 'I'
thus giving us the current Jehovah,
rather than the Old English
spelling of Iehovah.

August 19

"Search
the scriptures, for
in them ye think ye have
eternal life. And they are they
which testify of me. And yet will
ye not come to me, that ye might
have life. I receive not praise of
men. But I know you, that
ye have not the love
of God in you."
(John 5:39-42)

"It is verily as
good to preach the
word of God to swine
as to men, if thou preach
it in a tongue they understand
not. How shall I prepare myself to
God's commandments? How shall I be
thankful to Christ for his kindness? How
shall I believe the truth and promises
which God hath sworn, while thou
tellest them unto me in a tongue
which I understand not?"

August 20

"Let
us make man
in our similitude,
and after our likeness,
that he may have rule over
the fishes of the sea, and over
the fowls of the air, and over
cattle, and over all the earth,
and over all worms that
creep upon the earth."
(Genesis 1:26)

"The
scriptures can
represent divers things.
A serpent figureth Christ
in one place, and the devil in
another, and a lion doth likewise.
Christ, by leaven, signifieth God's
word in one place, and in another
the traditions of the Pharisees,
which soured and altered
God's word for their
advantage."

August 21

"Then the
Lord God cast
a slumber on Adam,
and he slept. And then he
took out one of his ribs, and
in stead thereof, he filled up
the place with flesh. And the Lord
God made of the rib which he took
out of Adam, a woman, and brought
her unto Adam. Then said Adam: This
is once bone of my bones, and flesh of
my flesh. This shall be called woman,
because she was taken of the man.
For this cause shall a man leave
father and mother and cleave
unto his wife, and they
shall be one flesh."
(Genesis 2:21-24)

"Obedience that is not of love
cannot long endure. Now then, if
disobedience rise, are ye not the
cause of it yourselves? Say not,
but that we be warned!"

August 22

"The Lord went by,
and a mighty strong wind rent
the mountains and brake the rocks
before him. But the Lord was not in
the wind. And after the wind, came
an earthquake. But the Lord was
not in the earthquake. And after
the earthquake, came fire. But
the Lord was not in the fire.
And after the fire, came
a small still voice."
(1 Kings 19:11-12)

"Christ
gave to his
apostles the key of
the knowledge of the
law of God, to bind all
sinners, and the key of the
promises, to loose all that
repent, and to let them
in to the mercy that
is laid up for us
in Christ."

August 23

"O generation
of vipers, how can ye
say well, when ye yourselves
are evil? For of the abundance of
the heart, the mouth speaketh. A good
man, out of the good treasure of his
heart, bringeth forth good things.
And an evil man, out of his
evil treasure, bringeth
forth evil things."
(Matthew 12:34-35)

"Many
things there be in
the scriptures, which have
a carnal fulfilling, even there
where they be spoken or done,
and yet have another spiritual
signification, to be fulfilled
long after in Christ and
his kingdom, and yet
never known till
the thing be
done."

August 24

"Once
justified by his
grace, (we) should be
heirs of eternal life, through
hope. ...Foolish questions, and
genealogies, and brawlings and
strife about the law avoid, for
they are unprofitable,
and superfluous."
(Titus 3:7 & 9)

"Let us, therefore,
look diligently whereunto
we are called, that we deceive
not ourselves. We are called, not to
dispute as the pope's disciples, but to
die with Christ, that we may live with
him, and to suffer with him, that we
may reign with him. We be called
unto a kingdom that must be won
with suffering only, as a sick man
winneth health. God is he that
doth all things for us, and
fighteth for us, and we
do but suffer only."

August 25

"I exhort
that above
all things, prayers,
supplications, petitions,
and giving of thanks be had
for all men, for kings, and for
all that are in preeminence, that
we may live a quiet and peaceable
life, in all godliness and honesty."
(1 Timothy 2:1-2)

"God
forbiddeth
all men to avenge
themselves, or to take
the authority and office of
avenging to himself, saying,
"Vengeance is mine, and I will
reward." For it is impossible that
a man should be a righteous, an
equal, or an indifferent judge
in his own cause, for our
lusts and appetites
so blind
us."

August 26

"Put thy trust in the Lord
with all thine heart, and lean not
unto thine own understanding. In
all thy ways have respect unto him, and
he shall order thy goings. Be not wise in
thine own conceit, but fear the Lord,
and depart from evil. So shall
thy navel be whole, and
thy bones strong."
(Proverbs 3:5-8)

"To them, sendeth he his Spirit, which
openeth their eyes, sheweth them their misery, and
bringeth them unto the knowledge of themselves, so
that they hate and abhor themselves, are astonished and
amazed, and at their wit's ends, neither wet what to do, or
where to seek health. Then, lest they should flee from God
by desperation, he comforteth them again with his sweet
promises in Christ, and certifieth their hearts that, for
Christ's sake, they are received to mercy, and their
sins forgiven, and they are the elect and made
the sons of God, and heirs with Christ of
eternal life, and thus through faith
are set at peace with God."

August 27

"Thou hast much
goods laid up in store
for many years; take thine ease.
Eat, drink and be merry. But God said
unto him: Thou fool, this night will they
fetch away thy soul again from thee.
Then, whose shall those things be
which thou hast provided?"
(Luke 12:19-20)

"What
will become
of us when we meet
with a subtle philosopher
and antichristian head who will
frame an argument against the truth,
unanswerable by our logic? Where shall a
man ever consist, if he must live on the terms
of the world? Besides, every one to whom the
Gospel of Christ is preached is not headstrong
enough to grapple with the bigness and depth
of some kinds of arguments. They may have
their hearts truly mortified in this world,
and are thereby transformed by love to
the person and nature of our Lord."

August 28

"They mocked
the messengers of God
and despised their words, and
misused his prophets until the
wrath of the Lord so arose
against his people that
it was past remedy."
(2 Chronicles 36:16)

Gordon Jackson
said: "The real mark of
the priesthood is that God's
human agent identifies with the
One he represents. He is, one could say,
God in metaphor. In bringing God, through
his word, to the people of England, Tyndale
undertook a task comparable to that of Christ.
The task had already been claimed by the one
who styled himself the Vicar of Christ, but
Tyndale made it his mission to take that
role on himself, not presumptuously,
as he was accused, but with the
full humility of a true priest, a
man prepared to lay down
his life for the sheep."

August 29

"Even unto
this day, we hunger
and thirst, and are naked,
and are buffeted with fists,
and have no certain dwelling
place, and labour, working with
our own hands. We are reviled, and
yet we bless. We are persecuted, and
suffer it. We are evil spoken of, and
we pray. We are made, as it were,
the filthiness of the world, the
offscouring of all things."
(1 Corinthians 4:11-13)

Tyndale
was forced to face
the authorities of the
diocese on trumped-up
charges of heresy. He
later recalled that he
was threatened,
and treated no
better than
a dog.

August 30

He
"would have all
men saved, and come
unto the knowledge of the
truth. For there is one God, and
one mediator between God and
man, which is the man Christ
Jesus, which gave himself a
ransom for all men, that
it should be preached
at his time."
(1 Timothy 2:4-6)

"There is no
other way to be saved
from condemnation than through
repentance toward the law, and faith
in Christ's blood, which are the very
inward baptism of our souls. Of
these, the washing and the
dipping of our bodies
in the water are
the outward
signs."

August 31

"Great
Babylon is fallen, is
fallen, and is become the
habitation of devils, and the
hold of all foul spirits, and a cage
of all unclean and hateful birds, for
all nations have drunken of the wine
of the wrath of her fornication. And
kings of the earth have committed
fornication with her, and her
merchants are waxed rich
of the abundance of
her pleasures."
(Revelation 18:2-3)

"Woe be to
you, scribes and
Pharisees, hypocrites!
For ye make clean the utter
side of the cup, and of the
platter, but within you
are full of bribery
and excess."

"I am the light of the world."
(John 9: 5)

September 1

"Ask, and
it shall be given you,
seek and ye shall find, knock
and it shall be opened unto you.
For whosoever asketh receiveth, and
he that seeketh, findeth, and to him that
knocketh, it shall be opened. Is there any
man among you which would proffer his
son an ibstone if he asked him bread? Or
if he asked fish, would he proffer him a
serpent? If ye then, which are evil, can
give to your children good gifts, how
much more shall your Father, which
is in heaven, give good things to
them that ask of him?"
(Matthew 7:7-11)

"A man ought to love his
neighbor as equally and fully
as he loves himself, because his
neighbor, be he ever so simple, is
equally created by God and as fully
redeemed by the blood of our
Savior Jesus Christ."

September 2

"With your
ears ye shall hear,
and shall not understand,
and with your eyes ye shall
see, and shall not perceive. For
this people's heart is waxed gross,
and their ears were dull of hearing,
and their eyes have they closed, lest
they should see with their eyes, and
hear with their ears, and should
understand with their hearts."
(Matthew 13:14-15)

"Now,
when thou
absolvest in Latin, the
unlearned heareth not, for
how, when thou blessest in
an unknown tongue, shall
the unlearned say Amen
unto thy thanksgiving?
For he wotteth not
what thou
sayest."

September 3

"Strait
is the gate,
and narrow is
the way, which
leadeth unto life,
and few there be
that find it."
(Matthew 7:14)

"In all my doings, I must
have the law before me to condemn
my imperfectness. For all I do is yet damnable
sin when compared to the law, which requires the
ground and bottom of my heart. I must, therefore, always
have the law in my sight so I may be meek in the spirit
and give God all the laud and praise, ascribing to him
all righteousness and to myself all unrighteousness
and sin. I must also have the promises before my
eyes so I do not despair, in which promises
I see the mercy, favor, and good-will of
God upon me in the blood of his Son
Christ, who has made satisfaction
for my imperfectness and has
fulfilled for me that which
I could not do."

September 4

"Men's hearts
shall fail them for fear, and
for looking after those things
which shall come on the earth. For the
powers of heaven shall move. And then shall
they see the Son of Man come in a cloud with
power and great glory. When these things
begin to come to pass, then look up,
and lift up your heads, for your
redemption draweth nye."
(Luke 21:26-28)

"Let every man,
therefore, wait on the
office wherein Christ hath put
him, and therein serve his brethren.
If he be of low degree, let him patiently
therein abide, till God promote him, and
exalt him higher. Remember that we are
members of one body, and ought to
minister one to another mercifully,
and that whatsoever we have
is given of God to bestow
on our brethren."

September 5

"A
bishop
may not be a
young man lest
he swell and fall
into the judgment
of the evil speaker.
He must also be well
reported of among them
which are without forth,
lest he fall into rebuke,
and into the snare of
the evil speaker."
(1 Timothy 3:6-7)

"A bishop
must be faultless,
the husband of one
wife. Nay, saith the
pope, the husband
of no wife, but the
holder of as many
whores as he
listeth."

September 6

"Thou
hast delivered
my soul from death,
mine eyes from tears,
and my feet from falling.
I will walk before the
Lord, in the land
of the living."
(Psalms 116:8-9)

"At the
beginning, miracles
were shewed through
such ceremonies, to move
the infidels to believe the word
of God; how the apostles anointed
the sick with oil, and healed them, and
Paul sent his pertelet or jerkin to the sick,
and healed them also. Yet was it not the
ceremony that did the miracle, but the
faith of the preacher and the truth
of God, which had promised to
confirm and establish his
Gospel with such
miracles."

September 7

"God spake unto Moses, saying unto him: I am the Lord, and I appeared unto Abraham, Isaac, and Jacob, an Almighty God, but in my name Jehovah, was I not known unto them."
(Exodus 6:2-3)

"While I am sowing in one place, they ravage the field I have just left. I cannot be everywhere. If Christians had the scriptures in their own tongue, they would have the means to withstand these sophists. Without their Bible, it is impossible to establish the laity in the truth." Of his translation efforts, Tyndale simply wrote: "All that I do and suffer is but the way to the reward, and not the deserving thereof."

September 8

"The king shall govern after the
rule of righteousness, and the princes
shall rule according to the balance of equity.
He shall be unto men as a defense for the wind, and
as a refuge for the tempest, like as a river of water
in a thirsty place, and the shadow of a great rock
in a dry land. The eyes of the seeing shall not be
dim, and the ears of them that hear shall take
diligent heed. The heart of the unwise
shall attain to knowledge, and the
unperfect tongue shall speak
plainly and distinctly."
(Isaiah 32:1-4)

"Expound the law
truly, as a faithful minister,
of the mercy of our Lord Jesus, and
let the wounded consciences drink of
the water of Him. And then shall your
preaching be with power, and not as the
hypocrites. And the Spirit of God shall
work with you, and all consciences
shall bear record unto you,
and feel that it is so."

September 9

"Our
rejoicing
is this, the
testimony of our
conscience, that we
with out doubleness,
but with godly pureness,
not in fleshly wisdom, but
by the grace of God, have
had our conversation in
the world, and most of
all to youwards."
(2 Corinthians 1:12)

"If a man put his
hand to the plough
of God's word to preach
it, and look also unto worldly
business, his plough will surely
go awry. Therefore, saith
Christ: Let the dead bury
the dead; but come
thou and preach
the kingdom
of God."

September 10

"As they spake
unto the people, the
priests and the ruler of the
temple and the saduces came
upon them, taking grievously
that they taught the people and
preached in the name of Jesus
the resurrection from death."
(Acts 4:1-2)

"Were scripture in the mother
tongue, then would the lay-people
understand it, every man after his own ways.
Why serveth the curate, but to teach him the right
way? Wherefore were the holy days made, but that the
people should come and learn? Are ye not abominable
schoolmasters, in that ye take so great wages, and will
not teach? If ye would teach, how could ye do it well,
and with great profit, as when the lay-people have
the scripture before them in their mother tongue?
For then should they see, by the order of the
text, whether thou jugglest or not, and then
would they believe it, because it is the
scripture of God, though thy living
be never so abominable."

September 11

"In the
beginning was that word,
and that word was with God, and
God was that word. The same was in the
beginning with God. All things were made by
it, and without it, was made no thing that
made was. In it was life, and life was the
light of men, and the light shineth in
the darkness, and darkness
comprehended it not."
(John 1:1-5)

"The
churches
in the beginning
were ordained that
the people should thither
resort, to hear the word of God
there preached only, and not for
the use wherein they now are.
The temple wherein God
will be worshipped
is the heart of
man."

September 12

"With
men it is
impossible, but
not with God, for
with God all things
are possible."
(Mark 10:27)

"Why suffered
the prophets? Because
they rebuked the hypocrites
which beguiled the world, and
namely princes and rulers, and taught
them to put their trust in things of vanity,
and not in God's word. As the weak powers
of the world defend the doctrine of the world, so
the mighty power of God defendeth the doctrine of
God, which thing thou shalt perceive, if thou call to
mind the wonderful deeds which God hath wrought
for his word since the world began, beyond all man's
reason, which are written for our learning and not
for our deceiving, that we through patience and
comfort of the scripture might have hope.
The nature of God's word is to fight
against hypocrites."

September 13

"Then came until him the
tempter, and said: If thou be
the son of God, command that
these stones be made bread. He
answered and said: It is written
that man shall not live only by
bread, but by every word
that proceedeth out of
the mouth of God."
(Matthew 4:3-4)

"To know
these things,
I say, is to have all
the scripture unlocked
and opened before you, so
that if you will go in and read,
you cannot but understand. And
to be ignorant in these things is to
have all the scripture locked up, so
that the more you read it, the blinder
you are, the more contrariety you find
in it, and the more tangled in it you
become, so that you are unable to
find the way through it."

September 14

"I saw the dead, both great
and small, stand before God. And
the books were opened, and another
book was opened, which is the book of
life, and the dead were judged of those
things which were written in the books
according to their deeds. And the sea
gave up her dead which were in her,
and death and hell delivered up the
dead which were in them. And they
were judged every man according
to his deeds… And whosoever
was not found written in the
book of life, was cast into
the lake of fire."
(Revelation 20:12-15)

"God looketh first on thy heart, and on what
faith thou hath to his words; how thou believeth
him, trusteth him, and how thou loveth him
for his mercy. He looketh with what heart
thou worketh, and not of what degree
thou art, whether thou be an
apostle or a shoemaker."

September 15

"Our Father, which
art in heaven, hallowed
be thy name. Let thy kingdom
come. Thy will be fulfilled, as well in
earth, as it is in heaven. Give us this
day our daily bread. And forgive us
our trespasses, even as we forgive
them which trespass us. Lead us
not in to temptation, but deliver
us from evil. For thine is the
kingdom, and the power,
and the glory for ever."
(Matthew 6:9-13)

"God hath
promised Christ's merits
unto all who will repent, so that
whosoever repenteth is immediately
heir of all Christ's merits, and beloved of
God, as Christ is. How then came this foul
monster of absolution to be lord over
Christ's merits, so that he hath
power to sell that which
God giveth freely?"

September 16

"This people honoureth me with their lips, but their hearts are far from me."
(Mark 7:6)

"The name of God is held in fear and reverence, and we are not to dishonor his name, swearing by it about light trifles or vanities, or call it to record for the confirming of wickedness, falsehood, or anything that would dishonor him; which is the breaking of his laws or doing what tends to hurt our neighbor."

September 17

"He
answered
and said: Whether
he be a sinner or no, I
cannot tell. One thing
I am sure of, that I
was blind, and
now I see."
(John 9:25)

"That thou
mayest perceive and feel
the Spirit in thine heart, and not be
a vain sophister, disputing about words
without perceiving, mark this. The root of
all evil, the greatest damnation and most
terrible wrath and vengeance of God, is
to suffer from blindness. We are out of
the right way when one judgeth this
best, and another that to be best,
when with craft and subtlety,
we seek to obtain that which
we judge falsely to be best.
As I err in my wit, so do
I err in my will."

September 18

"As much as ye
have purified your souls
through the Spirit, in obeying
the truth for to love brotherly
without feigning, see that ye love
one another with a pure heart
fervently. For ye are born a
new, not of mortal seed,
but of immortal seed,
by the word of God
which liveth, and
lasteth for ever."
(1 Peter 1:22-23)

"The Law of the Lord is
spiritual, and requireth the
heart, and is never fulfilled with the
deed, in the sight of God. With the deed,
thou fulfillest the law before the world, and
livest thereby. That is, thou enjoyest this present
life, and avoidest wrath and vengeance, death
and punishment, which the law threateneth
to them that break it. But before God, thou
keepest the law, if thou love only."

September 19

"Of
this
manner
shall ye eat
it: With your
loins girded, and
shoes on your feet,
and your staves in your
hands. And ye shall eat
it in haste, for it is the
Lord's Passover."
(Exodus 12:11)

"The
sacrament of the
body and blood of
Christ hath a promise
annexed, which the priest
should declare in the English
tongue: This is my body, that is
broken for you. This is my blood,
that is shed for many, unto the
forgiveness of sins. This do
in remembrance of me."

September 20

"He
giveth to
all men life and
breath everywhere,
and hath made of one
blood all nations of men
for to dwell on all the face
of the earth. And hath assigned
times appointed before, and the
ends of their inhabitation, that they
should seek God, if they might feel
and find him, though he be not far
from every one of us. For in him
we live, move, and have our
being, as certain of your
own poets said."
(Acts 17:25-28)

"And if thou canst find in thine heart
to do good unto him that rewardeth thee
evil again, then art thou sure that the same
Spirit is in thee that is in Christ. Therefore,
see that thou not once desire vengeance,
but remit all vengeance unto God."

September 21

"Bow down thine ear, and
harken unto the words of wisdom.
Apply thy mind unto my doctrine. For it is
a pleasant thing if thou keep it in thine heart,
and practice it in thy mouth, that thou mayest
always put thy trust in the Lord. Have not I
warned thee very oft with counsel and
learning, that I might shew thee the
truth and that thou with the verity
mightest answer them that lay
anything against thee?"
(Proverbs 22:17-21)

"In the heart of man,
there must first be a greater
thing than all the good works in
the world, to reconcile him to God,
to bring the love and favor of God to
him, to make him love God again, to
make him righteous in the sight of
God, to do away his sin, and to
deliver him from captivity.
That precious thing is
the word of God."

September 22

"But
one shall say:
Thou hast faith,
and I have deeds. Shew
me thy faith by thy deeds,
and I will shew thee my faith
by my deeds. Believest thou that
there is one God? Thou doest well.
The devils also believe and tremble.
Wilt thou understand O thou vain
man, that faith without deeds is
dead? …The body without the
spirit is dead, even so, faith
without deeds is dead."
(James 2:18-20 & 26)

"The blind
owls care not
what they howl,
seeing it is night,
and the daylight of
God's word shut up,
that no man can
see them."

September 23

"If
any man
say to you: Lo,
here is Christ; lo, he
is there, believe not. For
false Christs shall arise, and
false prophets, and shall show
miracles and wonders, to deceive
if it were possible, even the elect.
But take ye heed, behold I have
showed you all things."
(Mark 13:21-23)

"Let not your
hearts be glued to worldly things.
Study not to heap treasure upon treasure,
and riches upon riches, but study to bestow well
that which is gotten already, and let your abundance
succor the lack and need of the poor which have not.
Have an eye to good works, to which if ye have
power to do them, then are ye sure that
the Spirit of God is in you, to the
reward of eternal life, which
followeth good works."

September 24

"Thou hast
power over all
things, and…there
is no thought hid unto
thee. For who can keep
his own counsel so
secret, but it shall
be known?"
(Job 42:2-3)

"Happy are they
who search the testimonies
of the Lord; that is to say, that which
God testifieth and witnesseth unto us. But
how shall I do that, when ye will not let me
have his testimonies, or witnesses, in a tongue
which I understand? Will ye resist God? Will
ye forbid him to give his Spirit unto the lay
as well as unto you? Hath he not made
the English tongue? Why forbid ye
him to speak in the English
tongue then, as well as
in the Latin?"

September 25

"And he came into all the
coasts about Jordan, preaching the
baptism of repentance for the remission of
sins, as it is written in the book of the sayings of
Esayas the prophet, which sayeth: The voice of a
crier in wilderness, prepare the way of the Lord,
make his paths straight. Every valley shall be
filled, and every mountain and hill shall be
brought low. And crooked things shall
be made straight, and the rough
ways shall be made smooth.
And all flesh shall see the
Saviour sent of God."
(Luke 3:3-6)

"We will speak a word or two of the
sacraments which Christ left among us for our
comfort, that we may walk in light and in truth,
and in feeling of the power of God. For he that
walketh in the day stumbleth not; while
contrariwise he that walketh in the
night stumbleth, and they that
walk in darkness wot not
whither they go."

September 26

"At the first creation, God
made them man and woman,
saying: For this thing's sake shall
man leave father and mother, and
bide by his wife, and shall be made
one flesh. So then are they now not
twain, but one flesh, therefore that
which God hath coupled, let
not man separate."
(Mark 10:6-9)

"Wedlock
is a state or a
degree ordained
of God and an office
wherein the husband
serveth the wife, and the
wife the husband. It was
ordained for a remedy, and
to increase the world, and for
the man to help the woman,
and the woman the man,
with all love and
kindness."

September 27

"Jesus cried again with a
loud voice and yielded up the ghost. And
behold, the veil of the temple was rent in twain
from the top to the bottom, and the earth did
quake, and the stones did rent, and graves
did open, and the bodies of many saints
which slept, arose, and came out of the
graves after his resurrection, and
came into the holy city, and
appeared unto many."
(Matthew 27:50-53)

"Christ hath
brought us all into the
inner temple, within the
veil or forehanging, and unto
the mercy-stool of God, and hath
coupled us unto God, where we offer,
every man for himself, the desires and
petitions of our hearts, and sacrifice
and kill the lusts and appetites of
our flesh, with prayer, fasting,
and all manner of godly
living."

September 28

"Jesus then
said to his disciples:
If any man will follow
me, let him forsake himself
and take up his cross.... For
whosoever will save his life,
shall lose it. And whosoever
shall lose his life for my
sake, shall find it."
(Matthew 16:24-25)

"When Christ
is preached, and the
promises rehearsed which are
contained in the psalms, prophets,
and divers places in the five books
of Moses, which preaching is called
the Gospel or glad tidings, then the
hearts of those who are elect and
chosen begin to grow soft, and
to melt at the bounteous
mercy of God and the
kindness shown
in Christ."

September 29

"The
last shall
be first, and the
first shall be last. For
many are called, and
few be chosen."
(Matthew 20:16)

The
unbridled
enthusiasm and
the unconquerable
and indomitable spirit
of Tyndale were evident in
all of his writings. "Christ is
with us until the world's end,"
he declared. "Let his little flock
be bold, therefore. For if God
be on our side, what matter
maketh it who be against
us, be they bishops,
cardinals, popes,
or whatsoever
names they
will?"

September 30

"There is no thing so close,
that shall not be opened, and no
thing so hid, that shall not be known.
What I tell you in darkness, that
speak ye in light. And what ye
hear in the ear, that preach
ye on the house tops."
(Matthew 10:26-27)

"In the Gospel,
when we believe in the
promises, we receive the spirit of
life and are justified in the blood of Christ
from all things in which the law condemned us.
And we receive love for the law, and power to fulfill it,
and grow therein daily. Of Christ, it is written, this is he of
whose abundance, or fullness, we have all received, grace for
grace or favor for favor; that is to say, for the favor that God
has to his Son Christ, he gives to us his favor and goodwill,
and all gifts of his grace, like a father to his sons. Paul
affirms this, saying: 'He loved us in his beloved,
(that is, in Christ) before the creation of the
world.' Thus, it is Christ who brings the
love of God to us, and not our
own holy works."

"I was blind, and now I see."
(John 9:39)

October 1

"He that lacketh
these things is blind and
gropeth for the way with his hand,
and hath forgotten that he was purged
from his old sins. Wherefore, brethren, give the
more diligence for to make your calling and election
sure. For if ye do such things, ye shall never err. Yea,
and by this means an entering in shall be ministered
unto you abundantly into the everlasting kingdom
of our Lord and Saviour Jesus Christ. Wherefore,
I will not be negligent to put you always in
remembrance of such things, though
that ye know them yourselves
and be also established in
the present truth."
(2 Peter 1:9-12)

"See that thou have God's promises in
thine heart, and that thou believe them without
wavering. When temptation ariseth, and the devil
layeth the law and thy deeds against thee, answer him
with the promises, and turn to God, and confess thyself to
him, and say it is even so, or else how could he be merciful?
He is a God of mercy and of truth and will fulfill his promises."

October 2

"Finally,
my brethren, be
strong in the Lord, and in
the power of his might. Put on
the armour of God, that ye may stand
steadfast against the crafty assaults of the
devil. For we wrestle not against flesh and
blood, but against rule, against power,
and against worldly rulers of the
darkness of this world; against
spiritual wickedness in
heavenly things."
(Ephesians 6:10-12)

"Who slew
the prophets?
Who slew Christ?
Who slew his apostles,
the martyrs, and all the
righteous that ever were
slain? The kings and the
temporal sword at the
request of the false
prophets."

October 3

"These things
write I unto you, that
ye should not sin. And if
any man sin, yet we have
an Advocate with the Father,
Jesus Christ, which is righteous,
and he it is that obtaineth grace for
our sins; not for our sins only, but
also for the sins of all the world.
And hereby we know that we
have known him, if we keep
his commandments."
(1 John 2:1-3)

"Christ,
when he had
fulfilled his course,
anointed his apostles and
disciples with the same Spirit,
and sent them forth, without all
manner disguising, like other men
also, to preach the atonement and
peace, which Christ had made
between God and man."

October 4

"And
if any man
will sue thee at
the law, and take thy
coat from thee, let him
have thy cloak also. And
whosoever will compel thee
to go a mile, go with him
twain. Give to him that
asketh, and from him
that would borrow,
turn not away."
(Matthew 5:40-42)

"There is
no work better
than to please God.
To pour water, to wash
dishes, to be a cobbler or
to preach, or to be an
apostle, all are one;
as touching the
deed, all are
pleasing to
God."

October 5

"Thou
art Peter. And
upon this rock I will
build my congregation,
and the gates of hell shall not
prevail against it. And I will give
unto thee the keys of the kingdom of
heaven, and whatsoever thou bindest
upon earth, it shall be bound in
heaven, and whatsoever thou
lowsest on earth, it shall be
lowsed in heaven."
(Matthew 16:18-19)

"Lo, saith antichrist,
Peter is the rock whereon the
church of Christ is built, and I am
his successor, and therefore the head of
Christ's church. Not so! Faith is the rock
whereon Christ's church is built. Faith
is it against which hell-gates cannot
prevail. Faith is it which saveth
the congregation of Christ,
and not Peter."

October 6

"Behold, I set before you this
day, a blessing and a curse; a blessing
if ye hearken unto the commandments of the
Lord your God which I command you this day.
And a curse if ye will not hearken unto the
commandments of the Lord your God."
(Deuteronomy 11:26-28)

"God setteth before
us a blessing and also a curse:
a blessing, verily, and that a glorious
and an everlasting, if we suffer tribulation
and adversity with our Lord and Savior Christ;
and an everlasting curse, if, for a little pleasure sake,
we withdraw ourselves from the chastising and nurture
of God, wherewith he teacheth all his sons, and fashioneth
them after his godly will, and maketh them perfect, as he did
Christ, and maketh them apt and meet vessels to receive his
grace and his Spirit, that they might perceive and feel the
exceeding mercy which we have in Christ, and the
innumerable blessings and the unspeakable
inheritance, whereto we are called and
chosen, and sealed to our Savior
Jesus Christ, unto whom
be praise for ever."

October 7

"The
Lord shall
scatter you among
nations, and ye shall be
left few in number among
the people whither the Lord
shall bring you. And there ye
shall serve gods which are the
works of man's hand, wood and
stone, which neither see, nor
hear, nor eat, nor smell."
(Deuteronomy 4:27-28)

"Among
Christians, it is
love that maketh
all things common.
Every man is another's
debtor, and every man is
bound to minister to his
neighbor, and to supply
to his neighbor of that
wherewith God hath
endowed him."

October 8

"But
they were
not obedient. They
inclined not their ears there
unto, but went after their own
imaginations and after the motions
of their own wicked heart, and so
turned themselves away, and
converted not unto me."
(Jeremiah 7:24)

"The sermons
which thou readest in the
Acts of the Apostles, and all
that the apostles preached, were no
doubt preached in the mother tongue.
Why then might they not be written
in our mother tongue? As, if one of
us preach a good sermon, why
may it not be written? Saint
Jerome also translated the
Bible into his mother
tongue. Why may
we not also?"

October 9

"I
will put
my laws in their
minds and in their
hearts. I will write them,
and I will be their God, and
they shall be my people. And
they shall not teach every man his
neighbor, and every man his brother,
saying: Know the Lord. For they shall
know me, from the least to the most of
them. For I will be merciful over their
iniquities, and on their sins and on
their unrighteousness will
I not think any more."
(Hebrews 8:10-12)

"God
hath promised
mercy unto a contrite
heart, that is, to a
sorrowful and
a repenting
heart."

October 10

"Go
unto Pharaoh
and tell him: Thus
saith the Lord, let my
people go, that they
may serve me."
(Exodus 8:1)

"God
has ordained a
better way to convey
his truth into our hearts,
and that is by a renovation of our
minds and by the communication of a
divine nature. God has not let his people
remain in uncertainties in those things which
are material and necessary, but has given a
certainty of demonstration. Whatsoever
I do receive for truth on the account of
argumentive conclusions, that I am
bound to lay aside and disown
for error upon the same
account, when a more
probable argument
comes along."

October 11

> "I
> am filled
> with comfort, my
> joy exceeding in all
> our tribulations."
> (2 Corinthians 7:4)

> "To have
> faith or a trust in
> anything where God
> hath not promised, is plain
> idolatry, and a worshipping of thine
> own imagination instead of God. Mark this
> also, if God send thee to the sea, and promise
> to go with thee, and to bring thee safe to land, he
> will raise up a tempest against thee to prove whether
> thou wilt abide by his word, and that thou mayest feel
> thy faith, and perceive his goodness. For if it were
> always fair weather, and thou never brought
> into such jeopardy, whence his mercy only
> delivered thee, thy faith should be but a
> presumption, and thou shouldest
> be ever unthankful to God
> and merciless unto
> thy neighbor."

October 12

"When God doth once command a
thing, there should no man be curious, to search
whether it be right. In dreams and visions of the
night season, when slumbering cometh upon
men, that they fall a sleep in their beds, he
roundeth them in the ears, he informeth
them, and showeth them plainly."
(Job 33:14-16)

"Prepare
thy mind unto
this little treatise;
and read it discreetly,
and judge it indifferently.
When I allege any scripture,
look thou on the text, whether I
interpret it right, which thou shalt
easily perceive by their circumstance
and process. Make thou the Christ the
foundation and ground, and build all
on him, and referrest all to him, and
proveth also that my exposition
agreeth unto the common
articles of faith and the
open scriptures."

October 13

"Bring
hither that
fatted calf, and
kill him, and let us
eat and be merry, for
this my son was dead,
and is alive again. He
was lost, and is
now found."
(Luke 15:23-24)

"Learning
and comfort is the
fruit of the scripture, and
cause why it was written. And
with such a purpose read it, for it is
the way to everlasting life, and to those
joyful blessings that are promised unto
all nations in the seed of Abraham,
which seed is Jesus Christ our
Lord, to whom be honour
and praise forever, and
unto God our Father
through him."

October 14

"Salute
one another
among yourselves
with an holy kiss. The
congregations of
Christ salute
you."
(Romans 16:16)

"The
church
of Christ is
the multitude of
all those who believe
in him for the remission
of sins, and who are thankful
for that mercy and who love the law
of God purely, and who hate the sin in
this world and long for the life to come.
To then confess out of the heart that all
benefits come of God, even out of the
goodness of his mercy and not
the deservings of our deeds,
is the only sacrifice that
pleases God."

October 15

"Flesh and
blood cannot
inherit the kingdom of
God. Neither doth corruption
inherit uncorruption. Behold I show a
mystery unto you. We shall not all sleep, but
we shall all be changed, and that in a moment,
and in the twinkling of an eye, at the sound of
the last trumpet. For the trumpet shall blow,
and the dead shall rise incorruptible. And
we shall be changed. For this corruptible
must put on incorruptibility, and this
mortal must put on immortality."
(1 Corinthians 15:50-53)

"He that
doubteth, or
hath his conscience
tangled, ought to open his
mind unto some faithful
brother that is learned,
and he shall give him
faithful counsel to
help him."

October 16

"Blessed are the
pure in heart, for they
shall see God. Blessed are the
maintainers of peace, for they shall be
called the children of God. Blessed are
they which suffer persecution for
righteousness' sake, for theirs is
the kingdom of heaven."
(Matthew 5:8-10)

"The Evangelion is
a more gentle pastor, which
supples and assuages the wounds of
the conscience and brings health. It brings the
Spirit of God, which looses the bonds of Satan and
joins us to God and his will, through strong faith and
fervent love, with bonds too strong for the devil, the
world, or any creature, to loose. And the poor and
wretched sinner feels such great mercy, love,
and kindness in God, that he is sure in
himself that it is not possible that
God would forsake him, or
withdraw his mercy
and love from
him."

October 17

"Unto them
that are defiled, and
unbelieving, is nothing
pure, but even the very minds
and consciences of them are defiled.
They confess that they know God, but
with deeds they deny him and are
abominable, and disobedient,
and unto all good works
discommendable."
(Titus 1:15-16)

"Antichrist has
ordained bishops to
kill whosoever preaches
true faith in Christ. So are his
ceremonies ordained to quench
the faith which Christ's sacraments
preach. And hereby mayest thou know
the difference between Christ's signs
or sacraments, and antichrist's
signs or ceremonies; that
Christ's signs speak,
and antichrist's
be dumb."

October 18

"God
created man
after his likeness,
after the likeness of God
created he him, male and
female created he them. And
God blessed them, and God said
unto them: Grow, and multiply,
and fill the earth and subdue it,
and have dominion over the
fishes of the sea, and over
the fowls of the air, and
over all the beasts that
move on the earth."
(Genesis 1:27-28)

"I beseech
his grace to have
compassion on his subjects,
which have ever been unto his
grace both obedient, loving, and
kind, that the realm utterly perish
not with the wicked counsel
of our pestilent prelates."

October 19

"Judge
not, lest ye
be judged. For
as ye judge, so
shall ye be
judged."
(Matthew 7:1-2)

"If any
can say better,
or improve this with
God's word, no man shall
be better content therewith
than I. For I seek nothing but
the truth and to walk in the light.
I submit therefore this work and all
other that I have made or shall make
(if God will that I shall make more)
unto the judgments, not of them
that furiously burn all truth, but
of them which are ready with
God's word to correct, if any
thing be said amiss, and
to further God's
word."

October 20

"Israel loved
Joseph more than
all his children, because
he begat him in his old age,
and he made him a coat of many
colours. When his brethren saw that
their father loved him more than
all his brethren, they hated him
and could not speak one kind
word unto him. Moreover,
Joseph dreamed a dream
and told it his brethren.
Wherefore, they hated
him yet the more."
(Genesis 37:3-5)

"As thou
readest, therefore,
think that every syllable
pertaineth to thine own self,
and search out the pith
of the scriptures, and
arm thyself against
all assaults."

October 21

"Jesus
said unto him:
If thou wilt be perfect,
go and sell that thou hast,
and give it to the poor, and
thou shalt have treasure
in heaven. And come
and follow me."
(Matthew 19:21)

"By faith, we receive
from God, and by love, we
give out again. And this must we
do freely, after the example of Christ,
without any other consideration except our
neighbor's welfare alone. And we must not
look for reward in earth or in heaven based on
our merit, or deserving for our deeds, as friars
preach, but out of pure love we must bestow
ourselves all that we have, and all that
we are able, even on our enemies, to
bring them to God, considering
nothing but their welfare,
as Christ did
ours."

October 22

"God,
be merciful
unto me, for my soul
trusteth in thee, and under
the shadow of thy wings shall
be my refuge, until wickedness be
overpast. I call unto God the most
highest, even to the God that help
me up again. He shall send from
heaven, and save me from the
reproof of him that would
swallow me up."
(Psalms 57:1-3)

"The deeds
which we henceforth do,
do we not to make satisfaction,
or to obtain heaven, but to succor
our neighbor, to tame the flesh,
that we may wax perfect and
strong men in Christ, and to
be thankful to God again
for his mercy, and to
glorify his name."

October 23

"Every high
priest that is taken from
among men, is ordained for
men in things pertaining to God, to
offer gifts and sacrifices for sins, which
can have compassion on the ignorant, and
on them that are out of the high way, because
that he himself also is compassed with infirmity.
For the which infirmities sake, he is bound
to offer for sins, as well for his own part
as for the peoples. No man taketh
honour unto himself, but he
that is called of God,
as was Aaron."
(Hebrews 5:1-4)

"The ministers and
apostles of God preach
his word, and his signs or
sacraments signify his word
and put us in remembrance
of the promises which he
hath made unto us
in Christ."

October 24

"These are
wells without water, and
clouds carried about of a tempest, to
whom the mist of darkness is reserved
for ever. For when they have spoken the
swelling words of vanity, they beguile with
wantonness through the lusts of the flesh
them that were clean escaped, but now
are wrapped in errors. They promise
them liberty, and are themselves
the bondservants of corruption.
For of whomsoever a man is
overcome, unto the same
is he in bondage."
(2 Peter 2:17-19)

"If any person,
from impatience or a
stubborn and rebellious mind,
withdraw himself and get him to any
other order, let him not think thereby
to avoid the vengeance of God in
obeying rules and tradition of
man's imagination."

October 25

"O,
generation of
vipers, who hath
shewed the craft to fly
from wrath to come?
Bring forth due fruits
of repentance."
(Luke 3:7-8)

"Show
the pope a
little money, and God
is so merciful that there is
no purgatory. And why is not
the fire out as well, if I offer for
me the blood of Christ? If Christ
hath deserved all for me, who
gave the pope might to keep
part of his deservings from
me, and to buy and sell
Christ's merits, and to
make merchandise
over us with
contrived
words?"

October 26

"Blessed be
God, the Father of
our Lord Jesus Christ, which
hath blessed us with all manner of
spiritual blessings in heavenly things
by Christ, according as he had chosen us
in him through love, before the foundation
of the world was laid, that we should be saints,
and without blame in his sight. And ordained us
before unto him self that we should be chosen
as heirs through Jesus Christ, according to
the pleasure of his will, to the praise of
his glorious grace, wherewith he
hath made us accepted."
(Ephesians 1:3-6)

"Woe be to
you scribes and
Pharisees, hypocrites, for
ye shut up the kingdom of
heaven before men, that is,
as it is written: Ye have
taken away the key
of knowledge."

October 27

"How
sweet are thy
words unto my
throat! Yea, more
than honey unto
my mouth!"
(Psalm 119:103)

"It is through a holy
sympathy that a regenerate heart
entertains with infinite delight holy
truths. Arguments and syllogisms make
great noise in the world, like the appearance
to the prophet Elijah, when the great and strong
wind broke the mountains and broke in pieces all
the rocks. But it is said, the Lord was not found in
the wind, nor in the earthquake, nor in the fire,
but He was in the still, small voice. The Holy
Spirit doth gently hover over the soul and
brood upon it. Heavenly doctrine falls
down upon the spirits of men, not
like a mighty violent rain, but
like a shower of oil, like
a sweet honey
dew."

October 28

"The
Lord
bless thee
and keep thee.
The Lord make
his face shine upon
thee and be merciful
unto thee. The Lord lift
up his countenance
upon thee and give
thee peace."
(Numbers 6:24-26)

"Let
Christian
kings keep their
faith and all lawful
promises, not one with
another only, but even with
whatsoever infidel it be. For
so it is right before God,
as the scriptures and
ensamples of the
Bible testify."

October 29

"This
is the tidings
which we have heard of
him, and declare unto you,
that God is light, and in him is
no darkness at all. If we say that
we have fellowship with him, and
yet walk in darkness, we lie, and do
not the truth. But, and if, we walk
in light even as he is in light, then
have we fellowship with him,
and the blood of Christ his
Son cleanseth us from all
sin." (1 John 1:5-7)

"Do
not our blind
guides also stumble at a
straw, and leap over a
block, making narrow
consciences at trifles,
and at matters of
weight none
at all?"

October 30

"Ye blind guides, which
strain out a gnat, and swallow
a camel. Woe be to you scribes and
Pharises, hypocrites, for ye make clean the
outer side of the cup, and of the platter, but
within they are full of bribery and excess.
Thou blind Pharise, cleanse first that
which is within the cup and the
platter, that the outside
may also be clean."
(Matthew 23:24-26)

"Where faith is
mighty and strong,
there is love fervent,
and deeds plenteous,
and done with exceeding
meekness. Where faith
is weak, there is love
cold, and the deeds
few and seldom,
as flowers and
blossoms in
winter."

October 31

"The
gentiles
glorified
the word
of the Lord,
and believed,
even as many as
were ordained unto
eternal life. And the
word of the Lord was
published throughout
all the region."
(Acts 13:48-49)

"Christ
desires his mysteries
to be published abroad, as
widely as possible. I would that
the Gospels and the epistles of
Paul were translated into all
languages, of all Christian
people, and that they
might be read and
known."

"Wandering stars"
(Jude 1:13)

November 1

"Go unto this
people and say: With
your ears shall ye hear,
and shall not understand,
and with your eyes shall ye
see and shall not perceive. For
the heart of this people is waxed
gross, and their ears were thick of
hearing, and their eyes have they
closed, lest they should see with
their eyes, and hear with their
ears, and understand with
their hearts, and should be
converted, and I should
heal them."
(Acts 28:26-27)

"As the
circumcised in
the flesh, and not in the
heart, have no part in God's
promises, even so they that are
baptized in the flesh, and not in the
heart, have no part in Christ's blood."

November 2

"And
the devil took
him up into an high
mountain, and showed
him all the kingdoms
of the earth, even
in the twinkling
of an eye."
(Luke 4:5)

"The
task he
had undertaken
was a prophetic one,
and to achieve it called for
dedication. Tyndale was born to
give the English their Bible. We can
appreciate that, but Tyndale saw it before
there was much of a chance of its realization.
Indeed, he ventured on, not in the anticipation
of success, but on manly faith. He depended
on God to provide, and I suspect that he
was blessed with assistance from the
quarter to which he looked."
(Gordon Jackson)

November 3

"Ye
are the light
of the world. A
city that is set on an
hill cannot be hid, neither
do men light a candle and put it
under a bushel, but on a candlestick,
and it lighteth all them which are
in the house. See that your light
so shine before men that they
may see your good works,
and glorify your Father
which is in heaven."
(Matthew 5:14-16)

"I marvel,
dearly beloved in
Christ, that any man
would ever contend or
speak against having the
scriptures available in
every language,
for every
man."

November 4

"Thus is it
written, and
thus it behooved
Christ to suffer, and to
rise again from death the
third day. And that repentance,
and remission of sins, should be
preached in his name among all
nations. And the beginning
must be at Jerusalem. And
ye are witnesses of
these things."
(Luke 24:46-48)

"Our health is
the power or strength
to fulfill the law, or to keep
the commandments. Now, he that
longeth for health, that is to say, for
to do the law of God, is blessed in
Christ, and hath a promise that
his lust shall be fulfilled,
and that he shall be
made whole."

November 5

"If,
when we
were enemies,
we were reconciled
to God by the death of his
Son, much more, seeing we are
reconciled, we shall be preserved
by his life. Not only so, but we
also joy in God by the means
of our Lord Jesus Christ, by
whom we have received
this atonement."
(Romans 5:10-11)

"Neither do our
works justify us, for
except we were justified by
faith, we could do no good work
freely, without respect of some
profit, either in this world,
or in the world to come.
Neither could we have
spiritual joy in our
hearts in time of
affliction."

November 6

"Death,
where is
thy sting?
Hell, where
is thy victory?
The sting of
death is
sin."
(1 Corinthians 15:55-56)

"Be not easily
offended, that divers
things are overseen through
negligence in this little treatise.
For verily, the chance was such,
that I marvel that it is so well as it is.
It becometh the book even so to come
as a mourner, and in vile apparel to
wait on his master, which sheweth
himself now again, not in honor
and glory, but in rebuke and
shame, try his true friends,
and to prove whether
there be any faith
on the earth."

November 7

"So
likewise ye,
when ye have
done all those things
which are commanded
unto you, say, we are
unprofitable servants.
We have done that
which was our
duty to do."
(Luke 17:10)

"The
blood
of Christ
hath hired us
already. Thus, in
the deed delighteth
God, as far as we do it,
either to serve our neighbor,
or tame the flesh, that we may
fulfill the commandment
from the bottom of
our hearts."

November 8

"By their fruits ye shall know them. Not all they that say unto me, master, master, shall enter in to the kingdom of heaven, but he that fulfilleth my Father's will which is in heaven."
(Matthew 7:20 -21)

"The miracles done in Egypt, in the Red Sea, on mount Sinai, and so forth, were not done that men should go in pilgrimage unto the places, to pray there, but to provoke them unto the true knowledge of God, that afterward they might ever pray in the Spirit, wheresoever they were. Christ also did not his miracles that men should pray in the places where he did them, but to stir up the people to come and hear the word of their souls' health. And when Christ sent the blind thither to receive his sight, the miracle was so done in order to declare the obedient faith of the blind, that they might learn to know God."

November 9

"Ye, as living
stones, are made
a spiritual house, and
an holy priesthood, for to
offer up spiritual sacrifice,
acceptable to God by Jesus
Christ. Wherefore, it is
contained in the
scripture."
(1 Peter 2:5-6)

"If any
question arise, let
them judge by the manifest and
open scriptures, not excluding the lay
men, for there are many found among them
which are as wise as the officers. Or else, when the
officer dieth, how could we put another in his room?
Wilt thou so teach twenty, thirty, forty, or fifty years,
that no man shall have knowledge or judgment in
God's word, save thou only? Is it not a shame
that we Christians come so oft to church
in vain, when he of fourscore years
old knoweth no more than he
that was born yesterday?"

November 10

"And he
said unto them,
follow me, and I will
make you fishers of men.
And they straightway
left their nets, and
followed him."
(Mark 1:17-18)

"A Christian rejoiceth
not of his deeds, neither
counteth his merits, neither
seeketh a higher place in heaven
of them, neither maketh himself a
Savior of other men through his good
works, but giveth all honor to God,
and knowledgeth himself a sinner,
and is content with the place that
is prepared for him of Christ. His
good deeds are to him a sign
only that Christ's Spirit is
in him, and, through
Christ, he is elect
to eternal
life."

November 11

"This is
the testament
that I will make unto
them after those days,
saith the Lord. And I will
put my laws in their hearts,
and in their minds I will write
them, and their sins and iniquities
will I remember no more. And where
remission of these things is, there is no
more offering for sin. Seeing, brethren,
that by the means of the blood of Jesus,
we may be bold to enter into that holy
place by the new and living way,
which he hath prepared for
us, through the veil."
(Hebrews 10:16-20)

"The love
of Christ excludeth
no man. In Christ, we
are all of one degree,
without respect
of persons."

November 12

"Jesus said
unto her: I am the
resurrection and the life.
Whosoever believeth on
me, yea though he were
dead, yet shall he live,
and whosoever liveth,
and believeth on me,
shall never die."
(John 11:25-26)

"Scripture is
nothing else but that
which the Spirit of God
hath spoken by the mouth of
his prophets and apostles, and
it cannot be understood but of the
same Spirit. Let every man pray to God
to send him his Spirit, to loose him from
his natural blindness and ignorance, and
to give him understanding and feeling
of the things of God, and of the
speaking of the Spirit
of God."

November 13

"I sit not among
vain persons, and have no
fellowship with the deceitful. I
hate the congregation of the wicked,
and will not sit among the ungodly. I
wash my hands with innocency, O
Lord, and so go I to thine altar,
that I may show the voice of
thy praise and tell of all
thy wondrous works."
(Psalms 26:4-7)

"God's
word is hateful
and contrary unto
them. For it is impossible
to preach Christ, except thou
preach against antichrist; that is
to say, them which with their
false doctrine and violence
of sword enforce to
quench the true
doctrine of
Christ."

November 14

"Then
said Jesus to those
Jews which believed on
him: If ye continue in my
saying, then are ye my
very disciples, and ye
shall know the truth,
and the truth shall
make you free."
(John 8:31-32)

"When those who are
unexpert in the mysteries of
Christ and weak in the faith desire
us to pray for them, then ought we to
lead them to the truth of God, and teach them
to put their trust in his promises, in the love that he
hath to Christ and to us for his sake, and to strength their
weak consciences, showing and proving by the scripture,
that as long as they follow the Spirit and resist sin, it is
impossible they should fall so deep that God shall
not pull them up again, if they hold fast by
the anchor of faith, having trust and
confidence in Christ."

November 15

"We
rejoice
in tribulation.
For we know that
tribulation bringeth patience,
patience bringeth feeling, feeling
bringeth hope, and hope maketh
not ashamed, because the love
that God hath unto us is shed
abroad in our hearts by the
Holy Ghost, which is
given unto us."
(Romans 5:3-5)

"The Spirit,
through tribulation,
purgeth us, and killeth our
fleshly wit, our belly wisdom
and worldly understanding, and
filleth us full of the wisdom
of God. Tribulation is a
blessing that cometh
cometh of God."

November 16

"God said,
Let there be
light, and there
was light."
(Genesis 1:3)

"Those
involved in the
Restoration built upon
the foundation of Gospel
truth because they possessed
the English Bible. Joseph Smith
studied from the Bible that bore
the imprint of William Tyndale.
Other good men and women in
the early days of the Restoration
were prepared to embrace the
Gospel because they read and
studied God's word from the
English Bible, that similarly
taught them to ponder, to
pray, and to anticipate
God's involvement
in their lives."
(Jeff Marsh)

November 17

"I
will bring
you together,
and kindle the
fire of my cruel
displeasure under
you, that ye may
be melted."
(Ezekiel 22:21)

"If we be
worldly-minded, and
do our works as the world
doth, how shall we know that God
hath chosen us out of the world? But
if we work freely, without all manner of
worldly respect, to show mercy, and to do
our duty to our neighbor, and to be unto
him as God is to us, then are we sure
that the favor and mercy of God are
upon us, and that we shall enjoy
all the good promises of God
through Christ, who hath
made us heirs thereof."

November 18

"And when
your children ask you
what manner of service is
this ye do, ye shall say: It
is the sacrifice of the
Lord's Passover."
(Exodus 12:26-27)

"If our
children ask
what our ceremonies
mean, no one can tell. The
clergy will say the scriptures
requireth a pure and a quiet mind
and therefore no layman, for he that is
cumbered with worldly business cannot
understand them. If that be so, then it is clear
that our prelates understand not the scriptures
themselves, for no layman is so tangled with
worldly business as they are. The great
things of the world are ministered by
them; neither do the lay-people
any great thing, but their
assignment."

November 19

"My
sheep
hear my
voice, and
I know them,
and they follow
me, and I give unto
them eternal life, and
they shall never perish,
neither shall any man
pluck them out of
my hand."
(John 10:27-28)

"Within the books of
scripture, thou mayest learn
how to behave thyself. Cleave
unto the text and plain story, and
endeavor to search out the meaning
of all that is described therein, and the
true sense of all manner of speaking of
the scriptures, as things pertaining
unto thine own heart and soul."

November 20

"Whosoever hath this
world's goods and seeth
his brother in necessity, and
shutteth up his compassion from
him, how dwelleth the love of
God in him? My babes, let us
not love in word, neither in
tongue, but with deed,
and in verity."
(1 John 3:17-18)

"Behold the
monsters, how they are
disguised with crosses, pillars,
and poleaxes, with mitres, crosiers,
and hats, and with three crowns! What
names have they? My lord prior, my
lord abbot, my lord bishop, my lord
archbishop, cardinal, and legate;
if it please your fatherhood,
your lordship, your grace,
your holiness and
innumerable
such like."

November 21

"He
that hateth me,
hateth my Father. If
I had not done works
among them which none
other man did, they should be
without sin. But now have they
seen, and yet have hated both
me and my Father, even that
the saying might be fulfilled
that is written in their
law: They hated me
without a cause."
(John 15:23-25)

"Wherefore
slew they Christ?
Even for rebuking the
hypocrites. If he had not
rebuked the Pharisees,
he might have been
uncrucified unto
this day."

November 22

"And it
came to pass, that
when Jesus had ended
these sayings, the people
were astonished at his doctrine.
For he taught them as one having
power, and not as the scribes."
(Matthew 7:28-29)

"Whosoever
heareth and believeth
the word is righteous, and
thereby is given him the Spirit
of God, which leadeth him unto all
that is the will of God, and is loosed
from the captivity and bondage of the
devil, and his heart is free to love God,
and hath lust to do the will of God.
Thus, are the scriptures called the
word of life, the word of grace,
the word of health, the word
of redemption, the word of
forgiveness, and the
word of peace."

November 23

"Cast
thy burden
or care upon the
Lord. He shall nourish
thee, and not leave
the righteous in
unquietness."
(Psalms 55:22)

"Let
thy care be to
prepare thyself with
thy strength, for to walk
which way he will have thee,
and to believe that he will go with
thee, and assist thee, and strengthen
thee against all tyrants, and deliver
thee out of all tribulation. But what
way, or by what means he will
do it, that commit unto him
and his godly pleasure
and wisdom, and
cast that care
upon him."

November 24

"Faith is a sure confidence of things which are hoped for, and a certainty of things which are not seen."
(Hebrews 11:1)

"If thou have true faith, thou seest the exceeding and infinite love and mercy which God hath showed thee freely in Christ. Then must thou needs love again, and love cannot but compel thee to work, and boldly to confess and knowledge thy Lord Christ, and the trust which thou hast in his word."

November 25

"Then began he to
curse and to swear, that
he knew not the man. And
immediately the cock crew. And
Peter remembered the words of
Jesus, which he said unto him:
Before the cock crow, thou
shalt deny me thrice. And
went out at the doors
and wept bitterly."
(Matthew 26:74-75)

These
two words
"wept bitterly" are
still used by almost all
modern translations. They
have not been improved upon
for almost five centuries, in
spite of weak efforts like
the one that reduces
the expression to
"cried hard."

November 26

"For
ye were as
sheep which
go astray, but
are now returned
unto the shepherd
and bishop of
your souls."
(1 Peter 2:25)

"Repentance
goeth before faith,
and prepareth the way
to Christ, and to the promises.
For Christ cometh not but unto
them that see their sins in the law,
and then repent. This mourning of
the heart lasteth all our lives long,
for we find ourselves too weak
for God's law, and therefore
sorrow, longing for
strength."

November 27

"Blessed are they which do hunger and thirst after righteousness, for they shall be filled."
(Matthew 5:6)

"Christ did not do his deeds to obtain heaven thereby. He was heir thereof, and it was his by inheritance. But he did his deeds freely for our sakes, considering nothing but our welfare and to bring the favor of God to us again, and to bring us to God. No natural son who is his father's heir does his father's will because he wants to be heir, for he is already so by birth. Rather, it is from pure love that the son does what he does. Ask him why he does it and he answers: 'My father asked me to. It is my father's will. It pleases my father.' Bond servants work for hire, but children for love. For their father, with all he has, is theirs already."

November 28

"Jerusalem,
Jerusalem, which killest
the prophets, and stonest them
which are sent to thee, how often
would I have gathered thy children
together, as a hen gathereth her
chickens under her wings,
and ye would not!"
(Matthew 23:37)

"Notwithstanding, even
though the rulers which God has
set over us command us against God, or
do us open wrong and oppress us with cruel
tyranny, yet because they stand in God's stead,
we may not avenge ourselves except by the
process and order of God's law and laws
of man made by the authority of God's
law, which are also God's law, ever
by an higher power, leaving
vengeance to God and, in
the meantime, suffering
until the hour has
come."

November 29

"And
thou shalt love
thy Lord God with
all thy heart, and with
all thy soul, and with all thy
mind, and with all thy strength.
This is the first commandment.
And the second is like unto
this. Thou shalt love thy
neighbor as thy self."
(Mark 12:30-31)

"The
love that springeth
out of Christ excludeth no
man. In Christ, we are all of one
degree, without respect of persons.
Nevertheless, though a man's heart
be open to all, yet, because his
ability of goods extendeth not
so far, provision is made
that every man shall
care for his own
household."

November 30

"Many
that are
first shall be
last, and the last
shall be first."
(Matthew 19:30)

Reflecting on
Tyndale, Gordon Jackson
said: "His translation is so much
more than a shifting of words from one
language into another. It is the rendering of a
medium that can carry the fire of the divine. And
his work, which we honor today, goes beyond mere
human achievement. His is the work of a prophet and
apostle. His honest and unrewarded labour was to bring
every English speaking man, woman, and child into the
company of Christ, Who is the Truth. It is doubtful
if any man of this nation ever aimed higher. We
who share that goal have the most reason to
honour Master William Tyndale, because
by so doing, he has become to the
English-speaking world the
mouth of Christ."

"I am not ashamed
of the Gospel of Christ."
(Romans 1:16)

December 1

"The
eye hath
not seen, and
the ear hath not
heard, neither have
entered into the heart
of man, the things which
God hath prepared for
them that love him."
(1 Corinthians 2:9)

"Let us
receive all things
of God, whether it be good
or bad. Let us humble ourselves
under his mighty hand, and submit
ourselves unto his nurture and chastising,
and not withdraw ourselves from his
correction. Let us not take the staff
by the end, or seek to avenge
ourselves on his rod,
which is the evil
rulers."

December 2

"After this, will I
pour out my spirit upon all
flesh, and your sons and your
daughters shall prophesy. Your
old men shall dream dreams,
and your young men
shall see visions."
(Joel 2:28)

"Prosperity is a right
curse, and a thing that God
giveth to his enemies. 'Woe be
to you rich,' saith Christ. 'Lo, ye have
your consolation; woe be to you that are
full, for ye shall hunger; woe be to you that
laugh, for ye shall weep; woe be to you when
men praise you, for so did their fathers unto
the false prophets.' Yea, and so have our
fathers done unto the false hypocrites.
The hypocrites have gotten not the
praise only, but the possessions
and the dominion and the
rule of the whole
world."

December 3

"And
thou shalt
set upon the
table, shewbread
before me always."
(Exodus 25:30)

"Joseph
saw the sun and the
moon and the eleven stars
worship him. Nevertheless, ere
that came to pass, God laid him where
he could neither see sun nor moon, neither
any star of the sky, and that many years and
also undeserved, to nurture him, to humble,
to meek, and to teach him God's ways, and
to make him apt and meet for the room
and honor against he came to it, that
he might perceive and feel that it
came of God, and that he
might be strong in the
spirit to minister
it godly."

December 4

"Beware,
lest ye be also
plucked away with
the error of the wicked,
and own steadfastness."
(2 Peter 3:17)

"How do
we know that St.
Augustine, who is one
of the best that ever wrote
upon the scriptures, wrote many
things amiss at the beginning, as many
other doctors do? Verily, by the scriptures,
as he himself well-perceived afterward, when
he looked more diligently upon them, and revoked
many things again. He wrote of many things which
he understood not when he was newly converted,
ere he had thoroughly seen the scriptures, and
followed the opinions of Plato, and the
common persuasions of man's
wisdom that were then
famous."

December 5

"The God of
peace that brought
again from death our Lord
Jesus Christ, the great shepherd
of the sheep, through the blood of
the everlasting testament, make you
perfect in all works, to do his will, and
bring to pass, that whatsoever ye do
may be accepted in his sight, by the
means of Jesus Christ. To whom
be praise for ever, while the
world endureth."
(Hebrews 13:20-21)

"God's word
pertains unto all men. It
pertains unto all servants to
know their master's will
and pleasure, and to all
subjects to know the
laws of their
prince."

December 6

"For
whosoever will save
his life shall lose it, but
whosoever shall lose his
life for my sake and the
Gospel's, the same
shall save it."
(Mark 8:35)

"A
Christian man is
a spiritual thing, and hath
God's Word in his heart, and God's
Spirit to certify him of all things. At the
preaching of faith, the Spirit came and certified
their hearts, that they were justified thru believing
the promises. If a man feels that his heart consents
to the law of God and feels himself meek, patient,
courteous, and merciful to his neighbor, altered
and fashioned like unto Christ, why should
he doubt that God has forgiven him,
and chosen him, and put his
Spirit in him?"

December 7

"The
Lord God
hath given me a well
learned tongue, so that I
can comfort them which are
troubled… I turn not my face
from shame and spitting, for
the Lord God helpeth me.
Therefore shall I not be
confounded."
(Isaiah 50:4-7)

"Look on
the stories well,
and thou shalt find
very few kings, since the
beginning of the world,
that have not perished
from the right way,
and that because
they would not
be learned."

December 8

"Then
Jesus said
unto him, go,
and do thou
likewise."
(Luke 10:37)

"I am
coupled to
God by Christ's
blood. I do good,
not for heaven's sake,
although it is the reward of
well doing, but freely, because
I am heir of heaven by grace and
Christ's purchasing, and have the
Spirit of God, for so is my nature
as a good tree brings forth good
fruit and an evil tree brings
forth evil fruit. By the
fruits you will know
what the tree
is."

December 9

"And
though he
were God's
Son, yet learned
he obedience by
those things which
he suffered, and was
made perfect."
(Hebrews 5:8-9)

"Christ
himself taught
obedience, how that
it is not lawful to resist
wrong, and how a man must
love his very enemy, and pray
for them that persecute him, and
bless them that curse him; and how
that all vengeance must be remitted
to God, and that a man must forgive
if he will be forgiven of God. Yet
the people, for the most part,
received it not."

December 10

"If we
say that we
have no sin, we
deceive ourselves, and
truth is not in us. If we
knowledge our sins, he is
faithful and just, to forgive
our sins, and to cleanse us
from all unrighteousness.
If we say we have not
sinned, we make him
a liar, and his word
is not in us."
(1 John 1:8-10)

"The truth is,
when any man hath
trespassed against God, if
he repent and knowledge his
trespass, God promiseth him
forgiveness without
ear-shrift."

December 11

"Thou
shalt not
avenge thyself
nor bear hate in
thy mind against
the children of thy
people, but shalt love
thy neighbour even as
thyself. I am the Lord."
(Leviticus 19:18)

"If thou
loveth God, thou hath
a commandment to love thy
neighbor also, whom, if thou have
offended, thou must make him amends or
satisfaction, or at the leastway, if thou be
notable, ask him forgiveness. If he will
have mercy of God, he is bound to
forgive thee. If he will not, yet
God forgiveth thee, if
thou thus submit
thyself."

December 12

"Gird
up the
loins of your
minds, be sober,
and trust perfectly
on the grace that is
brought unto you.
...Be ye holy, for
I am holy."
(1 Peter 1:13 & 16)

"If thou
ask where might
scripture be found to
prove a point of doctrine,
they say: We be the church,
and cannot err. Therefore, say
they, what we conclude, though
there be no scripture to prove
it so, it is of equal authority
and must, therefore, be
believed, under pain
of damnation."

December 13

"Prove yourselves whether ye are in the faith or not. Examine your own selves. Know ye not your own selves, how that Jesus Christ is in you?"
(2 Corinthians 13:5)

"When they be admitted to study divinity, because the scripture is locked up with false expositions and principles of natural philosophy that they cannot enter in, they go about the outside, and dispute all their lives about words and vain opinions, pertaining as much unto the healing of a man's body, as health of his soul."

December 14

"For the Lord
Jesus, the same night in
the which he was betrayed, took
bread, and thanked and brake, and said:
Take ye, and eat ye. This is my body which is
broken for you. This do ye in the remembrance
of me. After the same manner he took the cup
when supper was done saying: This cup is
the New Testament in my blood, this
do as oft as ye drink it, in the
remembrance of me."
(1 Corinthians 11:23-25)

"Christ
made the bread the
sacrament of his body only;
wherefore, as the bread is no
similitude of his blood, so
am I not bound or ought
to affirm that his
blood is there
present."

December 15

"And they laughed
him to scorn."
(Matthew 9:24)

"Antichrist
sitteth on the
seat of Satan, whose
vicar he is, and on the seat
of his own laws, ceremonies,
and false doctrine, whereunto he
compelleth all men with violence of
sword. Let a man break any of their
traditions, and he shall not be loosed
until, with shame most vile, or death
most cruel, he has paid the uttermost
farthing. But hate thy neighbour as
much as thou wilt, and thou shalt
have no rebuke of them. Yea,
rob thy neighbour, murder
him, and then come to
them and they will
welcome thee."

December 16

"In the
beginning,
God created
heaven and
earth."
(Genesis 1:1)

"Who
dried up
the Red sea?
Who slew Goliath?
Who did all those deeds
which thou readest in the
Bible? What delivered Israel
evermore from thralldom and
bondage, as soon as they had
repented and turned to God?
Faith verily, and God's
truth, and the trust
in the promises
which he had
made."

December 17

"The Lord hath
given rest unto your brethren
as he promised them. Wherefore,
return and go unto your tents and unto
the land of your possession, which Moses
the servant of the Lord gave you on the other
side Jordan. But in any wise, take exceeding good
heed that ye do the commandment and law which
Moses the servant of the Lord charged you, which
is that ye love the Lord your God, and walk in
his ways, and keep his commandments, and
cleave unto him, and serve him with all
your hearts and all your souls."
(Joshua 22:4-5)

"The
law of love,
which Christ left
among us, is to
give, and not
to receive."

December 18

"Our Father
which art in heaven,
hallowed be thy name. Let
thy kingdom come, thy will be
fulfilled, even in earth as it is in
heaven. Our daily bread give us
this day, and forgive us our sins,
for even we forgive every man
that trespasseth us. And lead
us not into temptation, but
deliver us from evil."
(Luke 11:2-4)

"There was no heresy, or
diversity of opinion, or disputing
about the matter, till the pope had
gathered a council to confirm this
transubstantiation, wherefore
it is most likely that this
opinion came up by
them of latter
days."

December 19

"I
should be
the minister of
Jesus Christ among
the Gentiles, and should
minister the glad tidings
of God, that the Gentiles
might be an acceptable
offering, sanctified by
the Holy Ghost."
(Romans 15:16)

"There is
a word in Latin
sacerdos, in Greek
hiereus, in Hebrew cohan,
that is, a minister, an officer, a
sacrifice or a priest, as Aaron
was a priest, and sacrificed
for the people, and was
a mediator between
God and them."

December 20

"These are they which
came out of great tribulation
and made their garments large,
and made them white in the blood
of the lamb. Therefore, are they in the
presence of the seat of God and serve
him day and night in his temple,
and he that sitteth in the seat
will dwell among them."
(Revelation 7:14-15)

"Be ye
learned, lest
the hypocrites
bring the wrath of
God upon your heads,
and compel you to shed
innocent blood, as they have
compelled your predecessors to
slay the prophets, kill Christ
and his apostles, and all
the righteous that
since were
slain."

December 21

"Then
said Paul: John
verily baptized with
the baptism of repentance,
saying unto the people that
they should believe on him
which should come after him.
That is on Christ Jesus. When
they heard that, they were
baptized in the name of
the Lord Jesus."
(Acts 19:4-5)

"Repentance, and
all the good deeds
which accompany
repentance, that
slay the lusts of
the flesh, are
signified by
baptism."

December 22

"And the
temple was
full of the smoke
of the glory of God,
and of his power."
(Revelation 15:8)

"Let
God's word try
every man's doctrine,
and whomsoever God's word
proveth unclean, let him be taken
for a leper. One scripture will help to
declare another. And the circumstances,
that is to say, the places that go before
and after, will give light unto the
middle text. And the open and
manifest scriptures will ever
improve the false and
wrong exposition
of the darker
sentences."

December 23

"Honor
father and
mother, and
thou shalt love
thine neighbor
as thyself."
(Matthew 19:19)

"Parents: Love
thy children with
all thine heart, and fear
and dread them, and wait
on their commandments, and
seek their worship, pleasure, will,
and profit in all things, and give thy
life for them, counting them worthy
of all honor, remembering that thou
art their good and possession, and
that thou owest unto them thine
own self, and all thou art able,
yea, and more than thou
art able to do."

December 24

"And there were in
the same region shepherds
abiding in the field, and watching
their flock by night. And, lo, the angel of the
Lord stood hard by them, and the brightness of
the Lord shone round about them, and they were
sore afraid. And the angel said unto them: Be not
afraid. Behold I bring you tidings of great joy,
that shall come to all the people. For unto
you is born this day in the city of David
a Saviour, which is Christ the Lord.
And take this for a sign. Ye shall
find the child swaddled, and
laid in a manger."
(Luke 2:8-12)

"How
shalt thou
know whether the
prophet be true or false,
or whether he speak God's
word, or of his own head,
if thou cannot read
the scriptures?"

December 25

"For unto us a child shall be
born, and unto us a son shall be given.
Upon his shoulders shall the kingdom lie,
and he shall be called with his own name; the
Wondrous Giver of Counsel, the Mighty God, the
Everlasting Father, the Prince of Peace."
(Isaiah 9:6)

"Finally, when
they had done all they
could, and that they thought
sufficient, and when Christ was in
the heart of the earth, and so many
bills and poleaxes about him to keep
him down, and when it was past man's
help, then help God. When man could not
bring him again, God's truth fetched him
again. The oath that God had sworn to
Abraham, to David, and to other holy
fathers and prophets, raised him
up again, to bless and save all
that believe in him. Thus
became the wisdom
of the hypocrites
foolishness."

December 26

"Tell us by
what authority
thou doest these
things? Other, who
is he that gave thee
this authority?"
(Luke 20:2)

"The
scribes and the
Pharisees laid also to
his charge, that he moved
the people to sedition, and said
to Pilate: 'We have found this fellow
perverting the people, and forbidding
to pay tribute to Caesar, and he saith
that he is Christ a king.' And again,
said they: 'He moveth the people
throughout Jewry, and he
began at Galilee even
to this place.'"

December 27

"Woe is me, for I am astonished, that I which am a man of unclean lips and dwell among people that hath unclean lips also, should see the King and Lord of Hosts with mine eyes."
(Isaiah 6:5)

"A Christian man loveth that which before he hated, and hateth that which before he loved, and is clean altered, and changed, and contrary disposed, and is knit and coupled fast to God's will, and naturally bringeth forth good works, that is to say, that which God commandeth to do, and not things of his own imagination."

December 28

"Here
is wisdom.
Let him that
hath wit, count
the number of the
beast. For it is the
number of a man,
and his number
is six hundred,
threescore
and six."
(Revelation 13:18)

"The kings
are become nothing
but hangmen unto the
pope and bishops, to kill
whosoever they condemn
without so much as an ado.
As Pilate was to the scribes
and Pharisees, so are the
bishops, to hang our
Lord and Saviour
Jesus Christ."

December 29

"Then said
Jesus unto him:
Except ye see signs
and wonders, ye
believe not."
(John 4:48)

"The Gospel, or
the joyful tidings, is
called the New Testament.
Just like a man, who when he
dies, has directed his goods to be
dealt and distributed after his death
among all his named heirs, so Christ,
before his death, commanded that the
Gospel, or glad tidings, be declared
throughout all the world, that his
goods might thereby be given
to those who would repent
and believe."

December 30

"Unto whom
much is given, of
him shall be much
required. To whom
men much commit,
the more of him
will they ask."
(Luke 12:48)

"What
reason is it that
mine enemy should
cast me in prison at his
pleasure, and there diet me,
and handle me as he listeth,
and judge me secretly, and
condemn me by a law of
his own making, and
then deliver me to
Pilate to murder
me?"

December 31

"This is the people that
neither heareth the voice
of the Lord their God, nor
receiveth his correction.
Faithfulness and truth
is clean rooted out
of their mouth."
(Jeremiah 7:28)

"I submit this
book, and all others
that I have either made or
translated, unto all them that
submit themselves unto the word
of God, to be corrected of them. Yea,
and moreover to be disallowed and also
burnt, if it seem worthy, when they have
examined it with the Hebrew, so that
they first put forth of their own
translating another that
is more correct."

Consummatum est

Appendix One

Scripture citations listed
in the order in which they
appear in the 1526 Tyndale Bible,
with corresponding calendar dates.

"Now I know unperfectly: but then shall I know."
(Tyndale New Testament, 1 Corinthians 13:2)

Genesis 1:1 – December 16	Job 33:14-16 – October 12
Genesis 1:3 – November 16	Job 38:4-7 – January 20
Genesis 1:26 – August 20	Job 42:2-3 – September 24
Genesis 1:27-28 – October 18	Psalms 1:1-4 – August 8
Genesis 2:21-24 – August 21	Psalms 23:1-6 – June 7
Genesis 3:11 – March 8	Psalms 26:4-7 – November 13
Genesis 37:3-5 – October 20	Psalms 31:7-10 – July 4
Genesis 48:14 – March 28	Psalms 55:22 – November 23
Exodus 6:2-3 – September 7	Psalms 57:1-3 – October 22
Exodus 8:1 – October 10	Psalms 62:5-9 – March 21
Exodus 12:11 – September 19	Psalms 83:18 – August 18
Exodus 12:26-27 – November 18	Psalms 107:11-13 – January 15
Exodus 18:10-11 – March 2	Psalms 116:8-9 – September 6
Exodus 25:17 – February 10	Psalms 119:103 – October 27
Exodus 25:30 – December 3	Proverbs 3:5-8 – August 26
Leviticus 9:5 – April 28	Proverbs 3:11-12 – February 5
Leviticus 18:5 – May 31	Proverbs 22:17-21 – September 21
Leviticus 19:18 – December 11	Proverbs 24:10 – May 14
Numbers 6:24-26 – October 28	Proverbs 24:20-22 – January 7
Deuteronomy 4:27-28 – October 7	Ecclesiastes 3:2-8 – July 16
Deuteronomy 6:4-7 – April 24	Ecclesiastes 9:2 – March 25
Deuteronomy 8:5 – May 12	Isaiah 6:1-3 – April 10
Deuteronomy 11:26-28 – October 6	Isaiah 6:5 – December 27
Deuteronomy 13:4 – August 4	Isaiah 9:2 – April 25
Deuteronomy 27:2-3 – April 17	Isaiah 9:6 – December 25
Deuteronomy 30:19 – July 6	Isaiah 25:8 – July 28
Deuteronomy 30:20 – June 21	Isaiah 30:12-13 – July 29
Joshua 22:4-5 – December 17	Isaiah 32:1-4 – September 8
Joshua 24:15 – August 11	Isaiah 49:23 – March 5
Ruth 1:16-17 – May 7	Isaiah 50:4-7 – December 7
2 Samuel 23:2-4 – March 11	Isaiah 53:3 – January 22
1 Kings 18:21 – January 3	Isaiah 54:2 – March 10
1 Kings 19:11-12 – August 22	Isaiah 55:1-2 – April 3
2 Chronicles 14:11 - June 15	Isaiah 55:11-13 – January 21
2 Chronicles 36:16 – August 28	Isaiah 63:2-4 – May 6
Nehemiah 8:5-6 – May 25	Jeremiah 5:28-30 – June 10
Nehemiah 13:11 – July 11	Jeremiah 5:31 – February 14
Esther 8:6 – January 18	Jeremiah 7:24 – October 8

Jeremiah 7:28 – December 31
Jeremiah 14:14 – June 22
Jeremiah 31:34 – February 2
Jeremiah 32:17-18 – March 26
Ezekiel 22:21 – November 17
Ezekiel 22:26-27 – June 19
Daniel 5:12 – January 31
Joel 2:28 – December 2
Amos 8:11-12 – July 18
Micah 7:7-8 – January 24
Matthew 3:7-8 – August 17
Matthew 3:16-17 – July 21
Matthew 4:3-4 – September 13
Matthew 4:16 – April 6
Matthew 4:23-24 – February 27
Matthew 5:6 – November 27
Matthew 5:8-10 – October 16
Matthew 5:10-12 – April 16
Matthew 5:13 – August 9
Matthew 5:14-16 – November 3
Matthew 5:17-18 – April 1
Matthew 5:22 – April 12
Matthew 5:40-42 – October 4
Matthew 5:43-44 – June 3
Matthew 6:9-13 – September 15
Matthew 6:23 – August 1
Matthew 6:24 – August 16
Matthew 6:31 – July 9
Matthew 7:1-2 – October 19
Matthew 7:5 – April 19
Matthew 7:7-11 – September 1
Matthew 7:14 – September 3
Matthew 7:15-16 – January 14
Matthew 7:20-21 – November 8
Matthew 7:28-29 – November 22
Matthew 9:24 – December 15
Matthew 10:16-20 – July 7
Matthew 10:23-24 & 28 – August 15

Matthew 10:24 – July 31
Matthew 10:26-27 – September 30
Matthew 10:34-36 – March 3
Matthew 10:37-39 – July 13
Matthew 11:27-28 – March 7
Matthew 11:29 – January 28
Matthew 12:8 – June 2
Matthew 12:34-35 – August 23
Matthew 13:14-15 – September 2
Matthew 14:14 - April 9
Matthew 16:3 – February 7
Matthew 16:18-19 – October 5
Matthew 16:24-25 – September 28
Matthew 18:20 – April 18
Matthew 19:5 – June 8
Matthew 19:19 – December 23
Matthew 19:21 – October 21
Matthew 19:30 – November 30
Matthew 20:16 – September 29
Matthew 20:25-28 – June 24
Matthew 23:23 – February 3
Matthew 23:24-26 – October 30
Matthew 23:27 – May 2
Matthew 23:33-34 – April 22
Matthew 23:37 – November 28
Matthew 24:6-8 – March 13
Matthew 24:11-13 – July 5
Matthew 25:44-45 – March 16
Matthew 26:17-18 – January 10
Matthew 26:41 – March 17
Matthew 26:74-75 – November 25
Matthew 27:50-53 – September 27
Matthew 28:19-20 – June 11
Mark 1:17-18 – November 10
Mark 4:11 – April 30
Mark 6:50-51 – January 1
Mark 7:6 – September 16
Mark 8:29 – July 17

Mark 8:35 – December 6
Mark 10:6-9 – September 26
Mark 10:27 – September 12
Mark 12:30-31 – November 29
Mark 13:9 – May 19
Mark 13:21-23 – September 23
Mark 14:35-36 – July 26
Mark 16:15-18 – April 8
Luke 1:67-72 – June 30
Luke 2:8-12 – December 24
Luke 3:3-6 – September 25
Luke 3:7-8 – October 25
Luke 4:4 – July 12
Luke 4:5 - November 2
Luke 5:30-32 – June 18
Luke 8:8 – May 30
Luke 9:61-62 – March 1
Luke 10:37 – December 8
Luke 11:2-4 – December 18
Luke 12:19-20 – August 27
Luke 12:48 – December 30
Luke 15:21-22 – June 23
Luke 15:23-24 – October 13
Luke 17:10 - November 11
Luke 18:13-14 – August 13
Luke 20:2 – December 26
Luke 21:26-28 – September 4
Luke 22:19-20 – April 15
Luke 22:35 – August 3
Luke 24:45 – February 15
Luke 24:46-48 – November 4
John 1:1-5 – September 11
John 4:48 – December 29
John 5:19 – March 14
John 5:39-42 – August 19
John 6:32-33 – January 4
John 6:35 – January 23
John 6:66-69 – March 30

John 7:16-17 – June 6
John 8:12 – February 25
John 8:31-32 – November 14
John 9:25 – September 17
John 10:11 – July 15
John 10:27-28 – November 19
John 11:25-26 – November 12
John 14:26 – March 4
John 15:5 – March 20
John 15:23-25 – November 21
John 16:25-26 – May 9
John 21:15-17 – February 13
Acts 2:37-38 – March 19
Acts 4:1-2 – September 10
Acts 4:24 – January 6
Acts 5:31-32 – May 22
Acts 6:5-6 – August 10
Acts 8:18-22 – June 17
Acts 13:48-49 – October 31
Acts 17:11 – May 29
Acts 17:25-28 – September 20
Acts 19:4-5 – December 21
Acts 28:26-27 – November 1
Romans 2:14-16 – April 20
Romans 5:3-5 – November 15
Romans 5:10-11 – November 5
Romans 7:5-6 – February 24
Romans 8:35 – August 7
Romans 12:12-18 – January 27
Romans 12:19-21 – July 8
Romans 13:1 & 11-14 – June 28
Romans 15:16 – December 19
Romans 16:16 – October 14
1 Corinthians 2:9 – December 1
1 Corinthians 3:2-3 – July 2
1 Corinthians 4:11-13 – August 29
1 Corinthians 11:23-25 – December 14
1 Corinthians 13:1-3 – February 16

1 Corinthians 13:9-13 – July 30
1 Corinthians 14:16-19 – January 11
1 Corinthians 15:50-53 – October 15
1 Corinthians 15:55-56 – November 6
2 Corinthian 1:12 – September 9
2 Corinthians 3:5-6 – May 24
2 Corinthians 6:4-7 – July 20
2 Corinthians 7:4 – October 11
2 Corinthians 11:19 – January 19
2 Corinthians 13:5 – December 13
Galatians 3:24-29 – July 27
Galatians 5:4-5 – June 25
Galatians 6:2 – August 5
Ephesians 1:3-6 – October 26
Ephesians 1:17-20 – April 7
Ephesians 2:4-5 – July 3
Ephesians 2:8-10 – June 20
Ephesians 2:19-22 – June 1
Ephesians 3:8-12 – May 21
Ephesians 3:14-19 – June 12
Ephesians 4:1-6 – June 13
Ephesians 4:11-14 – March 12
Ephesians 4:29-32 – April 26
Ephesians 5:1-5 – January 5
Ephesians 5:6-8 – January 16
Ephesians 5:8-14 – June 14
Ephesians 5:15-20 – July 23
Ephesians 5:25 & 27-28 – May 20
Ephesians 6:10-12 – October 2
Philippians 1:9-11 – July 10
Philippians 1:27-30 – June 9
Philippians 2:7-11 – May 8
Philippians 2:14-16 – August 2
Philippians 2:17-18 – May 13
Philippians 3:18-21 – May 10
Philippians 4:8-9 – January 29
Colossians 1:10-12 – May 11
Colossians 2:8 & 12 – February 29

Colossians 3:12-15 – March 22
Colossians 3:16 – February 6
1 Thessalonians 3:11-12 – April 27
1 Thessalonians 4:16-18 – January 25
1 Thessalonians 5:2-3 – May 4
2 Thessalonians 2:2-3 – July 1
2 Thessalonians 2:15-17 – March 23
2 Thessalonians 3:11-13 – April 2
1 Timothy 1:12-14 – March 29
1 Timothy 1:15 – June 4
1 Timothy 2:1-2 – August 25
1 Timothy 2:4-6 – August 30
1 Timothy 3:1-5 – February 21
1 Timothy 3:6-7 – September 5
1 Timothy 3:8-13 – May 15
1 Timothy 3:15-16 – July 25
1 Timothy 4:10-11 – April 11
1 Timothy 6:8-12 - January 26
2 Timothy 1:13-14 – March 27
2 Timothy 2:10 – June 16
2 Timothy 3:1-5 – February 20
2 Timothy 3:12-14 – February 17
2 Timothy 3:16-17 – April 4
2 Timothy 4:2-5 –April 21
2 Timothy 4:7-8 – February 11
Titus 1:7 – May 23
Titus 1:10-11 – March 18
Titus 1:15-16 – October 17
Titus 2:1-2 – January 2
Titus 3:1-2 – June 29
Titus 3:7 & 9 – August 24
Hebrews 1:9 – July 22
Hebrews 4:14-16 – April 23
Hebrews 5:1-4 – October 23
Hebrews 5:8-9 – December 9
Hebrews 5:11-12 – February 28
Hebrews 6:1-2 – January 12
Hebrews 8:6 – June 5

Hebrews 8:10-12 – October 9
Hebrews 10:16-20 – November 11
Hebrews 10:21-25 – April 14
Hebrews 10:31 – February 12
Hebrews 11:1 – November 24
Hebrews 11:13-16 – January 30
Hebrews 12:1-3 – February 1
Hebrews 12:6 – July 24
Hebrews 13:1-2 – August 14
Hebrews 13:20-21 – December 5
James 1:2-4 – May 28
James 1:5-8 – February 4
James 1:22-25 – May 5
James 2:8-10 – February 8
James 2:14-17 – February 18
James 2:18-20 & 26 – September 22
James 2:22 & 24 – June 26
James 3:5-6 – February 22
James 4:7-10 – May 17
James 5:11 – January 13
1 Peter 1:13 & 16 – December 12
1 Peter 1:22-23 – September 18
1 Peter 2:5-6 – November 9
1 Peter 2:9 – February 26
1 Peter 2:25 – November 26
1 Peter 3:10-12 – March 6
1 Peter 3:18-20 – February 19
1 Peter 4:7-10 – May 3
1 Peter 5:5-6 – August 6
2 Peter 1:5-8 – March 24
2 Peter 1:9-12 – October 1
2 Peter 1:10-11 – May 26
2 Peter 1:19:21 – February 23
2 Peter 2:1-3 – July 14
2 Peter 2:17-19 – October 24
2 Peter 3:10 – May 16
2 Peter 3:17 – December 4
1 John 1:5-7 – October 29

1 John 1:8-10 – December 10
1 John 2:1-3 – October 3
1 John 2:8-10 – April 13
1 John 2:15-17 – March 15
1 John 3:17-18 – November 20
2 John 1:9 – June 27
Revelation 1:4-8 – January 17
Revelation 3:19-20 – July 19
Revelation 3:20 – January 8
Revelation 6:15-16 – March 9
Revelation 7:14-15 – December 20
Revelation 12:7-9 – April 29
Revelation 13:18 – December 28
Revelation 14:6-7 – May 1
Revelation 15:18 – December 22
Revelation 16:18-21 – May 27
Revelation 18:2-3 – August 31
Revelation 19:1-3 – January 9
Revelation 20:1-3 – August 12
Revelation 20:12-15 – September 14
Revelation 21:2-4 – March 31
Revelation 21:6-7 – May 18
Revelation 22:4-5 – April 5
Revelation 22:18-19 – February 9

Appendix Two

Equivalent scriptures
from the King James Version
of the Bible, for comparison by date.

Differences between
the Tyndale translation and the
King James Version are noted in bold face.

"Study to shew
thyself laudable unto God,
a workman that needeth not to be
ashamed, dividing the word of truth justly."
(Tyndale New Testament, 1 Timothy 2:15)

January 1: "Be of good cheer: it is I; be not afraid. And he went up unto them into the ship; and the wind ceased: and they were sore amazed in themselves beyond measure, and wondered." (Mark 6:50-51).

January 2: "Speak thou **the things which become sound doctrine**: That the **aged** men be sober, **grave**, **temperate**, sound in faith, in **charity**, in patience." (Titus 2:1-2).

January 3: "And **Elijah** came unto all the people, and said, **How long** halt ye between two opinions? if the Lord be God, follow him: but if Baal, then follow him. And the people answered him not a word." (1 Kings 18:21).

January 4: "I say unto you, Moses gave you not **that** bread from heaven; but my Father giveth you the true bread from heaven. For **the bread of God is he** which cometh down from heaven, and giveth life unto the world." (John 6:32-33).

January 5: "Be ye therefore followers of God, as dear children; And walk in love, as Christ also **hath** loved us, and **hath given** himself for us an offering and a sacrifice to God for a **sweetsmelling** savour. **But** fornication, and all uncleanness, or covetousness, **let it not** be once named among you, as becometh saints; Neither filthiness, **nor** foolish talking, **nor** jesting, which are not **convenient**: but rather giving of thanks. For this ye know, that no whoremonger, **nor** unclean person, **nor** covetous **man, who is an idolater**, hath any inheritance in the kingdom of Christ and of God." (Ephesians 5:1-5).

January 6: "Lord, thou art God, which hast made heaven, and earth, and the sea, and all that in them is." (Acts 4:24).

January 7: "**There shall be no reward to the evil man**; the candle of the **wicked** shall be put out. My son, fear thou the Lord and the king: and **meddle not with them that are given to change**: For their **calamity** shall **rise** suddenly; and who knoweth the **ruin** of them both?" (Proverbs 24:20-22).

January 8: "Behold, I stand at the door, and knock: if any man hear my voice, and open the door, I will come in to him, and will sup with him, and he with me." (Revelation 3:20).

January 9: "I heard **a great** voice of much people in heaven, saying, Alleluia; **Salvation**, and glory, and honour, and power, unto **the Lord our God**: For true and righteous are his judgments: for he hath judged the great whore, which did corrupt the earth with her fornication, and hath avenged the blood of his servants at her hand. And again they said, Alleluia. And her smoke rose up for **ever and ever**." (Revelation 19:1-3).

January 10: "The first day of the **feast of** unleavened bread the disciples came to Jesus, saying unto him, Where wilt thou that we prepare for thee to eat the passover? And he said, Go into the city **to** such a man, and say **unto** him, The Master saith, My time is **at hand**; I will keep **the passover** at thy house with my disciples." (Matthew 26:17-18).

January 11: "How shall he that occupieth the room of the unlearned say Amen at thy giving of thanks, seeing he understandeth not what thou sayest? **For** thou verily givest thanks well, but the other is not edified. I thank my God, I speak with tongues more than ye all: Yet **in the church I had rather speak** five words with my **understanding, that by my voice I might teach** others **also**, than ten thousand words **in an unknown** tongue." (1 Corinthians 14:16-19).

January 12: "**Therefore leaving the principles of the** doctrine **of Christ**, let us go **on** unto perfection; **not laying again** the foundation of repentance from dead works, and of faith toward God, Of **the doctrine** of baptisms, and of laying on of hands, and of resurrection **of the dead**, and of eternal judgment." (Hebrews 6:1-2).

January 13: "Ye have heard of the patience of Job, and have **seen the end of the Lord; that** the Lord is very pitiful, and **of tender mercy**." (James 5:11).

January 14: "Beware of false prophets, which come to you in sheep's clothing, but inwardly they are ravening wolves. Ye shall know them by their fruits." (Matthew 7:15-16).

January 15: "They **rebelled against the words** of God, **and contemned** the counsel of the most **High: Therefore he brought down** their heart with labour; they fell down, and there was none to help. **Then** they cried unto the Lord in their trouble, and he **saved** them out of their distresses." (Psalms 107:11-13).

January 16: "Let no man deceive you with vain words: for **because of these** things cometh the wrath of God upon the children of **disobedience**. Be not **ye** therefore **partakers** with them. **For** ye were **sometimes** darkness, but **now are ye** light in the Lord: walk as children of light." (Ephesians 5:6-8).

January 17: "Grace be **unto** you, and peace, from him which is, and which was, and which is to come… And from Jesus Christ, **who** is **the** faithful witness, and the first begotten of the dead, and the **prince of** the kings of the earth. Unto him that loved us, and washed us from our sins in his own blood, And **hath** made us kings and priests unto God **and** his Father; **to him** be glory and dominion for **ever and ever**. Amen. Behold, he cometh with clouds; and **every** eye shall see him, and they also which pierced him: and all kindreds of the earth shall wail **because of him**. Even so, Amen.

I am Alpha and Omega, the beginning and the ending, saith the Lord, which is, and which was, and which is to come." (Revelation 1:4-8).

January 18: "How can I **endure to** see the evil that shall **come** unto my people? **or** how can I **endure to see** the destruction of my kindred?" (Esther 8:6).

January 19: "For ye suffer fools gladly, **seeing** ye yourselves are wise." (2 Corinthians 11:29).

January 20: "Where wast thou when I laid the foundations of the earth? **Declare**, if thou hast understanding. Who hath **laid the measures thereof, if** thou knowest? or who hath **stretched** the line upon it? Whereupon **are the foundations thereof fastened**? or who laid the corner stone **thereof**; When the morning stars **sang** together, and all the sons of God **shouted for joy**?" (Job 38:4-7).

January 21: "So **shall my** word **be** that **goeth forth** out of my mouth shall…accomplish **that which I please**, and…shall go **out** with joy, and be led **forth** with peace: the mountains and **the** hills shall **break forth before** you **into singing**, and all the trees of the field shall clap their hands. **Instead of the** thorn shall **come up the** fir tree, and instead of **the** brier **shall come up** the myrtle tree: and **it** shall be to the Lord **for a name**, for an everlasting **sign** that shall not be **cut off**." (Isaiah 55:11-13).

January 22: "**He shall be the most simple, and despised of all, which yet hath good experience** of sorrows and **infirmities. We shall reckon him so simple and so vile, that we shall hide** our faces from him." (Isaiah 53:3).

January 23: "I am the bread of life: he that cometh to me shall **never** hunger; and he that believeth on me shall never thirst." (John 6:35).

January 24: "I will **wait for the God of my salvation**: my God **will** hear me. **Rejoice not against me, O mine** enemy: **when** I fall, I shall **arise**; when I sit in darkness, the Lord **shall be a light unto me**." (Micah 7:7-8).

January 25: "The Lord himself shall descend from heaven with a shout, **with** the voice of the archangel, and **with** the trump of God: and the dead in Christ shall **rise** first: Then we which **are alive** and remain **shall** be caught up **together** with them in the clouds, to meet the Lord in the air: and so shall we ever be with the Lord. Wherefore comfort one another with these words." (2 Thessalonians 4:16-18).

January 26: "**And having** food and raiment let us be therewith content. **But** they that will be rich fall into temptation and a snare, and into many foolish and **hurtful** lusts, which drown men in destruction and perdition. For **the love of money** is the root of all evil: which while **some coveted** after, they **have** erred from the faith, and **pierced themselves through** with many sorrows. **But thou, O man of God, flee these things; and** follow **after** righteousness, godliness, **faith**, love, patience, meekness. Fight the good fight of faith, lay hold on eternal life, whereunto thou art also called, and hast professed a good profession before many witnesses." (1 Timothy 6:8-12).

January 27: "Rejoic**ing** in hope; patient in tribulation; continu**ing instant** in prayer; Distribut**ing to** the necessity of saints; **given to hospitality**. Bless them which persecute you: bless, **and** curse not. **Rejoice** with them that **do rejoice, and** weep with them that weep. Be of **the same mind** one toward another. **Mind not high things, but condescend to men of low estate**. Be not wise in your own **conceits**. Recompense to no man evil for evil. Provide things honest in the sight of all men. If it be possible, **as much as lieth in you, live peaceably** with all men." (Romans 12:12-18).

January 28: "Take my yoke upon you, and learn of me; for I am meek and lowly in heart: and ye shall find **rest** unto your souls." (Matthew 11:29).

January 29: "**Finally**, brethren, whatsoever things are true, whatsoever things are honest, whatsoever things are just, whatsoever things are pure, whatsoever things **are lovely**, whatsoever things are of **good** report; if there be any **virtue**, and if there be any **praise, think on these things. Those things**, which ye have both learned, and received, and heard, and seen in me, do: and the God of peace shall be with you." (Philippians 4:8-9).

January 30: "These all died in faith, **not having received** the promises, but **having seen** them afar off, and **were persuaded of** them, and **embraced** them, and confessed that they were strangers and pilgrims on the earth. **For** they that say such things declare **plainly** that they seek a country. **And truly**, if they had been mindful of that country from whence they came **out**, they **might have had opportunity to have** returned. But now they desire a better **country**, that is, **an heavenly**: wherefore God is not ashamed to be called their God: for he hath prepared for them a city." (Hebrews 11:13-16).

January 31: "An **excellent** spirit, **and** knowledge, and **understanding, interpreting of** dreams, and shewing of hard sentences, and **dissolving** of doubts, **were found in the same** Daniel." (Daniel 5:12).

February 1: "Let us run with patience **the race** that is set before us, Looking unto Jesus the author and finisher of our faith; **who** for the joy that was set before him **endured** the cross, **despising** the shame, and is set down **at** the right hand of the throne of God. **For** consider **him** that endured such **contradiction** of sinners **against himself**, lest ye be wearied and faint in your minds." (Hebrews 12:1-3).

February 2: "And **they** shall teach no more **every man** his neighbour, **and every man** his brother, **saying**, Know the Lord: for they shall all know me, from the **least of them** unto the **greatest of them**, saith the Lord: for I will forgive their **iniquity**, and **I will** remember their sin **no** more." (Jeremiah 31:34).

February 3: "Woe unto you, scribes and Pharisees, **hypocrites**! for ye **pay** tithe **of** mint **and** anise and cummin, and **have omitted** the weightier matters of the law, judgment, mercy, and faith: these ought ye to have done, and not to **leave** the other undone." (Matthew 23:23).

February 4: "If any **of** you lack wisdom, let him ask of God, that giveth to all men **liberally, and upbraideth not**; and it shall be given him. But let him ask in faith, **nothing** wavering. For he that **wavereth** is like a wave of the sea **driven with** the wind **and tossed. For let not** that man think that he shall receive any thing of **the Lord**. A **double minded** man is unstable in all his ways." (James 1:5-8).

February 5: "Despise not the chastening of the Lord; neither be weary of his correction: For whom the Lord loveth he correcteth; **even as a father the son in whom he delighteth**." (Proverbs 3:11-12).

February 6: "Let the word of Christ dwell in you **richly** in all wisdom; teaching and **admonishing one another** in psalms and hymns and spiritual songs, **singing with grace** in your hearts to the Lord." (Colossians 3:16).

February 7: "**And** in the morning, It **will be** foul weather to day: **for** the sky is red and **lowring**. O ye hypocrites, ye can discern the **face** of the sky; **but** can ye not discern the signs of the times?" (Matthew 16:3).

February 8: "If ye fulfil the royal law according to the scripture, Thou shalt love **thy** neighbour as thyself, ye do well: But if ye **have respect to persons**, ye commit sin, and are **convinced** of the law as transgressors. **For** whosoever shall keep the whole law, and yet **offend** in one point, he is guilty of all." (James 2:8-10).

February 9: "I testify unto every man that heareth the words of **the** prophecy of this book, If any man shall add unto these things, God shall add unto him the plagues that are written in this book: And if any man shall **take away from** the words of the book of this prophecy, God shall take away his part out of the book of life, and out of the holy city, and from the things which are written in this book." (Revelation 22:18-19).

February 10: "And thou shalt make a mercy seat of pure gold: two cubits and a half **shall be the length thereof**, and a cubit and a half **the breadth thereof**." (Exodus 25:17).

February 11: "I have fought a good fight, **I have finished** my course, **I** have kept the faith: Henceforth **there** is laid up for me a crown of righteousness, which the Lord, **the** righteous judge, shall give me at that day: **and** not to me only, but unto all them **also** that love his **appearing**." (2 Timothy 4:7-8).

February 12: "It is a fearful thing to fall into the hands of the living God." (Hebrews 10:31).

February 13: "**So** when they had dined, Jesus saith to Simon Peter…lovest thou me more than these? He **saith** unto him, Yea, Lord; thou knowest that I love thee. He **saith** unto him, Feed my lambs. He **saith** to him again the second time… lovest thou me? He **saith** unto him, Yea, Lord; thou knowest that I love thee. He **saith** unto him, Feed my sheep. He **saith** unto him the third time, Simon, son of Jonas, lovest thou me? Peter was grieved because he said unto him the third time, Lovest thou me? And he said unto him, Lord, thou knowest all things; thou knowest that I love thee. Jesus **saith** unto him, Feed my sheep." (John 21:15-17).

February 14: "The prophets **prophesy** falsely, and the priests **bear rule by their means**; and my people **love to have it so: and what will ye do in the end thereof**?" (Jeremiah 5:31).

February 15: "Then opened he their **understanding**, that they might understand the scriptures." (Luke 24:45).

February 16: "Though I speak with the tongues of men and of angels, and have not **charity**, I **am become** as sounding brass, **or** a tinkling cymbal. And though I **have the gift of** prophecy, and understand all **mysteries**, and all knowledge; and though I have all faith, so that I could remove mountains, and **have not charity**, **I am** nothing. And though I bestow all my goods **to** feed the poor, and though I give my body **to be** burned, and have **not charity**, it profiteth me nothing." (1 Corinthians 13:1-3).

February 17: "Yea, and all that will live godly in Christ Jesus **shall** suffer persecution. But evil men and seducers shall wax worse and worse, **deceiving, and being** deceived. But continue thou in the things which thou hast learned." (2 Timothy 3:12-14).

February 18: "What **doth it profit**, my brethren, though a man say he hath faith, **and have not works**? can faith save him? If a brother or sister be naked, and destitute of daily food, And one of you say unto them, Depart in peace, **be ye warmed and filled**; notwithstanding ye give them not those things which are needful to the body; **what doth it profit**? Even so faith, if it hath **not works**, is dead, **being alone**." (James 2:14-17).

February 19: "For Christ also hath once suffered for sins, the just for the unjust, **that**

he might bring us to God, **being put to death in** the flesh, but quickened **by** the Spirit: **By which** also he went and preached unto the spirits in prison; Which **sometime** were disobedient, when once the longsuffering of God **waited** in the days of Noah, while the ark was a preparing, wherein few, that is, eight souls were saved by water." (1 Peter 3:18-20).

February 20: "In the last days perilous times shall come. For men shall be lovers of their own selves, covetous, boasters, proud, **blasphemers**, disobedient to **parents**, unthankful, unholy, **Without natural affection**, **trucebreakers**, false accusers, **incontinent**, fierce, despisers of those **that** are good, Traitors, heady, highminded, **lovers of pleasures** more than lovers of God; Having a **form of godliness**, but **denying** the power thereof." (2 Timothy 3:1-5).

February 21: "If a man **desire** the office of a bishop, he desireth a good work. A bishop then must be **blameless**, the husband of one wife, **vigilant**, sober, of good behaviour, **given to hospitality**, apt to teach; Not **given to wine**, no **striker**, not **greedy of** filthy lucre; but **patient, not a brawler, not** covetous; One that ruleth well his own house, having **his** children **in subjection with all gravity**; For if a man **know not how to** rule his own house, how shall he **take** care of the **church** of God?" (1 Timothy 3:1-5).

February 22: "Behold, how great a **matter** a little fire kindleth! And the tongue is a fire, a world of **iniquity**: so is the tongue among our members, that it defileth the whole body, and setteth on fire **the course** of nature; and it **is set on** fire of hell." (James 3:5-6).

February 23: "We have also a more sure word of prophecy; whereunto **ye do well that** ye take heed, as unto a light that shineth in a dark place, **until the day dawn**, and the day star arise in your hearts: **Knowing this first**, that no prophecy of the scripture **is of** any private interpretation. For the **prophecy** came **not in old time** by the will of man: but holy men of God spake as they were moved by the Holy Ghost." (2 Peter 1:19-21).

February 24: "**For** when we were in the flesh, the **motions** of sins, which were by the law, **did work** in our members to bring forth fruit unto death. But now we are delivered from the law, **that being** dead **wherein we were** held; that we should serve in **newness of spirit**, and not in the old**ness** of the letter." (Romans 7:5-6).

February 25: "I am the light of the world: he that followeth me shall not walk in darkness, but shall have the light of life." (John 8:12).

February 26: "But ye are a chosen generation, a royal priesthood, an holy nation, a peculiar people; that ye should shew **forth** the **praises** of him **who hath** called you out of darkness into his marvellous light." (1 Peter 2:9).

February 27: "And Jesus went about all Galilee, teaching in their synagogues, and preaching the Gospel of the kingdom, and healing all manner of sickness and all manner of disease among the people. And his fame went throughout all Syria: and they brought unto him all sick people that were taken with divers diseases and **torments**, and **those which** were possessed with devils, and those which were lunatic, and those that had the palsy; and he healed them." (Matthew 4:23-24).

February 28: "**Of whom** we have many things to say, **and** hard to be uttered, **seeing** ye are dull of hearing. For when **for the time** ye ought to be teachers, ye have need that **one** teach you **again which be** the first principles of the **oracles** of God; and are become such as have need of milk, and not of strong meat." (Hebrews 5:11-12).

February 29: "Beware lest any man spoil you through philosophy and **vain deceit**, **after** the tradition of men, **after the rudiments of** the world, and not after Christ… Buried with him in baptism." (Colossians 2:8 & 12).

March 1: "And another **also** said, Lord, I will follow thee; but let me first go bid them farewell, which are at home at my house. **And** Jesus said unto him, No man, **having put** his hand to the plough, and look**ing** back, is **fit** for the kingdom of God." (Luke 9:61-62).

March 2: "Jethro said, Blessed be the Lord, **who** hath delivered you out of the hand of the Egyptians, and out of the hand of Pharaoh, **who** hath delivered **the** people from under the **hand** of the Egyptians. Now I know that the Lord is greater than all gods." (Exodus 18:10-11).

March 3: "Think not that I am come to send peace on earth: I came not to send peace, but a sword. For I am come to set a man at variance against his father, and the daughter against her mother, and the daughter in law against her mother in law. And a man's foes shall be they of his own household." (Matthew 10:34-36).

March 4: "**The** Comforter, which is the Holy Ghost, whom **the** Father will send in my name, he shall teach you all things, and bring all things to your remembrance, whatsoever I have **said unto** you." (John 14:26).

March 5: "They shall **bow down** to thee with their face toward the earth, and lick up the dust of thy feet; and thou **shalt** know that I am the Lord." (Isaiah 49:23).

March 6: "**For he that will** love life, and see good days, let him refrain his tongue from evil, and his lips that they speak no guile: Let him eschew evil, and do good; let him seek peace, and ensue it. For the eyes of the Lord are over the righteous, and his ears are open unto their prayers." (1 Peter 3:10-12).

March 7: "All things are **delivered** unto me of my Father: and no man knoweth the Son, but the Father; neither knoweth any man the Father, save the Son, and he to whomsoever the Son will **reveal** him. Come unto me, all ye that labour and are **heavy** laden, and I will give you **rest**." (Matthew 11:27-28).

March 8: "And he said, Who told thee that thou wast naked? Hast thou eaten of the tree, **whereof** I commanded thee that thou shouldest not eat?" (Genesis 3:11).

March 9: "And the kings of the earth, and the great men, and the rich men, and the chief captains, and the mighty men, and every bondman, and every free man, hid themselves in the dens and in the rocks of the **mountains**; And said to the **mountains and rocks**, Fall on us, and hide us from the **face** of him that sitteth on the throne, and from the wrath of the Lamb." (Revelation 6:15:16).

March 10: "**Enlarge the place of thy tent, and let them stretch forth the curtains** of thine habitations: spare not, **lengthen** thy cords, and **strengthen** thy stakes." (Isaiah 54:2).

March 11: "The Spirit of the Lord spake by me, and his word **was in** my tongue. The God of Israel **said**, the **Rock** of Israel **spake to me**, He that **ruleth** over men **must be just, ruling** in the fear of God. And he shall be as the light of the morning, when the sun **riseth, even** a morning **without** clouds; as the **tender** grass **springing out of the earth by clear shining after rain.**" (2 Samuel 23:2-4).

March 12: "And **he gave** some, apostles; and some, prophets; **and** some, evangelists; **and** some, **pastors and** teachers; **For the perfecting of** the saints, **for the** work **of the ministry, for** the edifying of the body of Christ: Till we **all come** in the unity of **the** faith, and **of the** knowledge of the Son of God, unto a perfect man, **unto** the measure of **the stature of the** fulness of Christ: That we henceforth be no more children, **tossed to and fro, and** carried **about** with every wind of doctrine, by the **sleight** of men, and **cunning** craftiness, whereby they **lie in** wait to deceive." (Ephesians 4:11-14).

March 13: "Ye shall hear of wars and **rumours** of wars: see that ye be not troubled: for all these things must come to pass, but the end is not yet. For nation shall rise against nation, and **kingdom** against **kingdom**: and there shall be **famines**, and pestilences, and earthquakes, in **divers places**. All these are the beginning of sorrows." (Matthew 24:6-8).

424

March 14: "Then answered Jesus and said unto them, Verily, verily, I say unto you, The Son can do nothing of himself, but **what** he seeth the Father do: for what things soever he doeth, **these also** doeth the Son **likewise**." (Matthew 5:19).

March 15: "Love not the world, neither the things that are in the world. If any man love the world, the love of the Father is not in him. For all that is in the world, the lust of the flesh, and the lust of the eyes, and the pride of **life**, is not of the Father, but **is** of the world. And the world **passeth** away, and the lust thereof: but he that **doeth** the will of God abideth for ever." (1 John 2:15-17).

March 16: "Then shall they also answer him, saying, Lord, when saw we thee an hungred, or athirst, or **a stranger**, or naked, or sick, or in prison, and **did** not minister unto thee? Then shall he answer them, **saying**, Verily I say unto you, Inasmuch as ye did it not to one of the least of these, ye did it not to me." (Matthew 25:44-45).

March 17: "Watch and pray, that ye **enter** not into temptation: the spirit **indeed** is willing, but the flesh is weak." (Matthew 26:41).

March 18: "There are many **unruly and vain** talkers and deceivers, **specially** they of the circumcision: Whose mouths must be stopped, **who subvert** whole houses, teaching things which they ought not, for filthy lucre's **sake**." (Titus 1:10-11).

March 19: "When they heard this, they were pricked in their heart, and said unto Peter and to the **rest of the apostles**, Men and brethren, what shall we do? **Then** Peter said unto them, Repent, and be baptized every one of you in the name of Jesus Christ for the remission of sins, and ye shall receive the gift of the Holy Ghost." (Acts 2:37-38).

March 20: "I am the vine, ye are the branches: He that abideth in me, and I in him, the same bringeth forth much fruit: for without me ye can do nothing." (John 15:5).

March 21: "My soul, **wait thou only** upon God; **for my expectation is from him**. He only **is my rock and** my salvation: he is my defence; I shall not be moved. In God is my **salvation** and my glory: **the rock of my strength, and my refuge, is** in God. Trust in him **at all times**; ye people, pour out your heart before him: God is **a refuge for us**. Selah. Surely men **of low degree are vanity, and** men **of high degree are a lie: to be laid in the balance**, they are altogether lighter than vanity." (Psalms 62:5-9).

March 22: "Put on **therefore, as the elect of God, holy and beloved, bowels of mercies**, kindness, humbleness of mind, meekness, longsuffering; Forbearing one another, and forgiving one another, if any man have a quarrel **against any**: even as Christ forgave you, so **also** do ye. **And** above all these things put on charity, which is the bond of perfectness. And let the peace of God rule in your hearts, to the which **also** ye are called in one body; and be ye thankful." (Colossians 3:12-15).

March 23: "Therefore, brethren, stand fast, and **hold** the traditions which ye have **been taught**, whether by **word**, or our epistle. **Now** our Lord Jesus Christ himself, and God, **even** our Father, which hath loved us, and hath given us everlasting consolation and good hope through grace. Comfort your hearts, and stablish you in **every good word** and **work**." (2 Thessalonians 2:15-17).

March 24: "**Add to** your faith virtue; and to virtue knowledge; And to knowledge temperance; and **to** temperance patience; **and to** patience godliness; **And to** godliness brotherly kindness; **and to** brotherly kindness **charity**. For if these things be **in** you, and **abound**, they make you that ye shall neither be **barren** nor unfruitful in the knowledge of our Lord Jesus Christ." (2 Peter 1:5-8).

March 25: "**All things come alike to all: there is one event to** the righteous, **and to** the **wicked; to** the good and **to** the clean, **and to** the unclean; **to** him that **sacrificeth, and to** him that **sacrificeth** not: as **is the good, so is the sinner; and he that sweareth, as he that feareth an oath**." (Ecclesiastes 9:2).

March 26: "Lord God! **behold**, thou hast made **the** heaven and the earth **by** thy great power and **stretched out** arm, and there is nothing too hard for thee: Thou shewest **loving kindness** unto thousands, **and** recompensest the **iniquity** of the fathers into the bosom of their children after them: the Great, the Mighty God, the Lord of hosts, **is his** name." (Jeremiah 32:17-18).

March 27: "**Hold fast the form of sound** words, which thou **hast** heard of me, in faith and love which is in Christ Jesus. That good thing which was committed unto **thee** keep **by** the Holy Ghost which dwelleth in us." (2 Timothy 1:13-14).

March 28: "And Israel stretched out his right hand, and laid it upon Ephraim's head, **who** was the younger, and his left hand upon Manasseh's head, **guiding** his hands **wittingly**; for Manasseh was the **firstborn**." (Genesis 48:14).

March 29: "I thank **Christ Jesus our Lord, who hath enabled** me, for that he counted me **faithful**, putting **me into the ministry. Who was before** a blasphemer, and a persecutor, and **injurious: but** I obtained mercy, because I did it ignorantly in unbelief. **And** the grace of our Lord was **exceeding** abundant with faith and love which is in Christ Jesus." (1 Timothy 1:11-14).

March 30: "From that time many of his disciples went **back**, and **walked** no more

426

with him. Then said Jesus **un**to the twelve, Will ye also go away? Then Simon Peter answered him, **Lord**, to whom shall we go? thou hast **the** words of eternal life. And we believe and **are sure** that thou art **that** Christ, the Son of the living God." (John 6:66-69).

March 31: "And I John saw the holy city, new Jerusalem, coming down from God out of heaven, prepared as a bride **adorned** for her husband. And I heard a great voice **out of heaven** saying, Behold, the tabernacle of God is with men, and he will dwell with them, and they shall be his people, and God himself shall be with them, and be their God. And God shall wipe away all tears from their eyes; and there shall be no more death, neither sorrow, **nor** crying, neither shall there be any more pain: for the **former** things are **passed** away." (Revelation 21:2-4).

April 1: "Think **not** that I am come to **destroy** the law, **or** the prophets: I am not come to **destroy**, but to fulfil. For **verily** I say unto you, Till heaven and earth **pass**, one jot or one tittle shall **in no wise pass from the law**, till all be fulfilled." (Matthew 5:17-18).

April 2: "**We hear that** there are some which walk among you **disorderly**, working not at all, but are busybodies. **Now** them that are such we command and exhort **by** our Lord Jesus Christ, that with quietness they work, and eat their **own** bread. **But ye**, brethren, be not weary in well doing." (2 Thessalonians 3:11-13).

April 3: "Come **ye** to the waters, and **he** that **hath** no money; come **ye**, buy, **and** eat; **yea**, come, buy wine and milk without money **and without price**. Wherefore do ye **spend** money for **that which is not bread**? and your labour for **that which** satisfieth not? hearken **diligently** unto me, and eat **ye that which is good**, and let your soul **delight itself in fatness**." (Isaiah 55:1-2).

April 4: "All scripture **is** given by inspiration of God, and is profitable **for doctrine, for reproof, for correction, for** instruction in righteousness: That the man of God may be perfect, **throughly furnished** unto all good works." (2 Timothy 3:16-17).

April 5: "They shall see his face; and his name shall be in their foreheads. And there shall be no night there; and they need no candle, neither light of the sun; for the Lord God giveth them light: and they shall reign for ever **and ever**." (Revelation 22:4-5).

April 6: "The people which sat in darkness saw great light." (Matthew 4:16).

April 7: "That the God of our Lord Jesus Christ, the Father of glory, **may** give unto you the spirit of wisdom and **revelation** in the knowledge **of him**: The eyes of your understanding **being** enlightened; that ye **may** know what **is the** hope **of his calling**, and **what** the riches of the **glory** of his inheritance in the saints, And what is the exceeding greatness of his power to us-ward **who** believe, according to the working of his mighty power, Which he wrought in Christ, when he raised him from **the dead**, and set him **at** his **own** right hand in the heavenly **places**." (Ephesians 1:17-20).

April 8: "Preach the Gospel to **every** creature. **He that** believeth and is baptized shall be **saved**; **but he that** believeth not shall be damned. And these signs shall follow them that believe; In my name shall they cast out devils; **they** shall speak with new tongues; **They** shall **take up** serpents; and if they drink any deadly thing, it shall not hurt them; they shall lay hands on the sick, and they shall recover." (Mark 16:15-18).

April 9: "And Jesus went forth, and saw **a great multitude**, and **was moved with compassion toward** them, and he healed **their** sick." (Matthew 14:14).

April 10: "I saw also the Lord sitting upon **a throne**, high and **lifted up**, and his train filled the **temple**. Above **it stood** the seraphims: **each** one had six wings; with twain **he** covered his face, **and** with twain **he covered** his feet, and with twain he did fly. **And one** cried **unto a**nother, **and said**, Holy, holy, holy, is the Lord of hosts." (Isaiah 6:1-3).

April 11: "We **both** labour and suffer reproach, because we **trust** in the living God, **who** is the Saviour of all men, specially of those that believe." (1 Timothy 4:10).

April 12: "Whosoever shall say, Thou fool, shall be in danger of hell fire." (Matthew 5:22).

April 13: "A new commandment I write unto you, **which thing is true in him and in you: because the darkness is past, and the true light now shineth**. He that saith he is in the light, and hateth his brother, is in darkness even until now. He that loveth his brother abideth in the light, and there is none occasion of **stumbling** in him." (1 John 2:8-10).

April 14: "And **having** an high priest over the house of God; Let us draw **near** with a true heart in **full assurance of** faith, having our hearts **sprinkled** from an evil conscience, and our bodies washed with pure water. Let us **hold fast** the profession of our **faith** without wavering; (for he is faithful that promised;) And let us consider one another to provoke unto love and to good works: Not forsaking the **assembling of** ourselves **together**, as the manner of some is; but exhorting one another: and so much the more, as ye see the day **approaching**." (Hebrews 10:21-25).

April 15: "And he took bread, **and** gave thanks, and brake it, and gave unto them, saying, This is my body which is given for you: this do in remembrance of me.

Likewise also the cup **after supper**, saying, This cup is the new testament in my blood, which is shed for you." (Luke 22:19-20).

April 16: "Blessed are they which **are persecuted** for righteousness' sake: for theirs is the kingdom of heaven. Blessed are ye, when men shall revile you, and persecute you, and shall say all manner of evil against you falsely, for my sake. Rejoice, and be **exceeding** glad: for great is your reward in heaven: for so persecuted they the prophets which were before **you**." (Matthew 5:10-12).

April 17: "**On the day** when ye **shall pass** over Jordan unto the land which the Lord thy God giveth thee, **that thou shalt** set thee up great stones. …And **thou shalt** write upon them all the words of this law, when thou art **passed** over, that thou mayest **go** in unto the land which the Lord thy God giveth thee, a land that floweth with milk and honey; as the Lord God of thy fathers hath promised thee." (Deuteronomy 27:2-3).

April 18: "For where two or three are gathered together in my name, there am I in the **midst** of them." (Matthew 18:20).

April 19: "**Thou** hypocrite, first cast out the beam out of thine own eye; and then shalt thou see clearly to **cast** out the mote out of thy brother's eye." (Matthew 7:5).

April 20: "**For when** the Gentiles, which have not **the** law, do **by** nature the things contained in the law, **these**, having not the law, are a law unto themselves: Which shew the **work** of the law written in their hearts, their conscience **also** bear**ing** witness, and their thoughts **the mean while** accusing **or else excusing** one another;) **In** the day when God shall judge the secrets of men." (Romans 2:14-16).

April 21: "Preach the word; be **instant** in season, out of season; **reprove**, rebuke, exhort with all longsuffering **and doctrine**. For the time will come when they will not **endure sound** doctrine; but after their own lusts shall they heap **to themselves** teachers, having itching ears; And **they** shall turn **away** their ears from the truth, and shall be **turned unto** fables. But watch thou in all things, **endure afflictions**, do the work of an evangelist, **make full proof of thy ministry**." (2 Timothy 4:2-5).

April 22: "**Ye** serpents, **ye** generation of vipers, how **can** ye escape the damnation of hell? Wherefore, behold, I send unto you prophets, **and** wise men, and scribes: and some of them ye shall kill and crucify; and some **of them** shall ye scourge in your synagogues, and persecute **them** from city to city." (Matthew 23:33-34).

April 23: "Let us **hold fast** our profession. For we have not an high priest which cannot **be touched with the feeling of** our infirmities; but was in all points tempted like **as we**

are, yet without sin. Let us therefore **come** boldly unto the **throne** of grace, that we may **obtain** mercy, and find grace to help in time of need." (Hebrews 4:14-16).

April 24: "Hear, O Israel: The Lord **our** God is **one** Lord: And thou shalt love the Lord thy God with all thine heart, and with all thy soul, and with all thy might. And these words, which I command thee this day, shall be in thine heart: And thou shalt **teach** them **diligently unto** thy children." (Deuteronomy 6:4-7).

April 25: "The people that **walked** in darkness **have seen** a great light: **they** that dwell in the land of the shadow of death, upon them **hath** the light shined." (Isaiah 9:2).

April 26: "Let no **corrupt** communication proceed out of your mouth, but that which is good to **the use of** edify**ing**, that it may **minister grace unto** the hearers. And grieve not the holy Spirit of God, **whereby** ye are sealed unto the day of redemption. Let all bitterness, and wrath, and **anger, and clamour, and evil** speaking, be put away from you, with all malice: And be ye kind one to another, **tenderhearted**, forgiving one another, even as God for Christ's sake **hath forgiven** you." (Ephesians 4:29-32).

April 27: "**Now** God himself **and** our Father, and our Lord Jesus Christ, **direct our way** unto you. And the Lord **make you to** increase and **abound** in love one toward another, and toward all men." (1 Thessalonians 3:11-12).

April 28: "And they brought that which Moses commanded before the tabernacle of the congregation." (Leviticus 9:5).

April 29: "And there was **war** in heaven: Michael and his angels fought **against** the dragon; and the dragon fought and his angels, And prevailed not; neither was their place found any more in heaven. And the great dragon was cast out, that old serpent, called the Devil, and Satan, which deceiveth the **whole** world: he was cast out into the earth, and his angels were cast out **with him**." (Revelation 12:7-9).

April 30: "Unto you it is given to know the mystery of the kingdom of God: but unto them that are without, all **these** things **are** done in parables." (Mark 4:11).

May 1: "And I saw **another** angel fly in the midst of heaven, having **the** everlasting Gospel to preach unto them that dwell on the earth, and to **every** nation, **and** kindred, and tongue, and people, Saying with a loud voice, Fear God, and give **glory** to him; for the hour of his judgment is come: and worship him that made heaven, and earth, and the sea, and **the** fountains of waters." (Revelation 14:6-7).

May 2: "Woe unto you, scribes and Pharisees, hypocrites! for ye are like unto **whited**

sepulchres, which **indeed** appear beautiful outward, but are within full of dead men's bones, and of all **uncleanness**." (Matthew 22:27).

May 3: "Be ye therefore sober, **and watch unto** prayer. And above all things have fervent **charity** among yourselves: for **charity shall** cover the multitude of sins. **Use hospitality one to another** without grudging. As every man hath received the gift, even so minister the same one to another, as **good stewards** of the manifold grace of God." (2 Peter 4:7-10).

May 4: "The day of the Lord so cometh as a thief in the night. **For** when they shall say, Peace and **safety**; then sudden destruction cometh **up**on them, as travail **upon** a woman with child; and they shall not escape." (1 Thessalonians 5:2-3).

May 5: "**But** be ye doers of the word, and not hearers only, deceiving your own selves. For if any **be a** hear**er** of the word, and not **a doer**, he is like unto a man beholding his natural face in a glass: For he **beholdeth** himself, and goeth his way, and **straightway** forgetteth what **manner of man he** was. But whoso looketh into the perfect law of liberty, and continueth therein, he being not a forgetful hearer, but a doer of the work, **this man** shall be **blessed** in his deed." (James 1:22-25).

May 6: "Wherefore **art thou** red **in thine apparel, and thy garments** like **him** that treadeth in the winefat? I have trodden the winepress alone; and of **the** people there was none with me: **for** I **will tread** them in mine anger, and **trample** them in my **fury**; and their blood **shall be sprinkled** upon my **garments**, and I **will** stain all my raiment. For the day of vengeance **is in mine heart**, and the year of my **redeemed** is come." (Isaiah 63:2-4).

May 7: "**And** Ruth said, Entreat me not to leave thee, or to return from **following** after thee: for whither thou goest, I will go; and where thou **lodgest**, I will **lodge**: thy people **shall be** my people, and thy God my God: Where thou diest, will I die, and there will I be buried: the Lord do so to me, **and more also**, if **ought** but death part thee and me." (Ruth 1:16-17).

May 8: "**And** took upon him the **form** of a servant, and was **made in the likeness of** men: **And being found in fashion as a man**, he humbled himself, and became obedient unto death, even the death of the cross. Wherefore God **also** hath **highly** exalted him, and given him a name **which is** above **every** name: That **at** the name of Jesus every knee should bow, of things in heaven, and things in earth, and things under the earth; And that **every** tongue should confess that Jesus Christ is Lord, to the **glory** of God the Father." (Philippians 2:7-11).

May 9: "These things have I spoken unto you in proverbs: **but** the time come**th**, when

I shall no more speak unto you in proverbs, but I shall shew you plainly **of the** Father. At that day ye shall ask in **my** name." (John 16:25-26).

May 10: "For many walk, **of whom I have told you often**, and **now tell you even weeping**, that they are the enemies of the cross of Christ: Whose end is **destruction**, whose God is their belly, and **whose** glory **is in** their shame, **who mind earthly things. For** our conversation is in heaven; from whence **also** we look for the Saviour, **the Lord** Jesus Christ: **Who** shall change our vile body, that **it** may be fashioned like unto his glorious body, according to the working whereby he is able **even** to subdue all things unto himself." (Philippians 3:18-21).

May 11: "Walk worthy of the Lord **unto** all **pleasing**, being fruitful in **every** good work, and increasing in the knowledge of God; Strengthened with all might, **according to** his glorious power, unto all patience and longsuffering with joyfulness; Giving thanks unto the Father, which hath made us meet to be partakers of the inheritance of **the** saints in light." (Colossians 1:10-12).

May 12: "**Thou shalt also consider** in thine heart, that, as a man **chasteneth** his son, so the Lord thy God chasteneth thee." (Deuteronomy 8:5).

May 13: "**Yea, and if** I be offered upon **the** sacrifice and service of **your** faith, I **joy, and** rejoice with you all. For the same cause also **do** ye joy, and rejoice with me." (Philippians 2:17-18).

May 14: "If thou **faint in the day of adversity**, thy strength is small." (Proverbs 24:10).

May 15: "Likewise must the deacons be **grave**, not doubletongued, not given to much wine, **not greedy of** filthy lucre; **Holding** the mystery of the faith in a pure conscience. And let **these also** first be proved; then let them **use the office of a deacon, being** found **blameless**. Even so must their wives be **grave**, not **slanderers**, sober, faithful in all things. Let the deacons be the husbands of one wife, **ruling** their children and their own **houses** well. For they that **have used the office of a deacon** well **purchase to themselves a** good degree, and great **boldness** in the faith which is in Christ Jesus." (1 Timothy 3:8-13).

May 16: "The day of the Lord will come as a thief in the night; in the which the heavens shall **pass away** with **a great** noise, and the elements shall melt with fervent heat, the **earth also and** the works that are therein shall **be burned up.**" (2 Peter 3:10).

May 17: "Submit yourselves **therefore** to God. Resist the devil, and he will **flee** from you. Draw nigh to God, and he will draw nigh to you. Cleanse your hands, ye sinners; and **purify** your hearts, ye **double** minded. **Be afflicted, and mourn**, and weep: let your laughter be turned to mourning, and your joy to heaviness. **Humble yourselves in the sight of** the Lord, and he shall lift you up." (James 4:7-10).

May 18: "I am Alpha and Omega, the beginning and the end. I will give unto him that is athirst of the **fountain of the** water of life freely. He that overcometh shall inherit all things; and I will be his God, and he shall be my son." (Revelation 21:6-7).

May 19: "For they shall **deliver** you up to councils; and in the synagogues ye shall be beaten: and ye shall be brought before rulers and kings for my sake, for a **testimony against** them." (Mark 13:9).

May 20: "Husbands, love your wives, even as Christ also loved the **church**... **That he might present it to** himself a glorious **church, not having** spot, or wrinkle, or any such thing; but that it should be holy and without **blemish**. So ought men to love their wives as their own bodies." (Ephesians 5:25, 27-28).

May 21: "Unto me, **who am less than** the least of all saints, is this grace given, that I should preach among the Gentiles the unsearchable riches of Christ; **And to make** all men **see** what is the fellowship of the mystery, which from the beginning of the world hath been hid in God, **who created** all things **by** Jesus Christ: To the intent that now unto the **principalities and** powers in heaven**ly places** might be known by the **church** the manifold wisdom of God, According to **the** eternal purpose which he purposed in Christ Jesus our Lord: **In** whom we **have** bold**ness and access with confidence** by **the** faith of him." (Ephesians 3:8-12).

May 22: "Him hath **God** exalted with his right hand to be a **Prince** and a Saviour, for to give repentance to Israel, and forgiveness of sins. And we are his **witnesses** of these things." (Acts 5:31-32).

May 23: "A bishop must be **blameless**... **a lover of hospitality, a lover of good men, sober, just**, holy, temperate; **Holding fast the faithful** word **as he hath been taught**, that he may be able by **sound doctrine both** to exhort **and to convince the gainsayers**." (Titus 1:7-9).

May 24: "Our **sufficiency is** of God; **Who also** hath made us able ministers **of** the new testament; not of the letter, but of the spirit: for the letter killeth, but the spirit giveth life." (2 Corinthians 3:5-6).

May 25: "Ezra opened the book **in the sight of** all the people... and when he opened it, all the people stood up: And Ezra **blessed** the Lord, the great God. And all the people answered, Amen, Amen, with **lifting** up their hands: and **they** bowed **their heads**, and worshipped the Lord with their faces to the ground." (Nehemiah 8:5-6).

May 26: "Give diligence to make your calling and election sure: for if ye do **these** things, ye shall never **fall: For so** an **entrance** shall be ministered unto you abundantly into the everlasting kingdom of our Lord and Saviour Jesus Christ." (2 Peter 1:10-11).

May 27: "And there was a great earthquake, such as was not since men were upon the earth, so mighty an earthquake, and so great. And the great city was divided into three parts, and the cities of the nations fell: and great Babylon came in remembrance before God, to give unto her the cup of the wine of the fierceness of **his** wrath. **And** every **island** fled away, and the mountains were not found. And there fell **upon men** a great hail **out of heaven, every stone about the weight of a talent**: and men blasphemed God because of the plague of the hail; for the plague **thereof** was **exceeding** great." (Revelation 16:18-21).

May 28: "My brethren, count it all joy when ye fall into divers temptations; **Knowing this**, that the trying of your faith **worketh** patience. **But** let patience have her perfect work, that ye may be perfect and **entire, wanting** nothing." (James 1:2-4).

May 29: "These were **more noble than those in** Thessalonica, **in that they** received the word with all **readiness** of mind, and searched the scriptures daily, whether those things were so." (Acts 17:11).

May 30: "He that hath ears to hear, let him hear." (Luke 8:8).

May 31: "Keep my ordinances and **laws**; which if a man **keep**, he shall live therein. For I am the Lord." (Leviticus 18:5).

June 1: "Now therefore ye are no more strangers and foreigners, but **fellow**citizens with the saints, and of the household of God. And are built upon the foundation of the apostles and prophets, Jesus Christ himself being the **chief** corner stone; In whom **all the** building **fitly framed** together groweth unto an holy temple in the Lord: In whom ye also are **builded** together." (Ephesians 2:19-22).

June 2: "For the Son of man is Lord even of the sabbath day." (Matthew 12:8).

June 3: "Ye have heard that it hath been said, Thou shalt love thy neighbour, and hate thine enemy. But I say unto you, Love your enemies, bless them that curse you, do good to them that hate you." (Matthew 5:43-44).

June 4: "This is a **faithful** saying, and worthy **of all acceptation**, that Christ Jesus came into the world to save sinners; of whom I am chief." (1 Timothy 1:15).

June 5: "Now hath he obtained a more excellent **ministry, by how much also** he is the mediator of a better **covenant**, which was **established upon** better promises." (Hebrews 8:6).

June 6: "Jesus answered them, and said, My doctrine is not mine, but his that sent me. If any man will do his will, he shall know of the doctrine, whether it be of God, or whether I **speak** of myself." (John 7:16-17).

June 7: "The Lord is my shepherd; I **shall not** want. He **maketh** me **to lie down** in green pastures: **he** leadeth me **beside the still** waters. He **restoreth** my soul: **he leadeth** me in the paths of righteousness for his name's sake. **Yea**, though I walk **through** the valley of the shadow of death, I **will** fear no evil: for thou art with me; thy **rod** and thy staff **they** comfort me. Thou preparest a table before me **in the presence of** mine enemies: thou anointest my head with oil; my cup **runneth over. Surely goodness** and mercy **shall** follow me all the days of my life: **and** I **will** dwell in the house of the Lord for ever." (Psalms 23:1-6).

June 8: "For this **cause** shall a man leave father and mother, and **shall** cleave to his wife." (Matthew 19:5).

June 9: "**Stand fast** in one spirit, **with** one **mind striving together for** the faith of the Gospel; And in nothing **terrified by** your adversaries: which is to them an **evident** token of perdition, **but** to you of **salvation**, and that of God. For unto you it is given **in the behalf of Christ, not only to** believe on **him**, but also to suffer for his sake; **Having** the same **conflict** which ye saw in me, and now hear **to be in** me." (Philippians 1:27-30).

June 10: "They are waxen fat, **they shine: yea, they** overpass the deeds of the wicked: they **judge** not the **cause**, the cause of the fatherless, **yet they prosper; and the right of the needy do** they not judge. **Shall** I not **visit for** these things? saith the Lord: **shall not my soul** be avenged **on such a nation as this? A wonderful and** horrible thing **is committed** in the land." (Jeremiah 5:28-30).

June 11: "Go ye therefore, and teach all nations, baptizing them in the name of the Father, and of the Son, and of the Holy Ghost: Teaching them to observe all things whatsoever I have commanded you: and, lo, I am with you alway, even unto the end of the world." (Matthew 28:19-20).

June 12: "For this cause I bow my knees unto the Father of our Lord Jesus Christ,

Of whom the whole family in heaven and earth is named, That he would grant you, according to the riches of his glory, to be strengthened with might by his Spirit **in the inner man**; That Christ may dwell in your hearts by faith; that ye, being rooted and grounded in love, **May** be able to comprehend **with all saints** what is the breadth, and length, and depth, and height; And to know the love of Christ." (Ephesians 3:14-19).

June 13: "I therefore, **the prisoner of the Lord, beseech** you that ye walk worthy of the vocation wherewith ye are called, With all lowliness and meekness, with longsuffering, forbearing one another in love; **Endeavouring** to keep the unity of the Spirit in the bond of peace. **There is** one body, and one Spirit, even as ye are called in one hope of your calling; One Lord, one faith, one baptism, One God and Father of all, **who** is above all, **and** through all, and in **you** all." (Ephesians 4:1-6).

June 14: "Walk as children of light: (**For the fruit of the Spirit is in all goodness and righteousness and truth**;) **Proving what is acceptable** unto the Lord. And have no fellowship with the unfruitful works of darkness, **but rather reprove them. For it is a shame even to speak of those things which are done of them in secret. But all things that are reproved are made manifest by the light**: for whatsoever **doth make** manifest is light. Wherefore he saith, Awake thou that sleepest, and **arise from the dead**, and Christ shall give thee light." (Ephesians 58-14).

June 15: "Help us, O Lord our God; for we **rest on** thee, and in **thy** name we go against **this** multitude. O Lord, thou art our God; let not man prevail against thee." (2 Chronicles 14:11).

June 16: "I **endure** all things for the elect's sakes, that they **may** also obtain **the salvation** which is in Christ Jesus with eternal glory." (2 Timothy 2:10).

June 17: "Give me also this power, that…he may receive the Holy Ghost. **But** Peter said unto him, Thy money perish **with thee, because** thou **hast thought** that the gift of God may be **purchased** with money. Thou hast neither part nor **lot** in this **matter**: for thy heart is not right in the sight of God. Repent therefore of this thy wickedness, and pray God, **if perhaps** the thought of thine heart may be forgiven thee." (Acts 8:18-22).

June 18: "**But their** scribes and Pharisees murmured against his disciples, saying, Why **do** ye eat and drink with publicans and sinners. **And** Jesus answering said unto them, They that are whole need not a physician; but they that are sick. I came not to call the righteous, but sinners to repentance." (Luke 5:30-32).

June 19: "Her priests **have violated** my law, and **have profaned mine holy things**: they **have** put no difference between the holy and **profane**, neither **have they shewed difference** between the unclean and the clean, **and have hid** their eyes from my sabbaths, and I am **profaned** among them. **Her princes** in **the midst thereof** are like wolves, to shed blood, and to destroy souls, **to get dishonest gain**." (Ezekiel 22:26-27).

June 20: "For by grace are ye **saved** through faith; and that not of yourselves: it is the gift of God: Not of works, lest any man should boast. For we are his workmanship, created in Christ Jesus unto good works, which God **hath** before ordained that we should walk in them." (Ephesians 2:8-10).

June 21: "That thou **mayest** love the Lord thy God, **and that thou mayest obey** his voice, and **that thou mayest** cleave unto him: for he is thy life, and the length of thy days: that thou mayest dwell **in the land** which the Lord sware unto thy fathers, **to** Abraham, to Isaac, and to Jacob, to give them." (Deuteronomy 30:20).

June 22: "**Then** the Lord said unto me, The prophets **prophesy** lies in my name: I **sent them not**, neither **have I commanded them**, neither spake unto them: they **prophesy** unto you a false vision **and divination, and a thing of nought**, and the **deceit** of their heart." (Jeremiah 14:14).

June 23: "And the son said unto him, Father, I have sinned against heaven, and in thy sight, **and am no more** worthy to be called thy son. **But** the father said to his servants, Bring forth the best robe, and put it on him; and put a ring on his hand, and shoes on his feet." (Luke 15:21-22).

June 24: "But Jesus called them unto him, and said, Ye know that the **princes** of the Gentiles **exercise** dominion over them, and they that are great exercise **authority upon** them. **But** it shall not be so **among you**: but whosoever will be great among you, let him be your minister; And whosoever will be chief among you, let him be your servant: Even as the Son of man came not to be ministered unto, but to minister, and to give his life a **ransom for** many." (Matthew 20:25-28).

June 25: "Christ **is become of no effect unto you, whosoever of you** are justified by the law; ye are fallen from grace. For we through the Spirit **wait for the hope of righteousness** by faith." (Galatians 5:4-5).

June 26: "Seest thou how faith wrought with his **works**, and **by works** was faith made perfect? ...Ye see then how that **by works** a man is justified, and not by faith only." (James 2:22 & 24).

June 27: "He that **abideth** in the doctrine of Christ, he hath both the Father and the Son." (2 John 1:9).

June 28: "The powers that be are ordained of God. …it is **high** time **to** awake out of sleep: for now is our salvation nearer than when we believed. The night is **far spent**, the day is **at hand**: let us therefore cast **off the works** of darkness, and let us put on the armour of light. Let us walk honestly, as in the **day**; not in **rioting and drunkenness, not** in chambering and wantonness, **not** in strife and envying. But put ye on the Lord Jesus Christ, and make not provision for the flesh, to fulfil the lusts **thereof**." (Romans 13:1 & 11-14).

June 29: "**Put** them **in mind to be subject to principalities** and powers, to obey **magistrates, to be ready to every** good work, To speak evil of no man, to be no **brawlers**, but **gentle**, shewing all meekness unto all men." (Titus 3:1-2).

June 30: "And his father Zacharias was filled with the Holy Ghost, and prophesied, saying, Blessed be the Lord God of Israel; for he hath visited and redeemed his people, And hath raised up an horn of salvation **for** us in the house of his servant David; As he **spake** by the mouth of his holy prophets, which **have been** since the world began: That we should be saved from our enemies, and from the hand of all that hate us; To **perform the** mercy **promised to** our fathers, and to remember his holy **covenant**." (Luke 1:67-72).

July 1: "Be not **soon shaken in** mind, **or** be troubled, neither by spirit, **nor** by word, nor by letter **as from** us, as **that** the day of Christ **is** at hand. Let no man deceive you by any means: for **that day shall not come**, except there come **a falling away** first, and that man of sin be revealed, the son of perdition." (2 Thesalonians 2:2-3).

July 2: "I **have fed you with** milk, and not **with** meat: for **hitherto** ye were not **able to bear it**, neither yet **now are ye able**. For ye are yet carnal: **for whereas** there is among you envying, **and** strife, and **divisions**, are ye not carnal, and walk as men?" (1 Corinthians 3:2-3).

July 3: "But God, **who** is rich in mercy, **for** his great love wherewith he loved us, Even when we were dead **in** sins, hath quickened us **together** with Christ, (by grace ye are saved)." (Ephesians 2:4-5).

July 4: "I will be glad and rejoice in thy mercy: for thou hast considered my trouble; thou hast known my soul in adversi**ties; And hast not shut me up** into the hand of the enemy: **thou** hast set my feet in a large room. Have mercy upon me, O Lord, for I am in trouble: mine eye is consumed **with grief**, yea, my soul and my **belly. For** my life is **spent with grief**, and my years with **sighing**: my strength faileth because of mine **iniquity**." (Psalms 31:7-10).

July 5: "Many false prophets shall rise, and shall deceive many. And because iniquity shall **abound**, the love of many shall **wax cold**. But he that **shall** endure unto the end, **the same** shall be saved." (Matthew 24:11-13).

July 6: "I call **heaven and earth** to record this day **against** you, that I have set before you life and death, blessing and cursing: **therefore** choose life, that **both** thou and thy seed may live." (Deuteronomy 30:19).

July 7: "**Behold**, I send you forth as sheep **in the midst of** wolves: be ye therefore wise as serpents, and **harmless** as doves. **But** beware of men: for they **will** deliver you up to the councils, and **they will** scourge you... And ye shall be brought before **governors** and kings for my sake, **for a testimony against** them and the Gentiles. But when they deliver you up, take no thought how or what ye shall speak: for it shall be given you in that same hour what ye shall speak. For it is not ye that speak, but the Spirit of your Father which speaketh in you." (Matthew 10:16-20).

July 8: "Avenge not yourselves, but **rather** give **place** unto wrath: for it is written, Vengeance is mine; I will **repay**, saith the Lord. Therefore if thine enemy hunger, feed him; if he thirst, give him drink: for in so doing thou shalt heap coals of fire on his head. Be not overcome of evil, but overcome evil with good." (Romans 12:19-21).

July 9: "Therefore **take no thought, saying**, What shall **we** eat? or, What shall **we** drink?" (Matthew 6:31).

July 10: "And this I pray, that your love may **abound yet** more and more in knowledge and in all **judgment**; That ye may **approve things that are** excellent; that ye may be **sincere** and **without offence** till the day of Christ; **Being** filled with the fruits of righteousness, which are by Jesus Christ, unto the glory and **praise** of God." (Philippians 1:9-11).

July 11: "Then **contended** I with the rulers, and said, Why is the house of God forsaken? **And** I gathered them together, and set them in their place." (Nehemiah 13:11).

July 12: "It is written, **That** man shall not live by bread alone, but by every word of God." (Luke 4:4).

July 13: "He that loveth father or mother more than me is not worthy of me: and he that loveth son or daughter more than me is not **worthy of** me. And he that taketh not his cross, and followeth after me, is not **worthy of** me. He that findeth his life shall lose it: and he that loseth his life for my sake shall find it." (Matthew 10:37-39).

July 14: "There shall be false teachers among you, **who** privily shall bring in damnable **heresies**, even denying the Lord that bought them, and bring **upon themselves** swift **destruction**. And many shall follow their **pernicious** ways; by **reason of whom** the way of truth shall be evil spoken of. And through covetousness shall they with feigned words make merchandise of you: whose judgment **now of a long time lingereth not**, and their damnation **slumbereth** not." (2 Peter 2:1-3).

July 15: "I am a good shepherd, a good shepherd giveth his life for his sheep." (John 10:11).

July 16: "A time to plant, and a time to pluck up **that which** is planted; A time to **kill**, and a time to **heal**; a time to break down, and a time to build up; A time to weep, and a time to laugh; a time to mourn, and a time to dance; A time to cast away stones, and a time to gather stones together; a time to embrace, and a time to refrain from embracing; A time to **get**, and a time to lose; a time to **keep**, and a time to **cast away**; A time to rend, and a time to sew; a time to keep silence, and a time to speak; A time to love, and a time to hate; a time of war, and a time of peace." (Ecclesiastes 3:2-8).

July 17: "And he saith unto them, But whom say ye that I am? And Peter answereth and **saith** unto him, Thou art the Christ." (Mark 8:29).

July 18: "Behold, the days come, saith the Lord God, that I will send **a famine** in the land, not a famine of bread, nor **a thirst for** water, but **of** hearing the words of the Lord: **And** they shall **wander** from sea to **sea**, and from the north **even to** the east, they **shall run to and fro** to seek the word of the Lord, and shall not find it." (Amos 8:11-12).

July 19: "As many as I love, I rebuke and chasten: be zealous therefore, and repent. Behold, I stand at the door, and knock: if any man hear my voice, and open the door, I will come in to him, and will sup with him, and he with me." (Revelation 3:19-20).

July 20: "**But** in all things **approving** ourselves as the ministers of God, in much patience, in afflictions, in necessities, in **distresses**, In stripes, in imprisonments, in **tumults**, in labours, in watchings, in fastings; **By** pureness, **by** knowledge, **by** longsuffering, **by** kindness, **by** the Holy Ghost, **by** love unfeigned, **By** the word of truth, **by** the power of God, **by** the armour of righteousness on the right hand and on the left." (2 Corinthians 6:4-7).

July 21: "Jesus, **when** he was baptized, **went up** straight**way** out of the water: and, lo, **the** heavens **were** opened unto him, and he saw the Spirit of God descend**ing** like a dove, and light**ing** upon him: And lo a voice from heaven, saying, This is my **beloved** Son, in whom **I am well pleased**." (Matthew 3:16-17).

July 22: "God, **even** thy God, hath anointed thee with the oil of gladness above thy fellows." (Hebrews 1:9).

July 23: "**See then** that ye walk circumspectly, **not as fools, but as wise, Redeeming the time, because the days are evil**. Wherefore **be ye not unwise, but** understanding what the will of the Lord is. And be not drunk with wine, wherein is excess; but be **filled** with the Spirit; Speaking to yourselves in psalms and hymns and spiritual songs, singing and **making melody** in your heart to the Lord; Giving thanks always for all things unto God and the Father in the name of our Lord Jesus Christ." (Ephesians 5:15-20).

July 24: "For whom the Lord loveth he chasteneth, and scourgeth every son **whom** he receiveth." (Hebrews 12:6).

July 25: "Thou mayest **know** how thou oughtest to behave thyself in the house of God, which is the church of the living God, the pillar and ground of the truth. And without controversy great is the mystery of godliness: God was manifest in the flesh, justified in the Spirit, seen of angels, preached unto the Gentiles, believed on in the world, received up into glory." (1 Timothy 3:15-16).

July 26: "He went forward a little, and fell on the ground, and prayed that, if it were possible, the hour might pass from him. And he said, Abba, Father, all things are possible unto thee; take away this cup from me: nevertheless not what I will, but **what** thou wilt." (Mark 14:35-36).

July 27: "The law was our schoolmaster **to bring us** unto Christ, that we might be **justified** by faith. But after that faith is come, we are no longer under a schoolmaster. For ye are all the **children** of God by faith in Christ Jesus. For **as many of you as have been** baptized **into Christ** have put on Christ. There is **neither** Jew nor Greek, there is neither bond **nor** free, there is neither **male** nor **female**: for **ye** are all one in Christ Jesus. **And** if ye be Christ's, then are ye Abraham's seed, and heirs **according to the** promise." (Galatians 3:24-29).

July 28: "The Lord God **will** wipe away tears from **off** all faces; and the **rebuke** of his people **shall he** take away **from off all** the **earth**: for the Lord hath **spoken it**." (Isaiah 25:8).

July 29: "**Because ye despise this word**, and **trust in oppression and perverseness**, and **stay** there**on**: Therefore this **iniquity shall be to you as a breach ready to fall, swelling out in** a high wall, whose breaking cometh suddenly." (Isaiah 30:12-13).

July 30: "For **we know in part, and we prophesy in part**. But when that which is perfect is come, then that which is **in part** shall be done away. When I was a child, I spake as a child, I understood as a child, I **thought** as a child: but **when I became** a man, I put away childish things. **For** now we see **through** a glass, **darkly**; but then face to face: now I know **in part**; but then shall I know even as also I am known. **And** now abideth faith, hope, **charity**, these three; but the **greatest** of these is **charity**." (1 Corinthians 13:9-13).

July 31: "The disciple is not above his master, nor the servant above his lord." (Matthew 10:24).

August 1: "If **therefore** the light that is in thee be darkness, how great is that darkness!" (Matthew 6:23).

August 2: "Do all things without murmurings and disputings: That ye may be **blameless** and **harmless**, the sons of God, without rebuke, in the midst of a crooked and perverse nation, among **whom** ye shine as lights in the world; Holding **forth** the word of life; **that I may** rejoice in the day of Christ, that I have not run in vain, neither laboured in vain." (Philippians 2:14-16).

August 3: "And he said unto them, When I sent you without **purse**, and scrip, and shoes, lacked ye any thing? And they said, Nothing." (Luke 22:35).

August 4: "Ye shall walk after the Lord your God, and fear him, and keep his commandments, and **obey** his voice, and **ye shall** serve him, and cleave unto him." (Deuteronomy 13:4).

August 5: "Bear ye one another's burdens, and so fulfil the law of Christ." (Galatians 6:2).

August 6: "Submit yourselves un**to the elder. Yea, all of you be subject** one to another, **and be clothed with humility**: for God resisteth the proud, and giveth grace to the humble. **Humble** yourselves therefore under the mighty hand of God, that he may exalt you **in due** time." (1 Peter 5:5-6).

August 7: "Who shall separate us from **the love of Christ**? shall tribulation, or **distress**, or persecution, or **famine**, or nakedness, **or** peril, **or** sword?" (Romans 8:35).

August 8: "Blessed is the man that **walketh** not in the counsel of the ungodly, **nor**

standeth in the way of sinners, **nor** sitteth in the seat of the scornful. But **his delight is** in the law of the Lord; and in his law **doth he meditate day and night. And he shall be** like a tree planted by the rivers of water, that bringeth forth his fruit in **his** season; his **leaf also** shall not **wither**; and whatsoever he doeth shall prosper. The ungodly **are not so**: but are like the **chaff** which the wind **driveth away**." (Psalms 1:1-4).

August 9: "Ye are the salt of the earth: but if the salt have **lost his savour, wherewith shall it** be salted? It is thenceforth good for nothing, but to be cast out, and **to be trodden under foot of men**." (Matthew 5:13).

August 10: "And they chose Stephen, a man full of faith and of the Holy Ghost, and Philip. …**Whom** they set before the apostles: and **when** they had prayed, **they** laid their hands on them." (Acts 6:5-6).

August 11: "Choose you this day whom ye will serve; whether the gods which your fathers served that were on the other side of the flood, or the gods of the Amorites, in whose land ye **dwell: but** as for me and my house, we will serve the Lord." (Joshua 24:15).

August 12: "And I saw an angel come down from heaven, having the key of the bottomless pit and a great chain in his hand. And he **laid hold on** the dragon, that old serpent, which is the Devil, and Satan, and bound him a thousand years, And cast him into the bottomless pit, and **shut him up**, and set a seal **up**on him, that he should deceive the **nations** no more, till the **thousand** years **should be** fulfilled: and after that he must be loosed a little season." (Revelation 20:1-3).

August 13: "The publican, **standing** afar off, would not lift up **so much as** his eyes **un**to heaven, but smote **upon** his breast, saying, God be merciful to me a sinner. I tell you, this man **went down** to his house justified…for every **one** that exalteth himself shall be **abased**; and he that humbleth himself shall be exalted." (Luke 18:13-14).

August 14: "Let brotherly love continue. Be not forgetful to **entertain** strangers: for thereby **some** have **entertained** angels unawares." (Hebrews 13:1-2).

August 15: "When they persecute you in **this** city, **flee ye** into another: **for verily I say unto you**, Ye shall not **have gone over** the cities of Israel, till the Son of man be come. The disciple is not above his master, nor the servant above his lord. And fear not them which kill the body, **but are** not able to kill the soul." (Matthew 10:23-24 & 28).

August 16: "No man can serve two masters: for either he **will** hate the one, and love the other; or else he **will hold** to the one, and despise the other." (Matthew 6:24).

August 17: "O generation of vipers, who hath **warned** you to flee from the **wrath** to come? Bring forth therefore fruits **meet for** repentance." (Matthew 3:7-8).

August 18: "That **men** may know that thou, whose name **alone** is **Jehovah**, art the most high over all the earth." (Psalms 83:18).

August 19: "Search the scriptures; for in them ye think ye have eternal life: and they are they which testify of me. And ye will not come to me, that ye might have life. I receive not **honour** from men. But I know you, that ye have not the love of God in you." (John 5:39-42).

August 20: "Let us make man in our **image**, after our likeness: **and let them have dominion** over the fish of the sea, and over the fowl of the air, and over **the** cattle, and over all the earth, and over **every creeping thing that creepeth up**on the earth." (Genesis 1:26).

August 21: "**And** the Lord God **caused a deep sleep to fall** upon Adam, and he slept: and he took one of his ribs, and **closed up** the flesh **instead thereof**; And **the rib, which** the Lord God **had taken from man, made he** a woman, and brought her unto **the man. And** Adam said, This is **now** bone of my bones, and flesh of my flesh: **she** shall be called Woman, because she was taken **out** of Man. **Therefore** shall a man leave his father and his mother, and **shall** cleave unto his wife: and they shall be one flesh." (Genesis 2:21-24).

August 22: "The Lord **passed** by, and a **great and** strong wind rent the mountains, and brake **in pieces** the rocks before **the Lord**; but the Lord was not in the wind: and after the wind an earthquake; but the Lord was not in the earthquake: And after the earthquake a fire; but the Lord was not in the fire: and after the fire a still small voice." (1 Kings 19:11-12).

August 23: "O generation of vipers, how can ye, **being evil, speak good things**? for out of the abundance of the heart the mouth speaketh. A good man out of the good treasure of **the** heart bringeth forth good things: and an evil man out of **the** evil treasure bringeth forth evil things." (Matthew 22:34-35).

August 24: "**Being** justified by his grace, we should be **made** heirs **according to the hope** of eternal life. ...**But** avoid foolish questions, and genealogies, and **contentions**, and **strivings** about the law; for they are unprofitable and vain." (Titus 3:7 & 9).

August 25: "I exhort therefore, that, **first of all**, supplications, prayers,

intercessions, and giving of thanks, be **made** for all men; For kings, and for all that are in **authority**; that we may **lead** a quiet and peaceable life in all godliness and honesty." (1 Timothy 2:1-2).

August 26: "Trust in the Lord with all thine heart; and lean not unto thine own understanding. In all thy ways **acknowledge** him, and he shall **direct** thy **paths**. Be not wise in thine own **eyes**: fear the Lord, and depart from evil. **It shall be health to** thy navel, and **marrow to** thy bones." (Proverbs 3:5-8).

August 27: "Thou hast much goods laid up for many years; take thine ease, eat, drink, and be merry. But God said unto him, Thou fool, this night thy soul **shall be required of** thee: then whose shall those things be, which thou hast provided?" (Luke 12:19-20).

August 28: "They mocked the messengers of God, and despised his words, and misused his prophets, until the wrath of the Lord arose against his people, **till there was no** remedy." (2 Chronicles 36:16).

August 29: "Even unto this **present hour** we **both** hunger, and thirst, and are naked, and are buffeted, and have no certain dwelling place; And labour, working with our own hands: being reviled, we bless; **being** persecuted, we suffer it. **Being defamed**, we **entreat**: we are made as the filth of the world, **and are** the offscouring of all things." (1 Corinthians 4:11-13).

August 30: "**Who will** have all men **to be** saved, and to come unto the knowledge of the truth. For there is one God, and one mediator between God and **men**, the man Christ Jesus; **Who** gave himself a ransom for all, **to be testified in due** time." (1 Timothy 2:4-6).

August 31: "Babylon **the** great is fallen, is fallen, and is become the habitation of devils, and the hold of **every** foul spirit, and a cage of every unclean and hateful bird. For all nations have drunk of the wine of the wrath of her fornication, and the kings of the earth have committed fornication with her, and the merchants **of the earth** are waxed rich **through** the abundance of her delicacies." (Revelation 18:2-3).

September 1: "Ask, and it shall be given you; seek, and ye shall find; knock, and it shall be opened unto you: For **every one that** asketh receiveth; and he that seeketh findeth; and to him that knocketh it shall be opened. **Or what** man is there **of you, whom if** his son ask bread, **will he give him** a stone? Or if he **ask a fish, will he give** him a serpent? If ye then, **being** evil, **know how to** give good gifts **unto** your children, how much more shall your Father which is in heaven give good things to them that ask him?" (Matthew 7:7-11).

September 2: "**By hearing** ye shall hear, and shall not understand; and **seeing** ye shall see, and shall not perceive: For this people's heart is waxed gross, and their ears **are** dull of hearing, and their eyes they have closed; lest **at any time** they should see with their eyes, and hear with their ears, and should understand with their heart." (Matthew 13:14-15).

September 3: "Strait is the gate, and narrow is the way, which leadeth unto life, and few there be that find it." (Matthew 7:14).

September 4: "Men's hearts failing them for fear, and for looking after those things which **are** com**ing** on the earth: for the powers of heaven shall **be shaken**. And then shall they see the Son of man com**ing** in a cloud with power and great glory. **And** when these things begin to come to pass, then look up, and lift up your **heads**; for your redemption draweth nigh." (Luke 21:26-28).

September 5: "**Not a novice**, lest **being lifted up with pride** he fall into the **condemnation** of the **devil. Moreover** he must **have a good** report of them which are without; lest he fall into **reproach** and the snare of the **devil**." (1 Timothy 3:6-7).

September 6: "Thou hast delivered my soul from death, mine eyes from tears, and my feet from falling. I will walk before the Lord in the land of the living." (Psalms 116:8-9).

September 7: "God spake unto Moses, **and said** unto him, I am the Lord: And I appeared unto Abraham, **unto** Isaac, and **unto** Jacob, **by the name of** God Almighty, but **by** my name Jehovah was I not known to them." (Exodus 6:2-3).

September 8: "Behold, a king shall **reign in** righteousness, and princes shall rule **in judgment. And a man shall be as an hiding place from** the wind, and a **covert from** the tempest; as rivers of water in a **dry** place, **as** the shadow of a great rock in a **weary** land. And the eyes of **them that see** shall not be dim, and the ears of them that hear shall **hearken**. The heart **also** of the **rash** shall **understand** knowledge, and the tongue **of the stammerers** shall **be ready to** speak plainly." (Isaiah 32:1-4).

September 9: "Our rejoicing is this, the testimony of our conscience, that **in simplicity and** godly **sincerity**, not **with** fleshly wisdom, but by the grace of God, **we** have had our conversation in the world, and **more abundantly** to you-ward." (2 Corinthians 1:12).

September 10: "As they spake unto the people, the priests, and the **captain** of the temple, and the Sadducees, came upon them, **Being grieved** that they taught the people, and preached **through** Jesus the resurrection from the dead." (Acts 4:1-2).

September 11: "In the beginning was the Word, and **the** Word was with God, and **the** Word was God. The same was in the beginning with God. All things were made by **him**; and without **him** was not **any** thing made that was made. In **him** was life; and **the** life was the light of men. And the light shineth in darkness; and **the** darkness comprehended it not." (John 1:1-5).

September 12: "With men it is **im**possible, but not with God: for with God all things are possible." (Mark 10:27).

September 13: "**And when** the tempter came **to** him, **he** said, If thou be the Son of God, command that these stones be made bread. **But** he answered and said, It is written, Man shall not live by bread alone, but by every word that proceedeth out of the mouth of God." (Matthew 4:3-4).

September 14: "And I saw the dead, small and great, stand before God; and the books were opened: and another book was opened, which is the book of life: and the dead were judged out of those things which were written in the books, according to their **works**. And the sea gave up the dead which were in it; and death and hell delivered up the dead which were in them: and they were judged every man according to **their works**. …And whosoever was not found written in the book of life was cast into the lake of fire." (Revelation 20:12-15).

September 15: "Our Father which art in heaven, Hallowed be thy name. Thy kingdom come. Thy will be **done** in earth, as it is in heaven. Give us this day our daily bread. And forgive us our **debts**, as we forgive **our debtors**. **And** lead us not into temptation, but deliver us from evil: For thine is the kingdom, and the power, and the glory, for ever." (Matthew 6:9-13).

September 16: "This people honoureth me with their lips, but their heart is far from me." (Mark 7:6).

September 17: "He answered and said, Whether he be a sinner or no, I know not: one thing I **know**, that, **whereas** I was blind, now I see." (John 9:25).

September 18: "**Seeing** ye have purified your souls in obeying the truth through the Spirit **unto unfeigned love of the brethren**, see that ye love one another with a pure heart fervently: **Being** born **again**, not of **corruptible** seed, but of **incorruptible**, by the word of God, which liveth and **abideth** for ever." (1 Peter 1:22-23).

September 19: "**And thus** shall ye eat it; with your loins girded, **your** shoes on your feet, and your **staff** in your hand; and ye shall eat it in haste: it is the Lord's passover." (Exodus 12:11).

September 20: "He giveth to all life, and breath, **and all things**; And hath made of one blood all nations of men for to dwell on all the face of the earth, and hath **determined the** times before appointed, and the bounds of their habitation; That they should seek **the Lord**, if **haply** they might feel **after** him, and find him, though he be not far from every one of us: For in him we live, and move, and have our being; as certain also of your own poets have said." (Acts 17:25-28).

September 21: "Bow down thine ear, and **hear** the words **of the wise**, and apply **thine heart** unto my **knowledge**. For it is a pleasant thing if thou keep **them within thee; they shall withal be fitted in thy lips**. That thy trust **may be** in the Lord, I have **made known to thee this day, even to thee**. Have not I **written to thee excellent things in** counsels and **knowledge**, That I might **make** thee **know the certainty of the words of** truth?" (Proverbs 22:17-21).

September 22: "**Yea, a man** may say, Thou hast faith, and I have **works**: shew me thy faith **without thy works**, and I will shew thee my faith by my **works**. Thou believest that there is one God; thou doest well: the devils also believe, and tremble. **But** wilt thou **know**, O vain man, that faith without **works** is dead? … For as the body without the spirit is dead, so faith without works is dead also." (James 2:18-20 & 26).

September 23: "If any man **shall** say to you, Lo, here is Christ; or, lo, he is there; believe **him** not: For false Christs and false prophets shall rise, and shall shew signs and wonders, to seduce, if it were possible, even the elect. But take ye heed: behold, I have **foretold** you all things." (Mark 13:21-23).

September 24: "I know that thou **canst do every thing**, and that no thought **can be withholden from** thee. **Who is he that hideth** counsel **without knowledge**?" (Job 42:2-3).

September 25: "And he came into all the **country** about Jordan, preaching the baptism of repentance for the remission of sins; As it is written in the book of the **words** of Esaias the prophet, **saying**, The voice of **one crying** in the wilderness, Prepare ye the way of the Lord, make his paths straight. Every valley shall be filled, and every mountain and hill shall be brought low; and **the** crooked shall be made straight, and the rough ways shall be made smooth; And all flesh shall see the **salvation** of God." (Luke 3:3-6).

September 26: "**From the beginning of the** creation God made them **male and female**. For this **cause** shall **a** man leave **his** father and mother, and **cleave to** his wife; And they **twain** shall be one flesh: so then they are **no more** twain, but one flesh. **What** therefore God hath **joined together**, let not man **put asunder**." (Mark 10:6-9).

September 27: "Jesus, **when he had** cried again with a loud voice, yielded up the ghost. And, behold, the veil of the temple was rent in twain from the top to the bottom; and the earth did quake, and the **rocks** rent; And **the** graves **were** open**ed**; and many bodies of the saints which slept arose. And came out of the graves after his resurrection, and **went** into the holy city, and appeared unto many." (Matthew 27:50-53).

September 28: "Then said Jesus unto his disciples, If any man will **come after me**, let him **deny** himself, and take up his cross, and follow me. For whosoever will save his life shall lose it: and whosoever **will** lose his life for my sake shall find it." (Matthew 16:24-25).

September 29: "The last shall be first, and the first last: for many **be** called, **but** few chosen." (Matthew 20:16).

September 30: "There is nothing **covered**, that shall not be **revealed**; and hid, that shall not be known. What I tell you in darkness, that speak ye in light: and what ye hear in the ear, that preach ye **up**on the housetops." (Matthew 10:26-27).

October 1: "He that lacketh these things is blind, and **cannot see afar off**, and hath forgotten that he was purged from his old sins. Wherefore **the rather**, brethren, give diligence to make your calling and election sure: for if ye do **these** things, ye shall never **fall: For so an entrance** shall be ministered unto you abundantly into the everlasting kingdom of our Lord and Saviour Jesus Christ. Wherefore I will not be negligent to put you always in remembrance of these things, though ye know them, and be established in the present truth." (2 Peter 1:9-12).

October 2: "Finally, my brethren, be strong in the Lord, and in the power of his might. Put on the whole armour of God, that ye may **be able to** stand against the **wiles** of the devil. For we wrestle not against flesh and blood, but against **principalities**, against powers, against the rulers of the darkness of this world, against spiritual wickedness in **high places**." (Ephesians 6:10-12).

October 3: "These things write I unto you, that ye sin not. And if any man sin, we have an advocate with the Father, Jesus Christ **the** righteous: And he **is the propitiation** for our sins: and not for ours only, but also for the sins of **the whole** world. And hereby we **do** know that we **know** him, if we keep his commandments." (1 John 2:1-3).

October 4: "And if any man will sue thee at the law, and take **away** thy coat, let him have thy cloak also. And whosoever **shall** compel thee to go a mile, go with him twain. Give to him that asketh thee, and from him that would borrow **of thee** turn not **thou** away." (Matthew 5:40-42).

October 5: "Thou art Peter, and upon this rock I will build my **church**; and the gates of hell shall not prevail against it. And I will give unto thee the keys of the kingdom of heaven: and whatsoever thou **shalt bind** on earth shall be bound in heaven: and whatsoever thou **shalt loose** on earth shall be loosed in heaven." (Matthew 16:18-19).

October 6: "Behold, I set before you this day a blessing and a curse; A blessing, if ye **obey** the commandments of the Lord your God, which I command you this day: And a curse, if ye will not **obey** the commandments of the Lord your God." (Deuteronomy 11:26-28).

October 7: "The Lord shall scatter you among **the** nations, and ye shall be left few in number among the **heathen**, whither the Lord shall **lead** you. And there ye shall serve gods, the work of **men's** hands, wood and stone, which neither see, nor hear, nor eat, nor smell." (Deuteronomy 4:27-28).

October 8: "But they **hearkened not, nor** inclined their ear, but **walked in the counsels and in the** imagination of their **evil** heart, and **went backward, and not forward**." (Jeremiah 7:24).

October 9: "I will put my laws into their mind, and **write them** in their hearts: and I will be **to them a** God, and they shall be **to me a** people: And they shall not teach every man his neighbour, and every man his brother, saying, Know the Lord: for **all** shall know me, from the least to the **greatest**. For I will be merciful **to their unrighteousness**, and their sins and their **iniquities** will I **remember no** more." (Hebrews 8:10-12).

October 10: "Go unto Pharaoh, and **say unto** him, Thus saith the Lord, Let my people go, that they may serve me." (Exodus 8:1).

October 11: "I am filled with comfort, **I am exceeding joyful** in all our tribulation." (2 Corinthians 7:4).

October 12: "God **speaketh once, yea twice, yet man perceiveth it not**. In **a** dream, **in a** vision of the night, when **deep sleep falleth** upon men, **in slumberings upon the** bed; **Then** he **openeth the** ears of men, **and sealeth their instruction**." (Job 33:14-16).

October 13: "And bring hither the fatted calf, and kill it; and let us eat, and be merry: For this my son was dead, and is alive again; he was lost, and is found." (Luke 15:23-24).

October 14: "Salute one another with an holy kiss. The **churches** of Christ salute you." (Romans 16:16).

October 15: "Flesh and blood cannot inherit the kingdom of God; neither doth corruption inherit in**corruption**. Behold, I shew **you a mystery**; We shall not all sleep, but we shall all be changed, In a moment, in the twinkling of an eye, at the last trump: for the trumpet shall **sound**, and the dead shall **be raised** incorruptible, and we shall be changed. For this corruptible must put on **incorruption**, and this mortal must put on immortality." (1 Corinthians 15:50-53).

October 16: "Blessed are the pure in heart: for they shall see God. Blessed are the peacemakers: for they shall be called the children of God. Blessed are they which **are persecuted** for righteousness' sake: for theirs is the kingdom of heaven." (Matthew 5:8-10).

October 17: "Unto the pure all things are pure: but unto them that are defiled and unbelieving is nothing pure; but even **their** mind and conscience **is** defiled. They **profess** that they know God; but **in works** they deny him, **being** abominable, and disobedient, and unto every good work **reprobate**." (Titus 1:15-16).

October 18: "God created man **in his own image, in** the **image** of God created he him; male and female created he them. And God blessed them, and God said unto them, **Be fruitful**, and multiply, and **replenish** the earth, and subdue it: and have dominion over the fish of the sea, and over the fowl of the air, and over **every living thing** that moveth upon the earth." (Genesis 1:27-28).

October 19: "Judge not, **that** ye be **not** judged. For **with what judgment** ye judge, **ye** shall be judged." (Matthew 7:1-2).

October 20: "Israel loved Joseph more than all his children, because he **was the son of** his old age: and he made him a coat of many colours. **And** when his brethren saw that their father loved him more than all his brethren, they hated him, and could not speak **peaceably** unto him. **And** Joseph dreamed a dream, and **he** told it his brethren: **and** they hated him yet the more." (Genesis 37:3-5).

October 21: "Jesus said unto him, If thou wilt be perfect, go and sell that thou hast, and give to the poor, and thou shalt have treasure in heaven: and come and follow me." (Matthew 19:21).

October 22: "O God, be merciful unto me: for my soul trusteth in thee: **yea, in** the shadow of thy wings **will I make** my refuge, until **these calamities** be overpast. I will cry unto God most high; **unto** God that **performeth all things for me**. He shall send from heaven, and save me from the **reproach** of him that would swallow me up." (Psalms 57:1-3).

October 23: "Every high priest taken from among men is ordained for men in things pertaining to God, **that he may** offer **both** gifts and sacrifices for sins: Who can have compassion on the ignorant, and on them that are out of the way; **for** that he himself also is compassed with infirmity. **And by reason hereof he ought, as for the people, so also for himself**, to offer for sins. **And** no man taketh this honour unto himself, but he that is called of God, as was Aaron." (Hebrews 5:1-4).

October 24: "These are wells without water, clouds **that are** carried with a tempest; to whom the mist of darkness is reserved for ever. For when they **speak great** swelling words of vanity, they **allure** through the lusts of the flesh, **through much wantonness, those** that were clean escaped **from them who live** in error. **While** they promise them liberty, **they** themselves are the **servants** of corruption: for of whom a man is overcome, **of** the same is he **brought** in bondage." (2 Peter 2:17-19).

October 25: "O generation of vipers, who hath **warned you** to **flee** from **the** wrath to come? Bring forth **therefore** fruits **worthy** of repentance." (Luke 3:7-8).

October 26: "Blessed be **the God and** Father of our Lord Jesus Christ, **who** hath blessed us with all spiritual blessings in heavenly **places in** Christ: According as he **hath** chosen us in him before the foundation of the world, that we should be **holy** and without blame **before him in love: Having predestinated us unto the adoption of children by** Jesus Christ to himself, according to the good pleasure of his will, To the praise of **the glory of his grace, wherein** he hath made us accepted in the beloved." (Ephesians 1:3-6).

October 27: "How sweet are thy words unto my **taste**! yea, **sweeter** than honey to my mouth!" (Psalms 119:103).

October 28: "The Lord bless thee, and keep thee: The Lord make his face shine upon thee, and be **gracious** unto thee: The Lord lift up his countenance upon thee, and give thee peace." (Numbers 6:24-26).

October 29: "This **then** is the **message** which we have heard of him, and declare unto you, that God is light, and in him is no darkness at all. If we say that we have fellowship with him, and walk in darkness, we lie, and do not the truth: But if we walk in the light, as he is in the light, we have fellowship **one with another**, and the blood of Jesus Christ his Son cleanseth us from all sin." (1 John 1:5-7).

October 30: "Ye blind guides, which strain at a gnat, and swallow a camel. Woe unto you, scribes and Pharisees, hypocrites! For ye make clean the **outside** of the cup and of the platter, but within they are full of **extortion** and excess. Thou blind Pharisee, cleanse first that which is within the cup and platter, that the outside **of them** may be clean also." (Matthew 23:24-26).

October 31: "The Gentiles...glorified the word of the Lord: and as many as were ordained to eternal life believed. And the word of the Lord was published throughout all the region." (Acts 13:48-49).

November 1: "Go unto this people, and say, Hearing ye shall hear, and shall not understand; and **seeing** ye shall see, and not perceive: For the heart of this people is waxed gross, and their ears **are dull** of hearing, and their eyes have they closed; lest they should see with their eyes, and hear with their ears, and understand with their heart, and should be converted, and I should heal them." (Acts 28:26-27).

November 2: "And the devil, taking him up into an high mountain, shewed unto him all the kingdoms of the **world** in **a moment of time**." (Luke 4:5).

November 3: "Ye are the light of the world. A city that is set on an hill cannot be hid. Neither do men light a candle, and put it under a bushel, but on a candlestick; and it **giveth light unto** all that are in the house. **Let** your light so shine before men, that they may see your good works, and glorify your Father which is in heaven." (Matthew 5:14-16).

November 4: "Thus it is written, and thus it behoved Christ to suffer, and to rise from the dead the third day: And that repentance and remission of sins should be preached in his name among all nations, beginning at Jerusalem. And ye are witnesses of these things." (Luke 24:46-48).

November 5: "For if, when we were enemies, we were reconciled to God by the death of his Son, much more, **being** reconciled, we shall be **saved** by his life. **And** not only so, but we also joy in God **through** our Lord Jesus Christ, by whom we have **now** received **the** atonement." (Romans 5:10-11).

November 6: "Death, where is thy sting? **O grave**, where is thy victory? The sting of death is sin." (1 Corinthians 15:55-56).

November 7: "This is the **covenant** that I will make with them after those days, saith the Lord, I will put my laws into their hearts, and in their minds will I write them; And their sins and iniquities will I remember no more. **Now** where remission of these is, there is no more offering for sin. **Having therefore**, brethren, **boldness to enter into** the holiest by the blood of Jesus, By **a** new and living way, which he hath **consecrated** for us, through the veil." (Hebrews 10:16-20).

November 8: "Wherefore by their fruits ye shall know them. Not **every one** that saith unto me, **Lord, Lord**, shall enter into the kingdom of heaven; but he that **doeth the** will of my Father which is in heaven." (Matthew 7:20-21).

November 9: "Ye **also**, as lively stones, are **built up** a spiritual house, an holy priesthood, to offer up spiritual sacrifices, acceptable to God by Jesus Christ. Wherefore **also** it is contained in the scripture." (1 Peter 2:5-6).

November 10: "And Jesus said unto them, Come **ye after me**, and I will make you **to become** fishers of men And straightway they **forsook** their nets, and followed him." (Mark 1:17-18).

November 11: "So likewise ye, when ye **shall** have done all those things which are commanded you, say, We are unprofitable servants: we have done that which was our duty to do." (Luke 17:10).

November 12: "Jesus said unto her, I am the resurrection, and the life: **he that** believeth in me, though he were dead, yet shall he live: And whosoever liveth and believeth **in** me shall never die." (John 11:25-26).

November 13: "I **have not sat with** vain persons, **neither will I go in** with **dissemblers**. I **have** hated the congregation of **evil doers**; and will not sit **with** the **wicked**. I will wash mine hands in innocency: so **will** I **compass** thine altar, O Lord: That I may **publish with** the voice of **thanksgiving**, and tell of all thy wondrous works." (Psalms 26:4-7).

November 14: "Then said Jesus to those Jews which believed on him, If ye continue in my word, then are ye my disciples **indeed**; And ye shall know the truth, and the truth shall make you free." (John 8:31-32).

November 15: "We **glory** in tribulations **also**: know**ing** that tribulation **worketh** patience; **And** patience, **experience**; **and experience**, hope: And hope maketh not ashamed; because the love of God is shed abroad in our hearts by the Holy Ghost which is given unto us." (Romans 5:3-5).

November 16: "And God said, Let there be light: and there was light." (Genesis 1:3).

November 17: "I will **gather** you, and **blow upon you in** the fire of my **wrath**, and ye **shall** be melted **in the midst thereof**." (Ezekiel 22:21).

November 18: "And **it shall come to pass**, when your children **shall say unto** you, What **mean ye by this** service? **That** ye shall say, It is the sacrifice of the Lord's Passover." (Exodus 12:26-27).

November 19: "My sheep hear my voice, and I know them, and they follow me: And I give unto them eternal life; and they shall never perish, neither shall any man pluck them out of my hand." (John 10:27-28).

November 20: "**Whoso** hath this world's good, and seeth his brother **have need**, and shutteth up his **bowels of** compassion from him, how dwelleth the love of God in him? My **little children**, let us not love in word, neither in tongue; but in deed and in **truth**." (1 John 3:17-18).

November 21: "He that hateth me hateth my Father **also**. If I had not done among them **the** works which none other man did, they **had not had** sin: but now have they **both** seen and hated both me and my Father. **But this cometh to pass, that the word** might be fulfilled that is written in their law, They hated me without a cause." (John 15:23-25).

November 22: "And it came to pass, when Jesus had ended these sayings, the people were astonished at his doctrine: For he taught them as one having **authority**, and not as the scribes." (Matthew 7:28-29).

November 23: "Cast thy burden upon the Lord, **and** he shall **sustain** thee: **he shall never suffer** the righteous **to be moved**." (Psalms 55:22).

November 24: "Faith is **the substance** of things hoped for, **the evidence** of things not seen." (Hebrews 11:1).

November 25: "Then began he to curse and to swear, saying, **I know** not the man. And immediately the cock crew. And Peter remembered the word of Jesus, which said unto him, Before the cock crow, thou shalt deny me thrice. And he went out, and wept bitterly." (Matthew 26:74-75).

November 26: "So likewise ye, when ye **shall** have done all those things which are commanded you, say, We are unprofitable servants: we have done that which was our duty to do." (Luke 17:10).

November 27: "Blessed are they which do hunger and thirst after righteousness: for they shall be filled." (Matthew 5:6).

November 28: "For ye were as sheep going astray; but are now returned unto the Shepherd and Bishop of your souls." (1 Peter 2:25).

November 29: "And thou shalt love thy Lord God with all thy heart, and with all thy soul, and with all thy mind, and with all thy strength. This is the first commandment. And the second is like unto this. Thou shalt love thy neighbor as thy self." (Mark 12:30-31)

November 30: "Many that are first shall be last; and the last shall be first." (Matthew 19:30).

December 1: "Eye hath not seen, nor ear heard, neither have entered into the heart of man, the things which God hath prepared for them that love him." (1 Corinthians 2:9).

December 2: "**And it shall come to pass afterward**, **that** I will pour out my spirit upon all flesh; and your sons and your daughters shall prophesy, your old men shall dream dreams, your young men shall see visions." (Joel 2:28).

December 3: "And thou shalt set upon the table shewbread before me alway." (Exodus 25:30).

December 4: "Beware lest ye also, **being led** away with the error of the wicked, fall from your own steadfastness." (2 Peter 3:17).

December 5: "The God of peace, that brought again from the dead our Lord Jesus, **that** great shepherd of the sheep, through the blood of the everlasting **covenant**, Make you perfect in **every** good work to do his will, **working in you that which is wellpleasing** in his sight, **through** Jesus Christ; to whom be **glory** for ever and ever. Amen." (Hebrews 13:20-21).

December 6: "For whosoever will save his life shall lose it; but whosoever shall lose his life for my sake and the Gospel's, the same shall save it." (Mark 8:35).

December 7: "The Lord God hath given me **the** tongue **of the** learned, that I **should know how to speak a word in season to him that is weary**… I **hid** not my face from shame and spitting. For the Lord God **will** help me; therefore shall I not be confounded." (Isaiah 50:4-7).

December 8: "Then said Jesus unto him, Go, and do thou likewise." (Luke 10:37).

December 9: "Though he were a Son, yet learned he obedience by **the** things which he suffered. And **being** made perfect." (Hebrews 5:8-9).

December 10: "If we say that we have no sin, we deceive ourselves, and the truth is not in us. If we **confess** our sins, he is faithful and just to forgive **us** our sins, and to cleanse us from all unrighteousness. If we say that we have not sinned, we make him a liar, and his word is not in us." (1 John 1:8-10).

December 11: "Thou shalt not avenge, nor bear **any grudge** against the children of thy people, but thou shalt love thy neighbour as thyself: I am the Lord." (Leviticus 19:18).

December 12: "Gird up the loins of your mind. Be sober, and **hope to the end for** the grace that is **to be** brought unto you.... Be ye holy; for I am holy." (1 Peter 1:13 & 16).

December 13: "**Examine** yourselves, whether ye **be** in the faith; **prove** your own selves. Know ye not your own selves, how that Jesus Christ is in you?" (2 Corinthians 13:5).

December 14: "The Lord Jesus the same night in which he was betrayed took bread: And **when he had given thanks, he** brake **it**, and said, Take, eat: this is my body, which is broken for you: this do in remembrance of me. After the same manner **also he** took the cup, when **he had supped**, saying, This cup is the new testament in my blood: this do **ye**, as oft as ye drink it, in remembrance of me." (1 Corinthians 11:23-25).

December 15: "And they laughed him to scorn." (Matthew 9:24).

December 16: "In the beginning God created **the** heaven and **the** earth." (Genesis 1:1).

December 17: "The Lord **your God** hath given rest unto your brethren, as he promised them: **therefore now** return **ye**, and **get you** unto your tents, and unto the land of your possession, which Moses the servant of the Lord gave you on the other side Jordan. But take **diligent heed to** do the commandment and the law, which Moses the servant of the Lord charged you, **to** love the Lord your God, and **to** walk in **all** his ways, and to keep his commandments, and to cleave unto him, and to serve him with all your heart and with all your soul." (Joshua 22:4-5).

December 18: "Our Father which art in heaven, Hallowed **be** thy name. Thy kingdom come. Thy will be **done**, as in heaven, so in earth. Give us day **by day** our daily bread. And forgive us our sins; for we **also** forgive every one that **is indebted** to us. And lead us not into temptation; but deliver us from evil." (Luke 11:2-4).

December 19: "I should be the minister of Jesus Christ to the Gentiles, ministering the **Gospel** of God, that the offering **up** of the Gentiles might be acceptable, **being** sanctified by the Holy Ghost." (Romans 15:16).

December 20: "These are they which came out of great tribulation, and **have washed their robes**, and made them white in the blood of the Lamb. Therefore are they **before the throne** of God, and serve him day and night in his temple: and he that sitteth **on the throne shall** dwell among them." (Revelation 7:14-15).

December 21: "Then said Paul, John verily baptized with the baptism of repentance, saying unto the people, that they should believe on him which should come after him, that is, on Christ Jesus. When they heard **this**, they were baptized in the name of the Lord Jesus." (Acts 19:4-5).

December 22: "And the temple was filled with smoke **from** the glory of God, and **from** his power." (Revelation 15:8).

December 23: "Honour **thy** father and **thy** mother: and, Thou shalt love **thy** neighbour as thyself." (Matthew 19:19).

December 24: "And there were in the same **country** shepherds abiding in the field, **keeping watch over** their flock by night. And, lo, the angel of the Lord **came upon** them, and the **glory** of the Lord shone round about them: and they were sore afraid. And the angel said unto them, **Fear** not: **for**, behold, I bring you **good** tidings of great joy, **which** shall **be** to all people. For unto you is born this day in the city of David a Saviour, which is Christ the Lord. And this **shall be** a sign **unto you**; Ye shall find the **babe** wrapped in swaddling clothes, **lying** in a manger." (Luke 2:8-12).

December 25: "For unto us a child is born, unto us a son is given: and the **government** shall be upon his shoulder: and **his name** shall be called Wonderful, **Counsellor**, The mighty God, The everlasting Father, The Prince of Peace." (Isaiah 9:6).

December 26: "Tell us, by what authority doest thou these things? **or** who is he that gave thee this authority?" (Luke 20:2).

December 27: "Woe is me! For I am **undone; because** I am a man of unclean lips, and I dwell **in the midst of a** people **of** unclean lips: for **mine eyes** have seen the King, **the** Lord of hosts." (Isaiah 6:5).

December 28: "Here is wisdom. Let him that hath **understanding** count the number of the beast: for it is the number of a man; and his number is Six hundred threescore and six." (Revelation 13:18).

December 29: "Then said Jesus unto him, Except ye see signs and wonders, ye **will** not believe." (John 4:48).

December 30: "Unto whomsoever much is given, of him shall be much required: and to whom men **have** committed much, of him they will ask the more." (Luke 12:48).

December 31: "This is **a nation** that **obeyeth not** the voice of the Lord their God, nor receiveth correction. Truth **is perished, and is cut off from** their mouth." (Jeremiah 7:28).

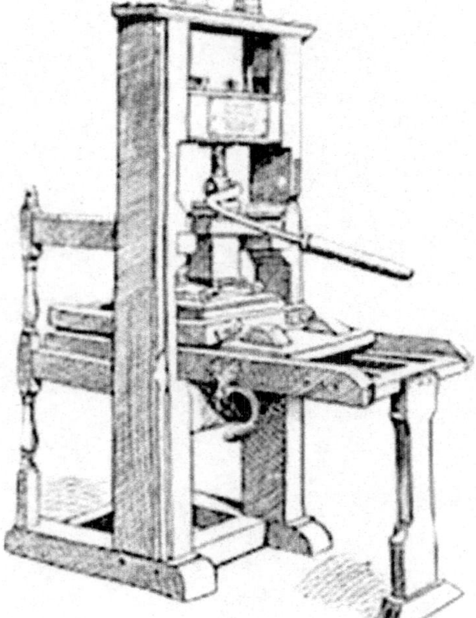

Appendix Three

This
appendix
represents just a
small sampling of well
known expressions found
in Tyndale's Bible, primarily
from the four Gospels, that were
received under inspiration, and that
were used by the King James Translators
when creating the King James Version of the
Bible. Students of the scriptures who are familiar
with the King James Version will recognize that some
of these are verbatim K.J.V., while others contain subtle
variations from the K.J.V.. The challenge for readers
is to compare the scriptures and to find additional
examples. A good source for comparison is
www.faithofgod.net.

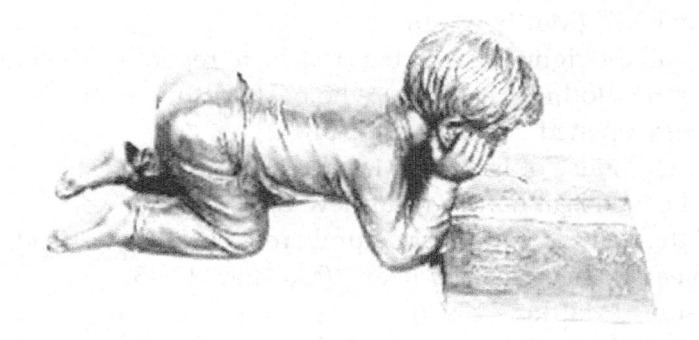

"Search the scriptures, for in them ye
think ye have eternal life: And they
are they which testify of me."
(Tyndale New Testament, John 5:39)

"My brother's keeper" (Genesis 4:9)
"A pillar of salt" (Genesis 19:26)
"Held his peace" (Genesis 34:5)
"Let my people go" (Exodus 5:1)
"A stranger in a strange land" (Exodus 2:22)
"Still as a stone" (Exodus 15:16)
"Flesh pots" (Exodus 16:3)
"Take the name of the Lord thy God in vain" (Deuteronomy 5:11)
"House of bondage" (Deuteronomy 6:12)
"A dreamer of dreams" (Deuteronomy 13:1)
"Atonement" (Leviticus 16:33)
"Tender mercies" (Psalms 51:1)
"Stiff-neck" (Psalms 75:5)
"The apple of his own eye" (Zechariah 2:8)
"Save his people from their sins" (Matthew 1:21)
"Born King of the Jews" (Matthew 2:2)
"Thou shalt not tempt thy Lord God" (Matthew 4:7)
"The poor in spirit" (Matthew 5:3)
"An eye for an eye: a tooth for a tooth" (Matthew 5:38)
"He maketh his sun to rise on the evil and on the good, and sendeth his rain on the just and unjust" (Matthew 5:45)
"Be perfect, even as your heavenly father is perfect" (Matthew 5:48)
"Thy father which seeth in secret, shall reward thee openly" (Matthew 6:4)
"No man can serve two masters" (Matthew 6:24)
"Behold the lilies of the field, how they grow" (Matthew 6:28)
"Neither cast ye your pearls before swine" (Matthew 7:6)
"Enter in at the strait gate" (Matthew 7:13)
"Arise, take up thy bed" (Matthew 9:6)
"I am not come to call the righteous, but the sinners, to repentance" (Matthew 9:13)
"If I may but touch his clothing, I shall be whole" (Matthew 9:21)
"And their eyes were opened" (Matthew 9:30)
"The lost sheep of the house of Israel" (Matthew 10:6)
"The kingdom of heaven is at hand" (Matthew 10:7)
"And now are all the hairs of your heads numbered" (Matthew 10:30)
"Whosoever hath ears to hear, let him hear" (Matthew 13:43)
"The carpenter's son" (Matthew 13:55)
"There is no prophet without honour, save in his own country" (Matthew 13:57)
"He stretched forth his hand" (Matthew 14:31)
"O ye of little faith" (Matthew 16:8)
"Faith as a grain of mustard seed" (Matthew 17:20)
"Seventy time seven" (Matthew 18:22)
"Suffer the children, and forbid them not to come to me" (Matthew 19:14)
"It is easier for a camel to go through the eye of a needle" (Matthew 19:24)
"Ye have made it a den of thieves" (Matthew 21:13)

"Many are called, but few are chosen" (Matthew 22:14)
"Give therefore to Caesar, that which is Caesar's" (Matthew 22:21)
"God is not the God of the dead, but the God of the living" (Matthew 22:32)
"Neither durst any from that day forth, ask him any more questions" (Matthew 22:46)
"There shall be weeping and gnashing of teeth" (Matthew 24:51)
"Thirty pieces of silver" (Matthew 26:15)
"Exceeding sorrowful" (Matthew 26:22)
"The king of the Jews" (Matthew 27:11)
"They parted his garments, and did cast lots" (Matthew 27:35)
"My God, my God, why hast thou forsaken me" (Matthew 27:46)
"Of a surety this was the son of God" (Matthew 27:54)
"His countenance was like lightning, and his raiment white as snow" (Matthew 28:3)
"He is not here: he is risen" (Matthew 28:6)
"I send my messenger before thy face" (Mark 1:2)
"The voice of one that crieth in the wilderness" (Mark 1:3)
"Make his paths straight" (Mark 1:3)
"The baptism of repentance, for the remission of sins" (Mark 1:4)
"The Holy Ghost descending upon him like a dove" (Mark 1:10)
"Son, thy sins are forgiven thee" (Mark 2:9)
"Publicans and sinners" (Mark 2:16)
"The Sabbath day was made for man, and not man for the sabbath day" (Mark 2:27)
"Is the candle lighted, to be put under a bushel" (Mark 4:21)
"What have I to do, with thee Jesus the son of the most highest God" (Mark 5:7)
"And Jesus immediately felt in himself, the virtue that went out of him" (Mark 5:30)
"And they anointed, many that were sick with oil and healed them" (Mark 6:13)
"What shall it profit a man" (Mark 8:36)
"He was transfigured before them" (Mark 9:2)
"They held their peace" (Mark 9:34)
"Suffer the children to come unto me and forbid them not" (Mark 10:14)
"The the eye of an needle" (Mark 10:25)
"A den of thieves" (Mark 11:17)
"The son of man coming in the clouds" (Mark 13:26)
"Couldest not thou watch with me one hour" (Mark 14:37)
"Art thou the Christ the son of the blessed" (Mark 14:61)
"They parted his garments, casting lots for them" (Mark 15:24)
"My God, my God, why hast thou forsaken me" (Mark 15:34)
"Truly this man was the son of God" (Mark 15:39)
"He is risen, he is not here" (Mark 16:6)
"Blessed art thou among women" (Luke 1:28)
"The son of the highest" (Luke 1:32)
"The power of the highest shall overshadow thee" (Luke 1:35)
"Blessed art thou among the women, and blessed is the fruit of thy womb" (Luke 1:28)
"Tender mercy" (Luke 1:78)
"Swaddling clothes" (Luke 2:6)

"And the child grew and waxed strong in spirit" (Luke 2:40)
"Jesus increased in wisdom and age, and in favour with God and man" (Luke 2:52)
"Physician, heal thyself" (Luke 4:23)
"I have not found so great faith, no not in Israel" (Luke 7:9)
"She hath washed my feet with tears" (Luke 7:44)
"Power and authority" (Luke 9:1)
"Let him deny himself" (Luke 9:23)
"Taste of death" (Luke 9:27)
"The harvest truly is great, but the labourers are few" (Luke 10:2)
"Exalted to heaven" (Luke 10:15)
"Go and do thou likewise" (Luke 10:37)
"He that is not with me is against me" (Luke 11:23)
"Where your treasure is, There will your hearts be also" (Luke 12:34)
"A grain of mustard seed" (Luke 13:19)
"The strait gate" (Luke 13:24)
"Workers of iniquity" (Luke 13:27)
"Riotous living" (Luke 15:13)
"Ninety and nine in the wilderness" (Luke 15:14)
"I have sinned against heaven and before thee" (Luke 15:18)
"That fatted calf" (Luke 15:23)
"This thy brother was dead, and is alive again: and was lost, and is found"
    (Luke 15:32)
"Children of light" (Luke 16:8)
"No servant can serve two masters" (Luke 16:13)
"The dogs came, and licked his sores" (Luke 16:21)
"A grain of mustard seed" (Luke 17:6)
"And the same was a Samaritan" (Luke 17:16)
"And he taught daily in the temple" (Luke 19:47)
"Men's hearts shall fail them for fear" (Luke 21:26)
"Pray lest ye fall into temptation" (Luke 22:40)
"Weep not for me: but weep for yourselves, and for your children" (Luke 23: 28)
"Today shalt thou be with me in paradise" (Luke 23:43)
"Into thy hands I commend my spirit" (Luke 23:46)
"Why seek ye the living among the dead" (Luke 24:5)
"And their eyes were opened" (Luke 24:31)
"Did not our hearts burn within us, while he talked with us by the way" (Luke 24:32)
"Born of water, and of the spirit" (John 3:5)
"The wind bloweth where he listeth" (John 3:8)
"The serpent in the wilderness" (John 3:14)
"God so loved the world, that he gave his only son for the intent, that none that
    believe in him, should perish: But should have everlasting life" (John 3:16)
"A well of water springing up into everlasting life" (John 4:14)
"Take up thy bed, and walk" (John 5:8)
"A shining light" (John 5:35)

"I am that living bread which came down from heaven" (John 6:51)
"Go hence and sin no more" (John 8:11)
"His time was not yet come" (John 8:20)
"Whosoever committeth sin, is the servant of sin" (John 8:34)
"There is no truth in him" (John 8:44)
"I am the light of the world" (John 9:5)
"I was blind, and now I see" (John 9:39)
"I am come that they might have life, and have it more abundantly" (John 10:10)
"There shall be one flock, and one shepherd" (John 10:16)
"I and my father are one" (John 10:30)
"And Jesus wept" (John 11:35)
"Lazarus come forth" (John 11:43)
"Blessed is he that in the name of the Lord cometh" (John 12:13)
"The servant is not greater than his master" (John 13:16)
"He was troubled in the spirit" (John 13:21)
"Have love one to another" (John 13:34)
"Let not your hearts be troubled" (John 14:1)
"In my father's house are many mansions" (John 14:2)
"I am the way, the verity, and life" (John 14:6)
"He that hath seen me, hath seen the father" (John 14:9)
"Another comforter" (John 14:16)
"Not as the world giveth, give I unto you" (John 14:27)
"Greater love than this hath no man, than that a man bestow his life for his friends" (John 15:13)
"Ye have not chosen me, but I have chosen you" (John 15:16)
"This is life eternal that they might know thee that only very God: and whom thou hast sent Jesus Christ" (John 17:3)
"I have finished the work which thou gavest me to do" (John 17:4)
"And that glory that thou gavest me, I have given them, that they may be one, as we are one" (John 17:24)
"For this cause was I born, and for this cause came I into the world, that I should bear witness unto the truth" (John 18:37)
"Gave up the ghost" (John 19:30)
"In the place where Jesus was crucified, was a garden, and in the garden a new sepulchre, wherein was never man laid" (John 19:41)
"Sir if thou have borne him hence, tell me where thou hast laid him" (John 20:15)
"I ascend unto my Father, and your Father: my God and your God" (John 20:17)
"Jesus is the Christ the Son of God" (John 20:31)
"I go a fishing" (John 21:3)
"The world could not contain the books that should be written" (John 21:25)
"Ye shall be baptized with the Holy Ghost" (Acts 1:5)
"The times, or the seasons" (Acts 1:7)
"And they continued in the Apostles' doctrine and fellowship" (Acts 2:42)
"Silver and gold have I none, such as I have give I thee" (Acts 3:6)

"God hath spoken by the mouth of all his holy prophets since the world began" (Acts 3:21)
"Them that believed, were of one heart, and of one soul" (Acts 4:32)
"If this counsel or work be of men, it will come to nought" (Acts 5:38)
"Put off thy shoes from thy feet, for the place where thou standest is holy ground" (Acts 7:33)
"He being full of the Holy Ghost looked up with his eyes into heaven and saw the majesty of God, and Jesus standing on the right hand of God" (Acts 7:55)
"And they went down both into the water: both Philip and also the gelded man" (Acts 8:38)
"Saul, Saul, why persecutest thou me" (Acts 9:4)
"Judge of quick and dead" (Acts 10:42)
"A mist and a darkness" (Acts 13:11)
"Sorcerer" (Acts 13:16)
"They shook off the dust off their feet against them" (Acts 13:51)
"Whom ye then ignorantly worship, him shew I unto you" (Acts 17:23)
"In him we live, move, and have our being" (Acts 17:28)
"Have ye received the holy ghost after ye believed" (Acts 19:2)
"Great is Diana of the Ephesians" (Acts 19:28)
"I am Iesus of Nazareth, whom thou persecutest" (Acts 22:8)
"So must thou bear witness at Rome" (Acts 23:11)
"Thou hast appealed unto Cesar: unto Cesar shalt thou go" (Acts 25:12)
"I saw in the way a light from heaven, above the brightness of the sun" (Acts 26:13)
"Somewhat thou bringest me in mind for to become christen" (Acts 26:28)
"Paul entered in and prayed, and laid his hands on him and healed him" (Acts 28:8)
"We have heard of this sect, that everywhere it is spoken against" (Acts 28:22)
"I am not ashamed of the Gospel of Christ" (Romans 1:16)
"It is the power of God unto salvation" (Romans 1:16)
"The riches of his goodness and patience and longsuffering" (Romans 2:4)
"There is no partiality with God" (Romans 2:11)
"Written in their hearts" (Romans 2:15)
"A man is justified by faith" Romans 3:28)
"Tribulation bringeth patience" (Romans 5:3)
"We are buried with him by baptism for to die" (Romans 6:4)
"Walk in a new life" (Romans 6:4)
"The servants of sin" (Romans 6:17)
"The reward of sin is death" (Romans 6:23)
"O wretched man that I am" (Romans 7:24)
"To be carnally minded is death; and to be spiritually minded is life and peace" (Romans 8:6)
"We are the sons of God" (Romans 8:16)
"The children of the promise" (Romans 9:8)
"Stumblingstone" (Romans 9:32)
"Christ is the end of the law to justify all that believe" (Romans 10:4)

"How shall they preach, except they be sent" (Romans 10:15)
"All tongues shall bow to me, and all tongue shall give knowledge to God"
    (Romans 14:11)
"God, the Father of our Lord Jesus" (Romans 15:6)
"A minister of the circumcision for the truth of God" (Romans 15:8)
"Signs and wonders" (Romans 15:19)
"Infidel" (2 Corinthians 6:15)
"Fallen from grace" (Galatians 5:4)
"Bear his own burden" (Galatians 6:5)
"Harden not your hearts" (Hebrews 3:15)
"Fathers of our flesh" (Hebrews 12:9)
"Wandering stars" (Jude 1:13)
"Ungodly" (Jude 1:15)
"Bottomless pit" (Revelation 9:2)

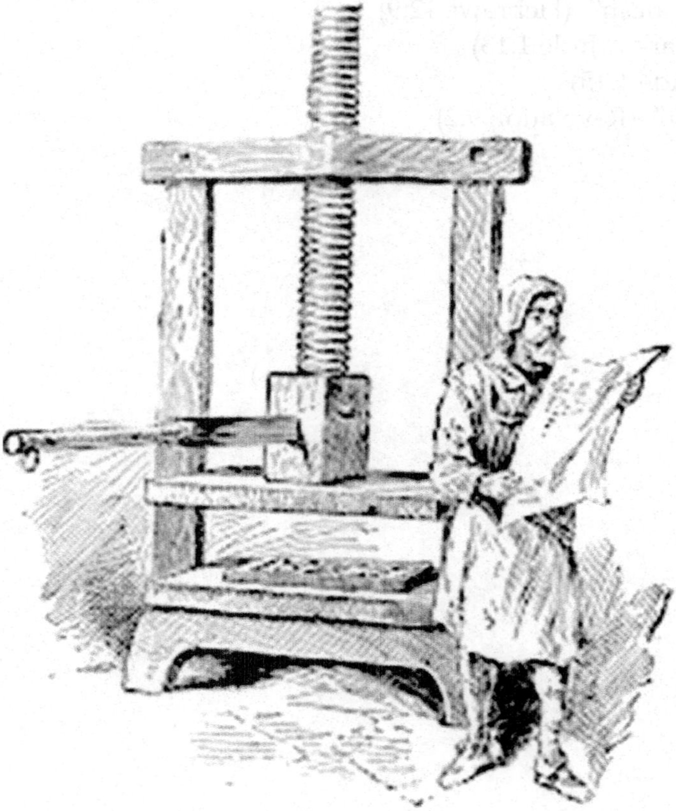

Appendix Four

In April, 2007, Moira Goff,
head of the British Section 1501-1800 at
the British Library, provided a wonderful
personal glimpse into its copy of Tyndale's New
Testament. The following is an adaptation of her remarks.

(Reprinted by Permission)

"It's a small, pocket sized book. The old-spelling edition that was published by the Library a few years ago is the same size as the original. Technically, it's what they call an octavo book, which means it's small enough to go into your pocket. It's quite a thick book, although it's only the New Testament. It's not the whole Bible.

Printed in 1526, it's the first New Testament printed in English. It was intended as a book that people could hold in their hands and read. It wasn't one of those large folio volumes that would stand on lecterns and be read in churches.

Our copy is very pretty. It's bound in red leather and it has gold tooling, but that was done much later. Originally, it probably would have had a plain brown leather binding, although again our copy is very nicely illuminated. There's only one other complete copy that survives, and that's much plainer. The initials at the beginning of each book are not illuminated, as they are in our copy, so our copy must have been someone's prized possession. It was a small personal book, very much intended for somebody to read to themselves or perhaps to hold and read to others who couldn't read as fluently as they could, so that they, too, could hear the Bible in English. It's very much a personal book.

Tyndale was writing from the spoken English that he knew. He was very concerned to provide a translation that people could read. And although a very long time has passed, I think once we get through the old spelling - and the spelling's changed quite a lot - you find so many phrases, so many expressions, with which you are familiar. They may not be quite the same, but they've passed into the English language, nevertheless.

So, in a sense, he was part way between the Wycliffe Bible, which is really the first Bible in English, which was circulated in manuscript form only, and which is much earlier, in the 1380s, and is recognizably English, but not quite as English as Tyndale is. Of course, Tyndale was drawing on Wycliffe, and so some expressions in the earlier version do come out in Tyndale. He adds others. The expressions in the Wycliffe Bible had probably passed into common parlance, and Tyndale picked up on that because he was working with the everyday language that people used in conversation.

This was not high-flown literary language. This was meant to be a direct language, translating words from the Greek New Testament, so that ordinary everyday literate people could read and understand. It was part of vernacular and everyday language that was straightforward and simply expressed so that people could repeat it. They would remember the expressions. They passed into common parlance through later editions of the Bible, in English. They are found in the writings of Shakespeare, in particular.

Not directly, however. We think that Shakespeare's Bible was the Geneva Bible (1560), which was itself based largely on Tyndale's translations. His language has become ours, so the unfamiliarity that you see when you look at the spelling very soon evaporates when you look at it more closely or hear it spoken.

I have to say that I've got quite a funny approach to this! It interests me that if you open and read some passages, the things that come to mind are the passages in Handel's Messiah, because in some of those passages, you can find phrases and expressions that are Tyndale's.

If you look, you see so much that's familiar; for example, the beginning of the Gospel of St John: "And the light shineth in darkness, and the darkness comprehended it not..." That's a sentence that is very familiar to all of us, although how many of us would recognize it as Tyndale?

And the very beginning of the Gospel of St John: "In the beginning was that word, and that word was with God." In this case, it's "...and God was that word," which still provides the feelings of rhythm. The meaning is there, even if the words are not quite the same as we're used to. "There is no power but of God; the powers that be are ordained of God." It's not quite the context that we're used to!

I think there was a business about love and charity, and it's right at the end of the 13th chapter of the First Epistle of St. Paul to the Corinthians: "Now abideth faith, hope and love, even these three; but the chief of these is love." In his revision of the translation, Tyndale changed that to "...and the greatest of these is love", but in the 1526 New Testament, we read: "But the chief of these is love." Not "charity," which is what we find elsewhere, and what had previously been used, but "love," which is a much more human and more personal word.

His choice of words says something about Tyndale's aim to bring the Gospel closer to the people so that they could read it for themselves and enter into a direct dialogue with God, which I think is what got him into trouble! Tyndale was ultimately burnt for doing this work.

Once you translate a Bible into English, and the people can interpret the Bible for themselves, what need is there for the clergy? How can the ecclesiastical establishment continue to manage the people's understanding? It's really about control. The church was anxious to maintain its authority through the hierarchy of cardinals, bishops and priests, and they did that by managing the Latin Bible.

Tyndale wasn't only about translation; he was about belonging to a group of people who criticized church hierarchy, control, and corruption. His approach to translation was influenced by Lutheranism, which is very much about a personal relationship with God without a need for the clergy. Tyndale wanted people, instead, to look to the scriptures to give them guidance for the conduct of their everyday lives, rather than to spiritual advisers to to tell them how to behave. This is dangerous!

It seems quite strange to us now. What's even more strange to me is that after all the prohibitions, the burning of Tyndale himself did not take place before we had the Coverdale Bible, which is in English, in 1535. That's the year before Tyndale was burnt at the stake. And the difference with the Coverdale Bible, as far as I can see, is that it was a large Bible to be put in churches. It wasn't a small Bible to be given to people to read themselves.

Tyndale himself had done a revision of his New Testament in 1534, and we have a copy of that here in the Library, as well, that belonged to Queen Anne Boleyn, who could not have been closer to the king! Yet, she had a Bible in English. She's said to have recommended Tyndale's Bible to Henry VIII, and he is said to have commended it. It was only a couple of years afterward that Tyndale was burned at the stake.

Anne Boleyn got into trouble for her Reformist sympathies. One of the reasons that she was executed was that she was caught in a conspiracy because she had sympathy for the Protestant religion, as opposed to Catholicism. She was executed in 1536, before Tyndale's martyrdom, but for a very different reason. And by that time, the Bible in English had been established.

I find that strange, and difficult to understand: How you can have one course of events unfolding which is against the Bible in English, and another course of events unfolding at almost exactly the same time whose purpose is to establish the Bible in English. We have a succession of Bibles in the English language, from Tyndale's New Testament, his production of further translations of books of the Old Testament, and the Coverdale Bible and the Geneva Bible, until we get to the King James Version, which is the one that so many people now know, much of which is based on Tyndale's own translations.

I think the estimate is that 84 per cent of the New Testament in the King James Version is from Tyndale. We're talking about something close to a hundred years between the two, but there was a succession of Bibles that used Tyndale's translation.

That the Bible in English was quickly established indicates that there must have been a wide readership. The so-called Wycliffe Bible, (1382 – 1395), had been circulating in manuscript form for well over a hundred years. But 3,000 copies of Tyndale's New Testament (1526) were smuggled in to the country, and then disseminated to people who would read it to themselves and to each other. There must have been copies at all levels of society, from the highest to the lowest. There must have been copies available at court, where intrigue was rife.

The background to this is the 'King's Great Matter,' that he wanted to divorce his wife Catherine of Aragon, who was supported by the Holy Roman Emperor, in favour of Anne Boleyn, who was within a circle of people who were interested in Reformed religion. Henry was moving in the direction of solving this dilemma by becoming the supreme head of the church in England.

One of those who spoke out against Tyndale most vociferously was Sir Thomas More, the Lord Chancellor. In this hierarchy, you have the influential leaders of the kingdom speaking out against Tyndale, but at the same time, you have others at court who sympathize with what Tyndale is doing. Further down, there is a merchant class traveling on the continent, and seeing what's happening there. They are eager to get the Bible in their own language, because they have seen the New Testament in German. They can see that there has been a long tradition of vernacular Bibles on the Continent, and they're asking: Why can't we have that? They want to read the word of God in English. At the same time, there are staunch Catholics who don't want things to change because they are certain that it would be wrong. To them, the Bible was the word of God, and that meant that it was written and recited in Latin!

The Latin Vulgate Bible was not what Tyndale used to produce his translation. He used the Greek New Testament. The 1526 New Testament translation represents just the first stage of his work. As he goes back to Hebrew, as well as to Greek, he refines and extends it, (1534 & 1536), and he goes on to translate the Old Testament (1530 – 1534).

I must emphasize that the beautiful copy that we have is only the New Testament. Tyndale does go on to translate the Old Testament, as well. He draws on Hebrew sources, as he's an extraordinarily good linguist. The sources he used are not the same as the Vulgate.

The Library's copy has been beautifully decorated, which is quite unusual. The illuminations must have been done early in the life of this particular copy, and are probably one of the reasons why it has survived. It was obviously a prized copy that belonged to somebody who could afford to have it illuminated. One wonders if it was a wealthy merchant who had a copy smuggled in, early on. We just don't know. Our first notice of it comes in the first half of the 18th century when it surfaced in the library of Queen Anne's first minister, Robert Harley.

The British Library acquired it for one million pounds (1.32 million U.S. dollars) in 1994. It got extensive media coverage at the time, and there was a lot of excitement surrounding it. It's been one of our great treasures ever since. It's one of three surviving copies, and each one is unique in its own way as a repository of English history.

I have to say that I have a very special affection for it. I think it's a very beautiful volume. I've had the privilege of handling it on various occasions. It's very precious and very wonderful."

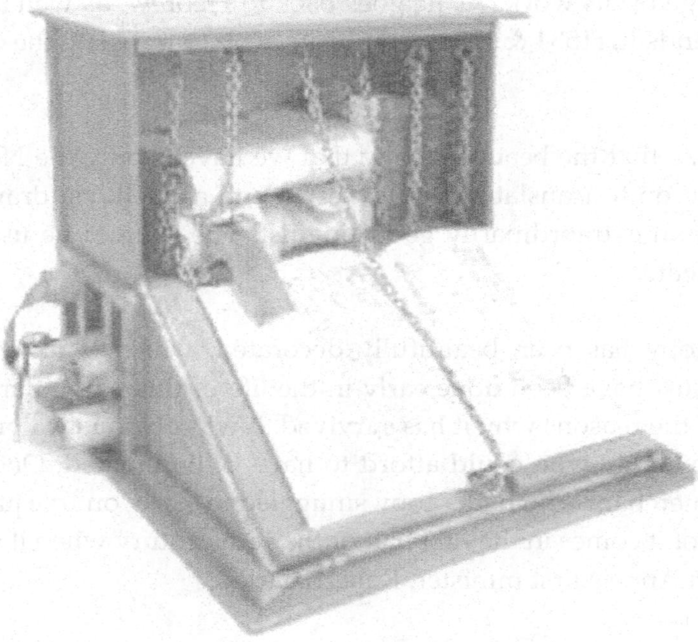

About the Author

Phil Hudson and his wife Jan, have been married nearly 50 years, and have 7 children and over 20 grandchildren. They enjoy whiling away summer days with their family at their cabin, on the shores of Priest Lake, the crown jewel of North Idaho. Phil had a successful family dental practice in Spokane, Washington for 43 years, before retiring in 2015. In his free time, if he and Jan are not visiting their loved ones, he can be found roaming through Pacific Northwest woods, boating on the lake, cycling up mountain passes, riding his motorcycle along forest trails, or snowbiking in winters' deep powder along the Selkirk Crest. He always seems to find the time to write down his thoughts on his laptop, but appreciates Isaac Asimov's frustration when he was asked: "If you knew that you only had 10 minutes left to live, what would you do?" Without hesitation, Asimov answered: "I'd type faster."

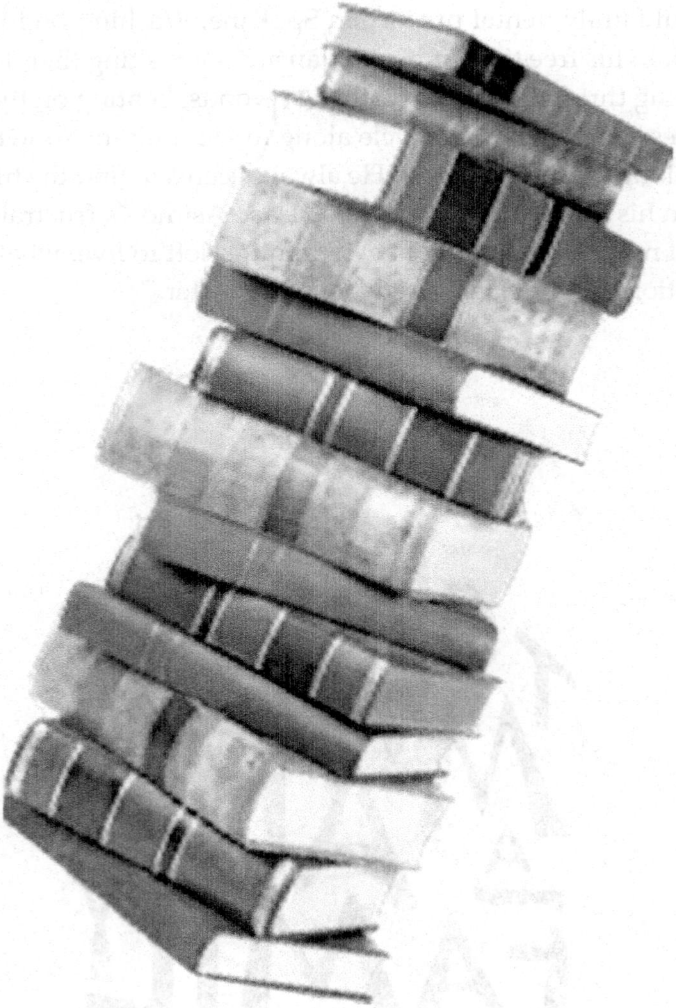

Also by the Author

Essays: Spray From The Ocean Of Thought
Essays: Ripples On A Pond
Essays: Serendipitous Meanderings
Essays: Presents Of Mind
Essays: Mental Floss
Essays: Fitness Training For The Mind And Spirit

Book of Mormon Commentary: Born In The Wilderness
Book of Mormon Commentary: Voices From The Dust
Book of Mormon Commentary: Journey To Cumorah

As I Think About my Savior

Minute Musings: Volume One
Minute Musings: Volume Two
Minute Musings: Volume Three

Diode Laser Soft Tissue Surgery: Volume One
Diode Laser Soft Tissue Surgery: Volume Two
Diode Laser Soft Tissue Surgery: Volume Three

These, and other titles, are available at Online Retailers